NEW MUTANTS BY VITA AYALA VOL. 2. Contains material originally published in magazine form as NEW MUTANTS (2019) #19-24. First printing 2022. ISBN 978-1-302-93119-3. Published by MARVEL WORLDWIDE, INC., a subsidiary of MARVEL ENTERTAINMENT, LLC. OFFICE OF PUBLICATION: 1290 Avenue of the Americas, New York, NY 10104. © 2022 MARVEL No similarity between any of the names, characters, persons, and/or institutions in this book with those of any living or dead person or institution is intended, and any such similarity which may exist is purely coincidental. **Printed in Canada.** KEVIN FEIGE, Chief Creative Officer; DAN BUCKLEY, President, Marvel Entertainment; JOE QUESADA, EVP & Creative Director; DAVID BOGART, Associate Publisher & SVP of Talent Affairs; TOM BREVOORT, VP, Executive Editor; NICK LOWE, Executive Editor, VP of Content, Digital Publishing; DAVID GABRIEL, VP of Print & Digital Publishing; JEFF YOUNGQUIST, VP of Production & Special Projects; ALEX MORALES, Director of Publishing Operations; DAN EDINGTON, Managing Editor; RICKEY PURDIN, Director of Talent Relations; JENNIFER GRÜNWALD, Senior Editor, Special Projects; SUSAN CRESPI, Production Manager; STAN LEE, Chairman Emeritus. For information regarding advertising in Marvel Comics or on Marvel.com, please contact Vit DeBellis, Custom Solutions & Integrated Advertising Manager, at vdebellis@ marvel.com. For Marvel subscription inquiries, please call 888-511-5480. **Manufactured between 1/22/2022 and 2/22/2022 by SOLISCO PRINTERS, SCOTT, QC, CANADA.**

10 9 8 7 6 5 4 3 2 1

NEW MUTANTS

Vol. 2

Writer:	Vita Ayala
Artists:	Alex Lins (#19-20),
	Rod Reis (#21-23)
	& Danilo Beyruth (#24)
Color Artists:	Matt Milla (#19-20),
	Rod Reis (#21-23)
	& Dan Brown (#24)
Letterer:	VC's Travis Lanham
	with Joe Caramagna (#21)
Cover Art:	Martin Simmonds
Head of X:	Jonathan Hickman
Design:	Tom Muller
Assistant Editor:	Anita Okoye
Editors:	Annalise Bissa
	& Sarah Brunstad
Senior Editor:	Jordan D. White
Collection Editor:	Jennifer Grünwald
Assistant Editor:	Daniel Kirchhoffer
Assistant Managing Editor:	Maia Loy
Associate Manager, Talent Relations:	Lisa Montalbano
VP Production & Special Projects:	Jeff Youngquist
SVP Print, Sales & Marketing:	David Gabriel
Editor in Chief:	C.B. Cebulski

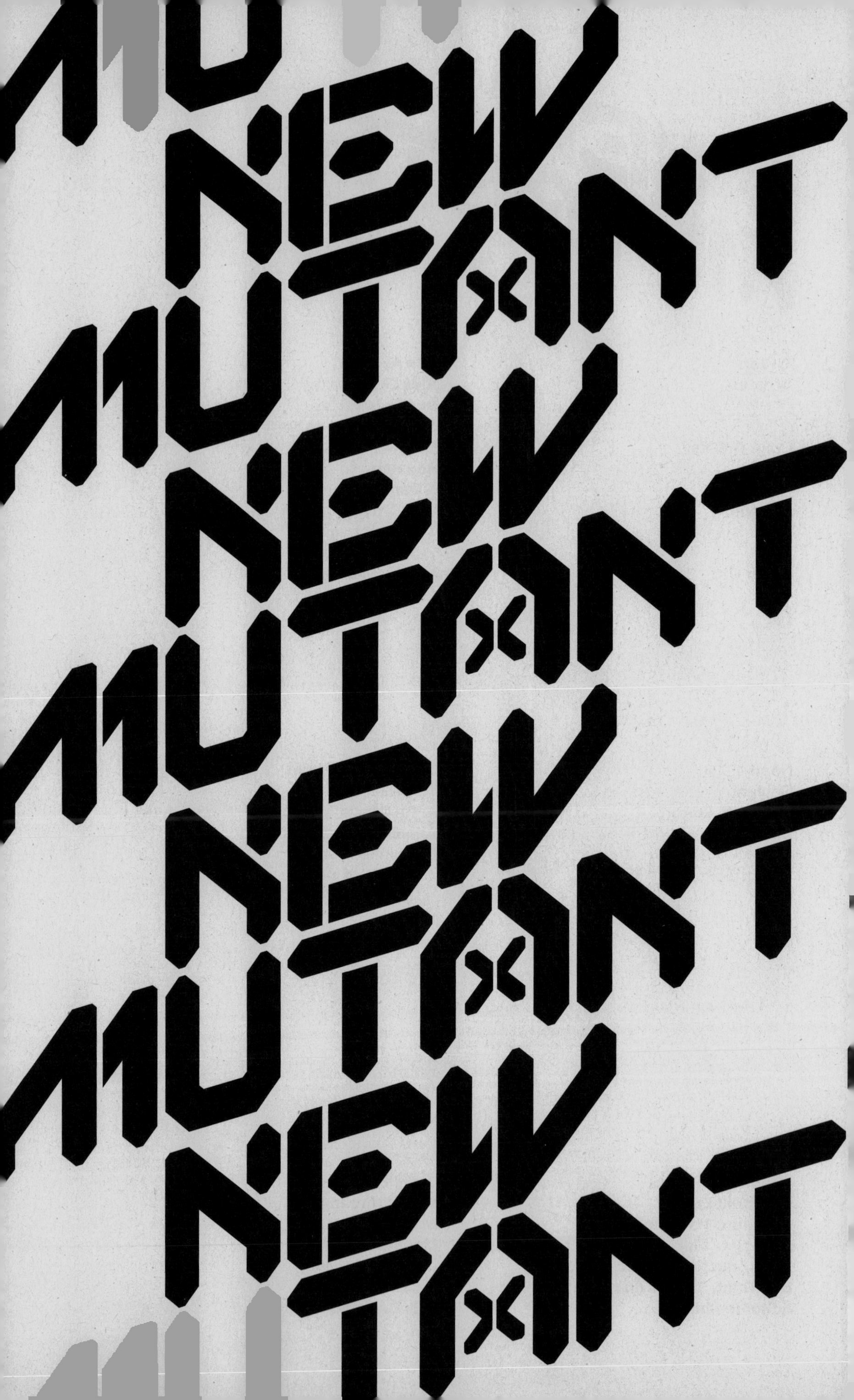
NEW
MUTANT
NEW
MUTANT
NEW
MUTANT
NEW

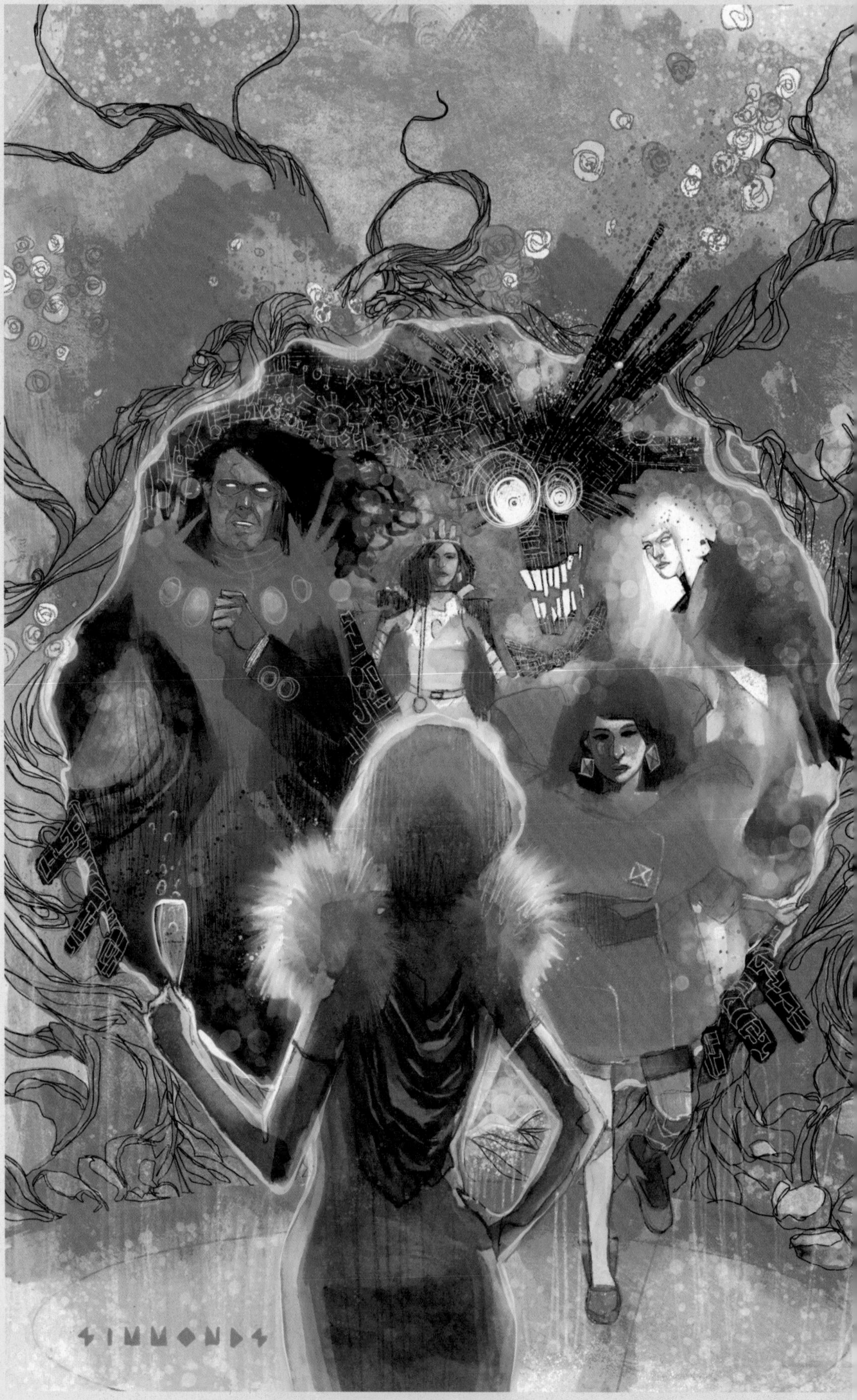
SIMMONDS

Party of the Century

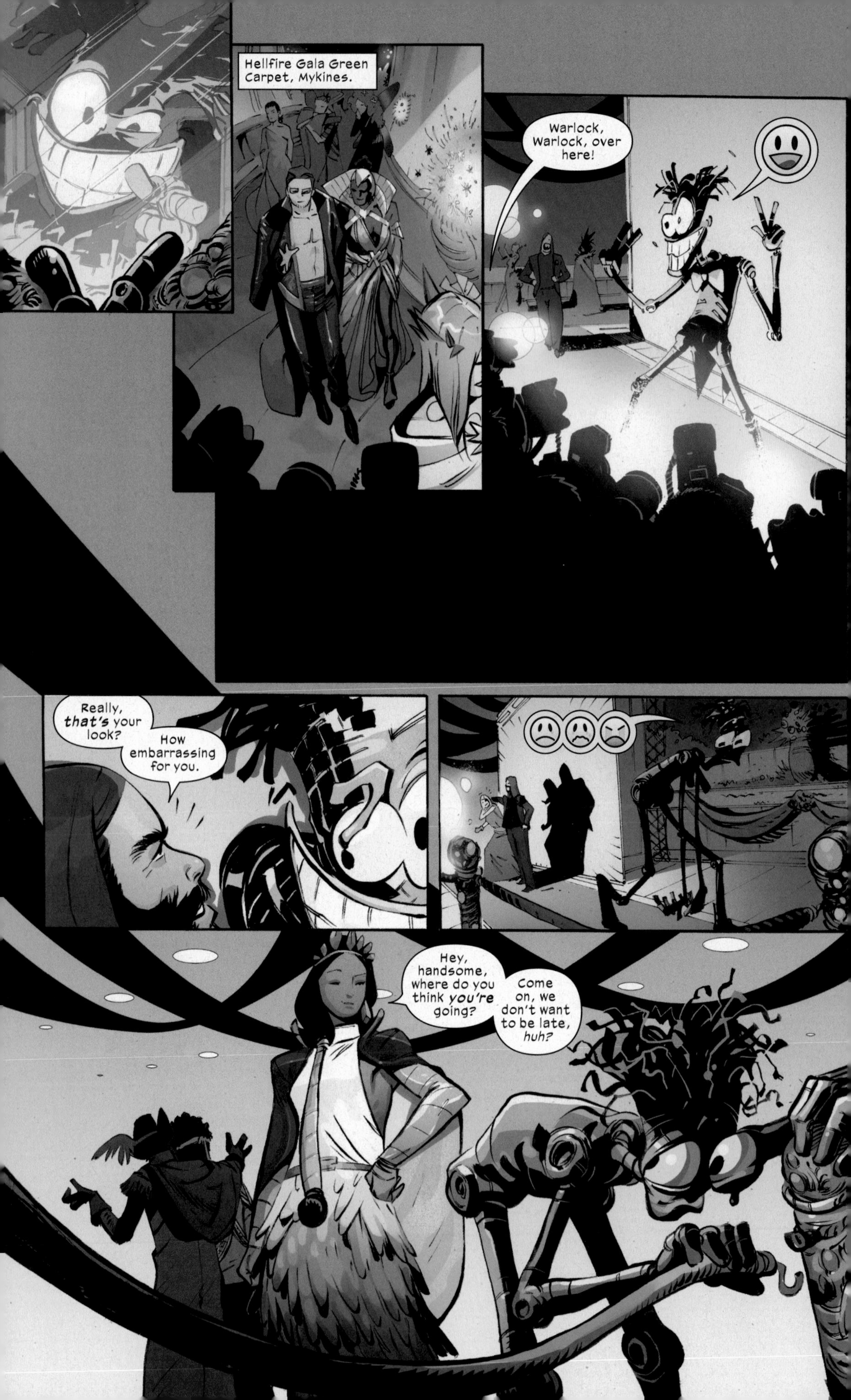
Hellfire Gala Green Carpet, Mykines.
Warlock, Warlock, over here!
Really, *that's* your look?
How embarrassing for you.
Hey, handsome, where do you think *you're* going?
Come on, we don't want to be late, *huh?*

GIVE ME MORE DREAMS

The NEW MUTANTS have been tasked with training the youth of Krakoa -- teaching them to use and combine their mutant abilities! But basic training isn't working for everyone -- a group of young mutants have fallen in with the Shadow King, though Scout became suspicious of his motives. Tonight, though, none of that matters -- it's time to party with all of Krakoa at the Hellfire Gala!

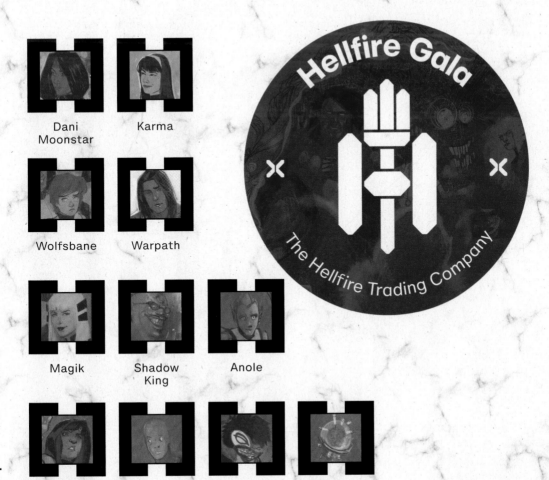

Dani Moonstar

Karma

Wolfsbane

Warpath

Magik

Shadow King

Anole

Scout

Rain Boy

Cosmar

No-Girl

Hellfire Gala

The Hellfire Trading Company

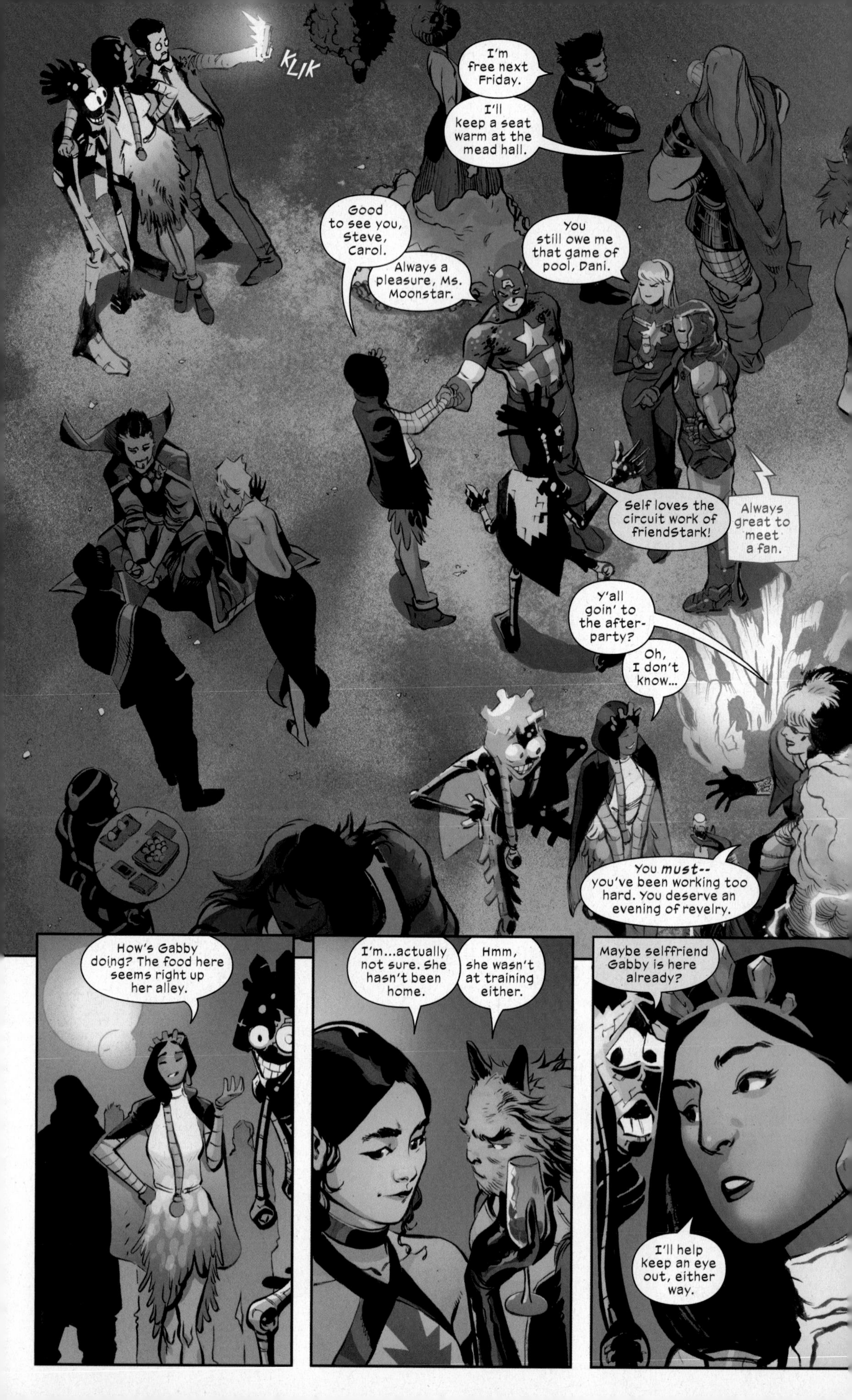
KLIK
I'm free next Friday.
I'll keep a seat warm at the mead hall.
Good to see you, Steve, Carol.
Always a pleasure, Ms. Moonstar.
You still owe me that game of pool, Dani.
Self loves the circuit work of friendStark!
Always great to meet a fan.
Y'all goin' to the after-party?
Oh, I don't know...
You must--you've been working too hard. You deserve an evening of revelry.
How's Gabby doing? The food here seems right up her alley.
I'm...actually not sure. She hasn't been home.
Hmm, she wasn't at training either.
Maybe selffriend Gabby is here already?
I'll help keep an eye out, either way.

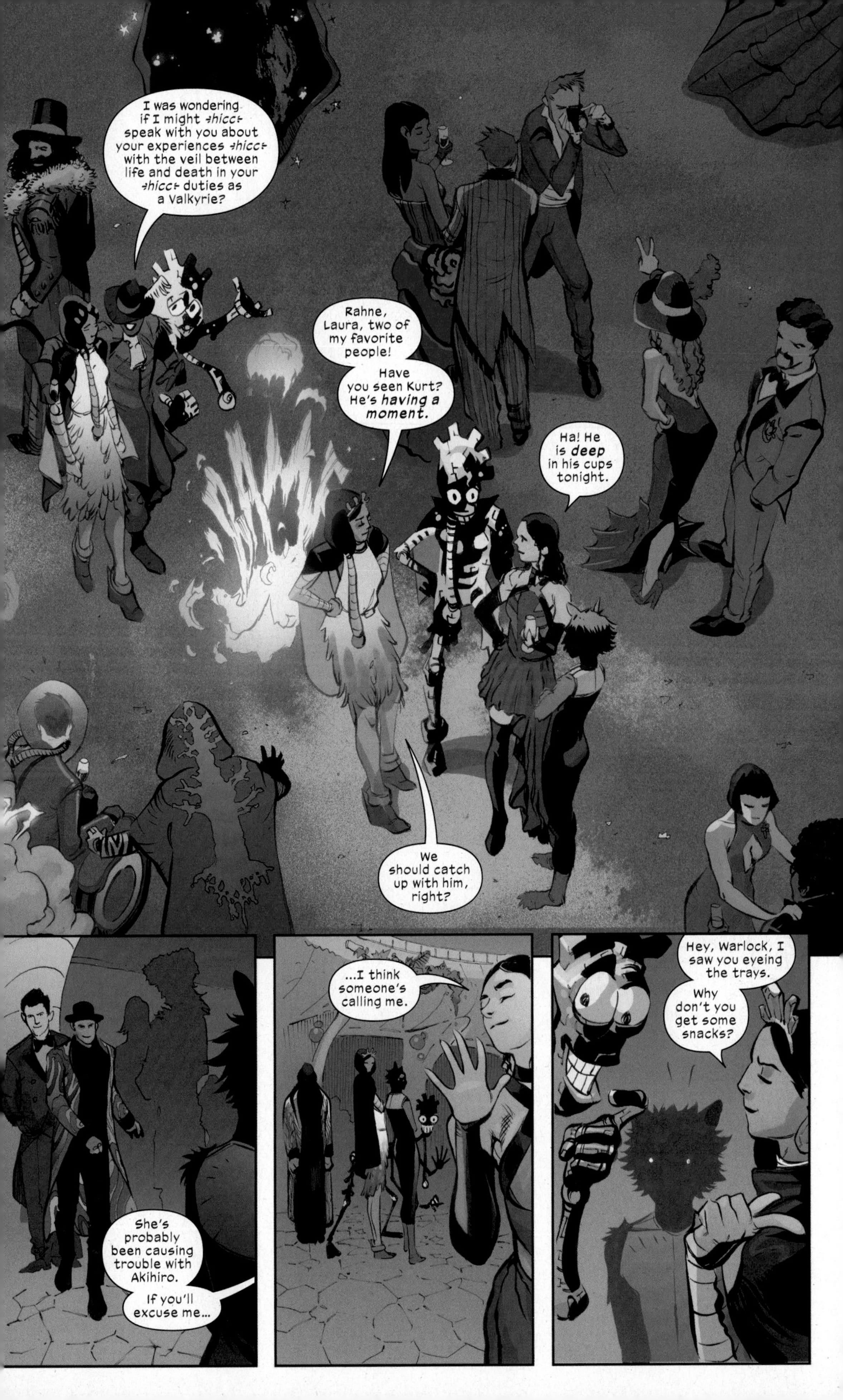

I was wondering if I might -hicc- speak with you about your experiences -hicc- with the veil between life and death in your -hicc- duties as a Valkyrie?
Rahne, Laura, two of my favorite people!
Have you seen Kurt? He's *having a moment.*
Ha! He is *deep* in his cups tonight.
We should catch up with him, right?
She's probably been causing trouble with Akihiro.
If you'll excuse me...
...I think someone's calling me.
Hey, Warlock, I saw you eyeing the trays.
Why don't you get some snacks?

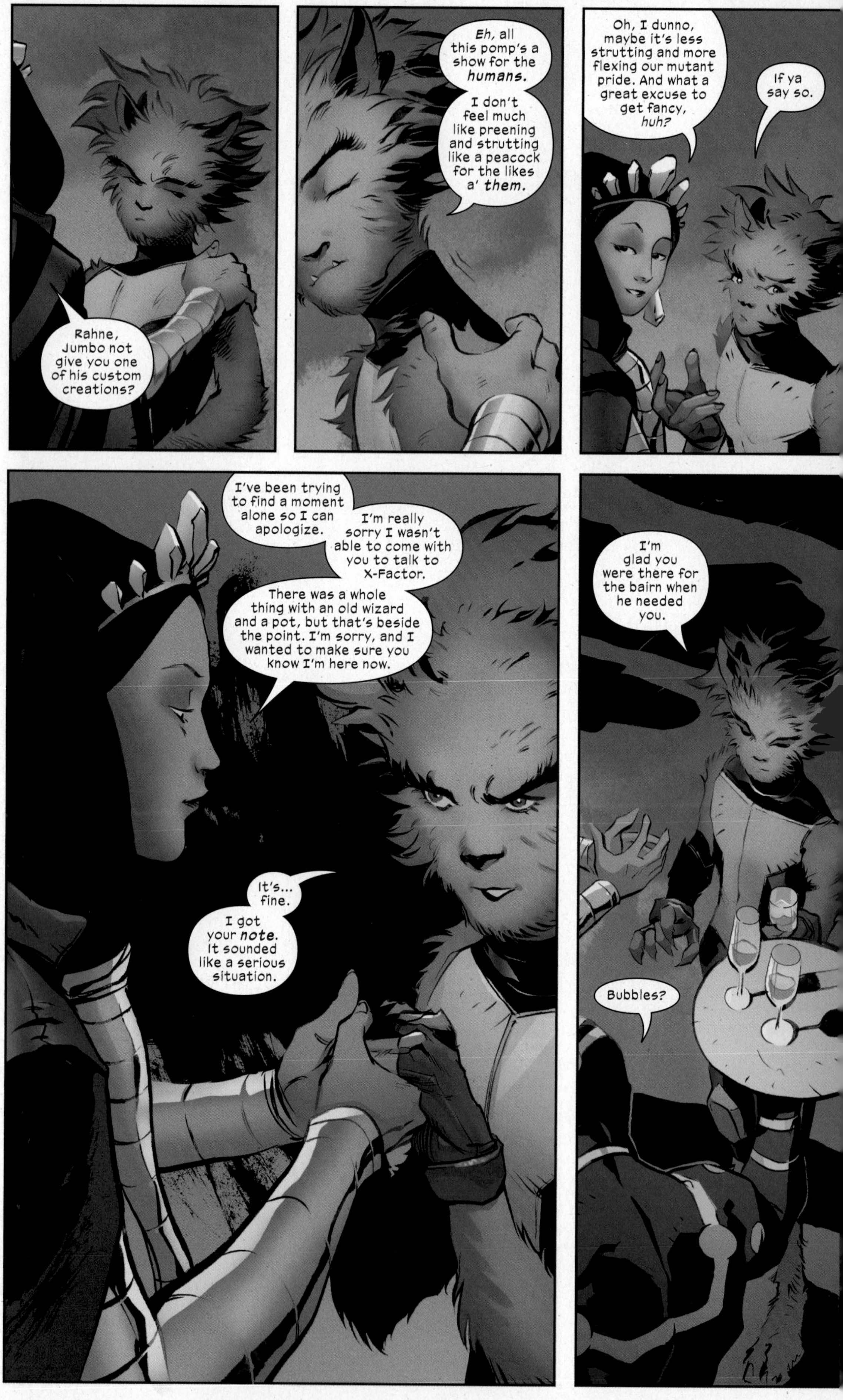
Rahne, Jumbo not give you one of his custom creations?
Eh, all this pomp's a show for the ***humans.***
I don't feel much like preening and strutting like a peacock for the likes a' ***them.***
Oh, I dunno, maybe it's less strutting and more flexing our mutant pride. And what a great excuse to get fancy, *huh?*
If ya say so.
I've been trying to find a moment alone so I can apologize.
I'm really sorry I wasn't able to come with you to talk to X-Factor.
There was a whole thing with an old wizard and a pot, but that's beside the point. I'm sorry, and I wanted to make sure you know I'm here now.
It's... fine.
I got your ***note***. It sounded like a serious situation.
I'm glad you were there for the bairn when he needed you.
Bubbles?

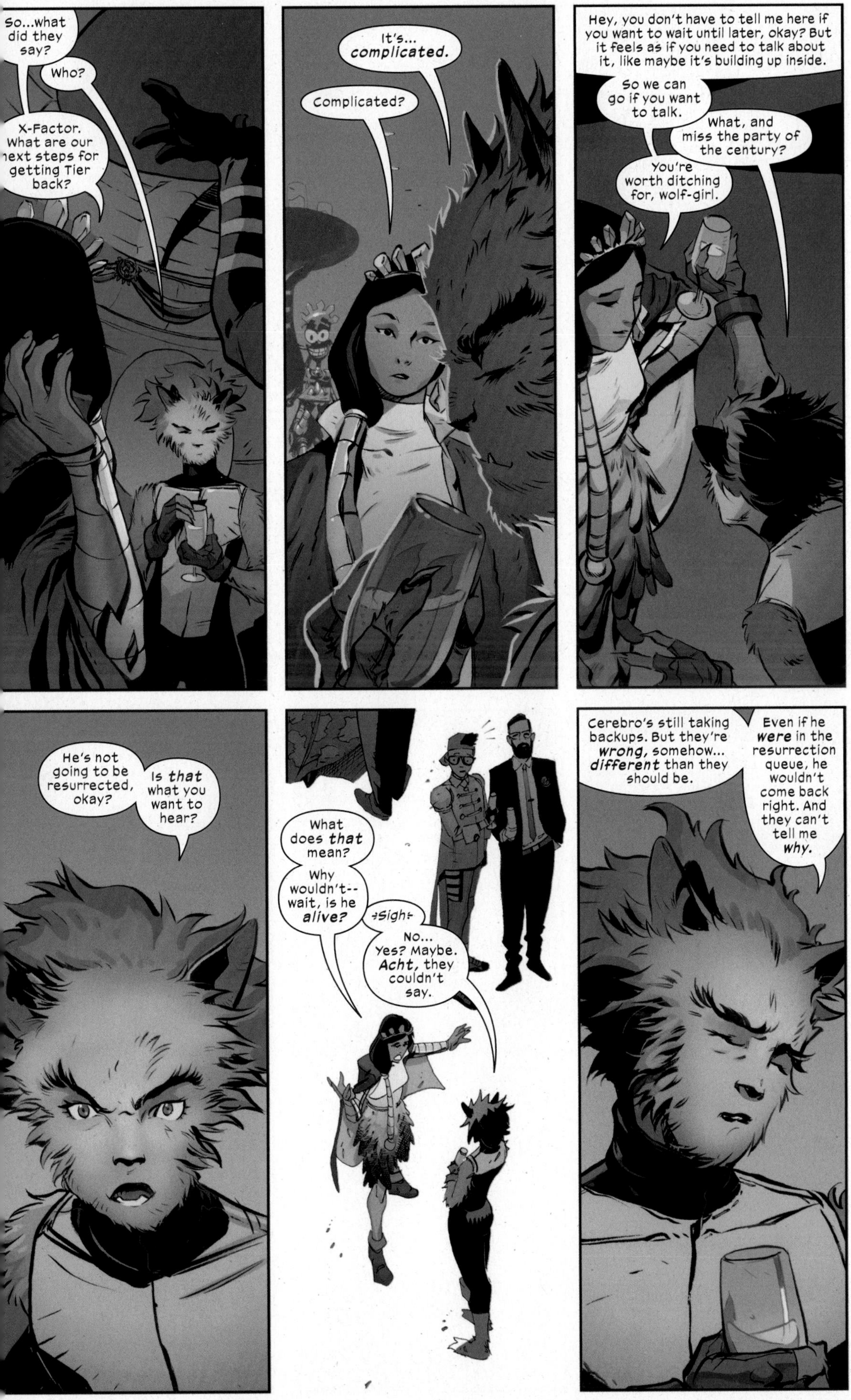
So...what did they say?
Who?
X-Factor. What are our next steps for getting Tier back?
It's... complicated.
Complicated?
Hey, you don't have to tell me here if you want to wait until later, okay? But it feels as if you need to talk about it, like maybe it's building up inside.
So we can go if you want to talk.
What, and miss the party of the century?
You're worth ditching for, wolf-girl.
He's not going to be resurrected, okay?
Is that what you want to hear?
What does that mean?
Why wouldn't-- wait, is he alive?
=Sigh=
No... Yes? Maybe. Acht, they couldn't say.
Cerebro's still taking backups. But they're wrong, somehow... different than they should be.
Even if he were in the resurrection queue, he wouldn't come back right. And they can't tell me why.

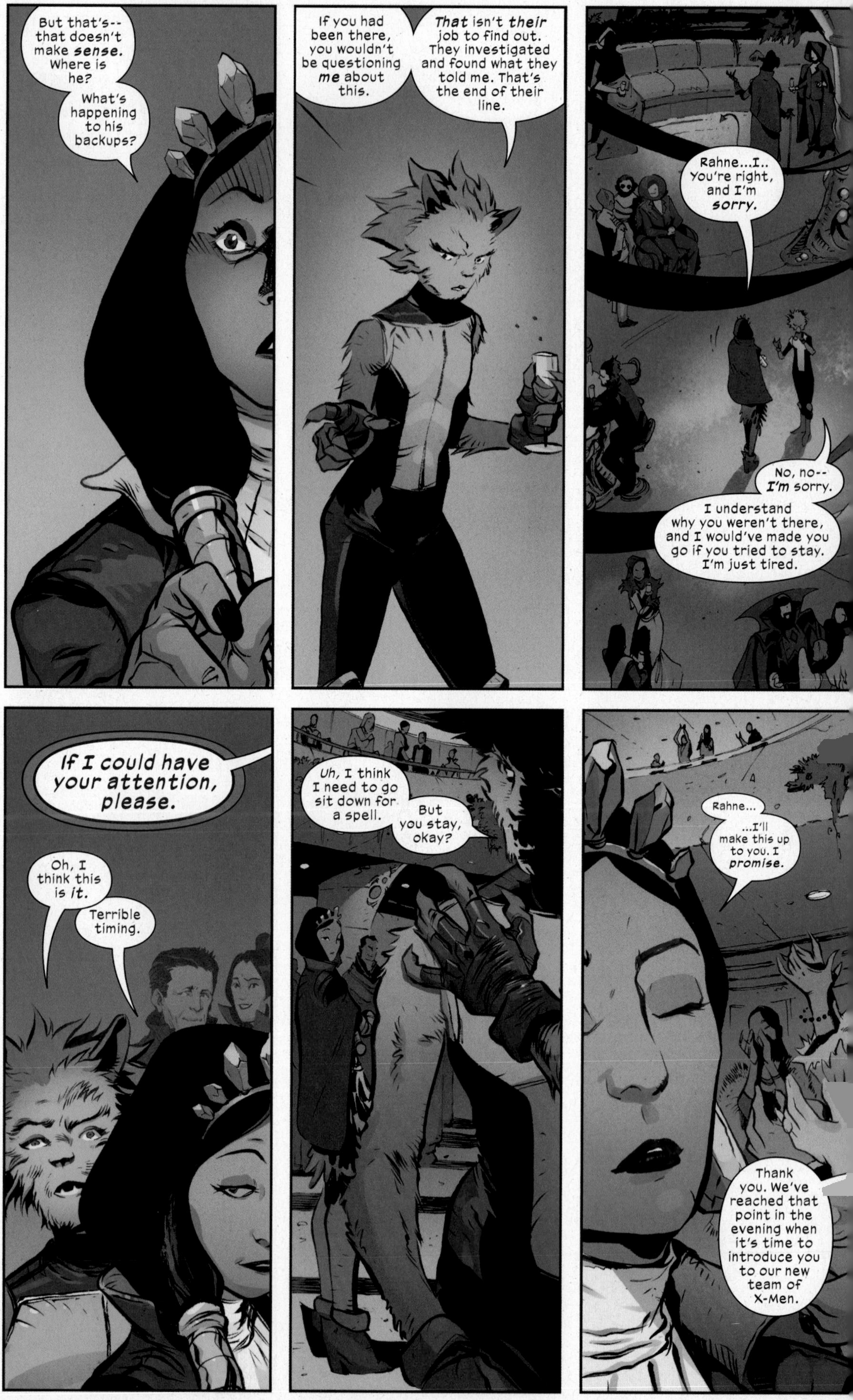
But that's--
that doesn't
make *sense*.
Where is
he?
What's
happening
to his
backups?
If you had
been there,
you wouldn't
be questioning
me about
this.
That isn't *their*
job to find out.
They investigated
and found what they
told me. That's
the end of their
line.
Rahne...I..
You're right,
and I'm
sorry.
No, no--
I'm sorry.
I understand
why you weren't there,
and I would've made you
go if you tried to stay.
I'm just tired.
If I could have
your attention,
please.
Oh, I
think this
is *it*.
Terrible
timing.
Uh, I think
I need to go
sit down for
a spell.
But
you stay,
okay?
Rahne...
...I'll
make this up
to you. I
promise.
Thank
you. We've
reached that
point in the
evening when
it's time to
introduce you
to our new
team of
X-Men.

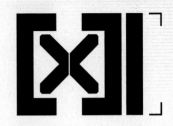

NEW MUTANTS FOREVER [GROUP CHAT]

// 8 Members
// Moonstar, Rahne, Sammonball, Berto, Karma, Magik, Dougie, Amara

KARMA: I still can't believe I missed the announcement!

BERTO: This was a *farce,* I demand a recount!!!

SAMMONBALL: Hey now, Roberto, at least this means you don't have to move back to Earth, right?

SAMMONBALL: Also, who changed my name to "Sammonball"??? That don't make any sense

MAGIK: ☺

DOUGIE: I think we should be happy for who won, it's a great team!

BERTO: I bet you voted for Sunfire, didn't you?

DOUGIE: 😬

BERTO: YOU DID, DIDN'T YOU?! BETRAYER!

BERTO: I'M THE BEST SUN-THEMED CANDIDATE!

MOONSTAR: Roberto, what did we say about all caps in the group chat?

MAGIK: 5 to 1 odds that Sunfire quits the first day anyway 😏

RAHNE: Don't be rude, Illyana

MAGIK: 🗡️ ☕

KARMA: If it helps, I heard Cyclops assuring Boom-Boom that there would be regular elections.

BERTO: >ahem< Well, that's good. It will give me time to find the perfect campaign manager

SAMMONBALL: 😀

BERTO: Amara, your upbringing included extensive training in oration and political dynamics, yes?

SAMMONBALL: 😐

BERTO: So, who *did* everyone vote for? 😶

BERTO: I'll start, I voted for myself, naturally

MAGIK: Marrow

MOONSTAR: Synch

RAHNE: Polaris

KARMA: Penance 😀

SAMMONBALL: Roberto

DOUGIE: Tempo! 😀

AMARA: ...Sunfire...

BERTO: I take back my offer to Amara, Sam is clearly the right choice to lead my campaign.

BERTO: Also know that I have noted how little faith you all have in me (except you Sam)

BERTO: You are all uninvited from my victory party!

KARMA: How can you have a victory party when you *lost.*

BERTO: ...

BERTO: ...

BERTO has left the chat

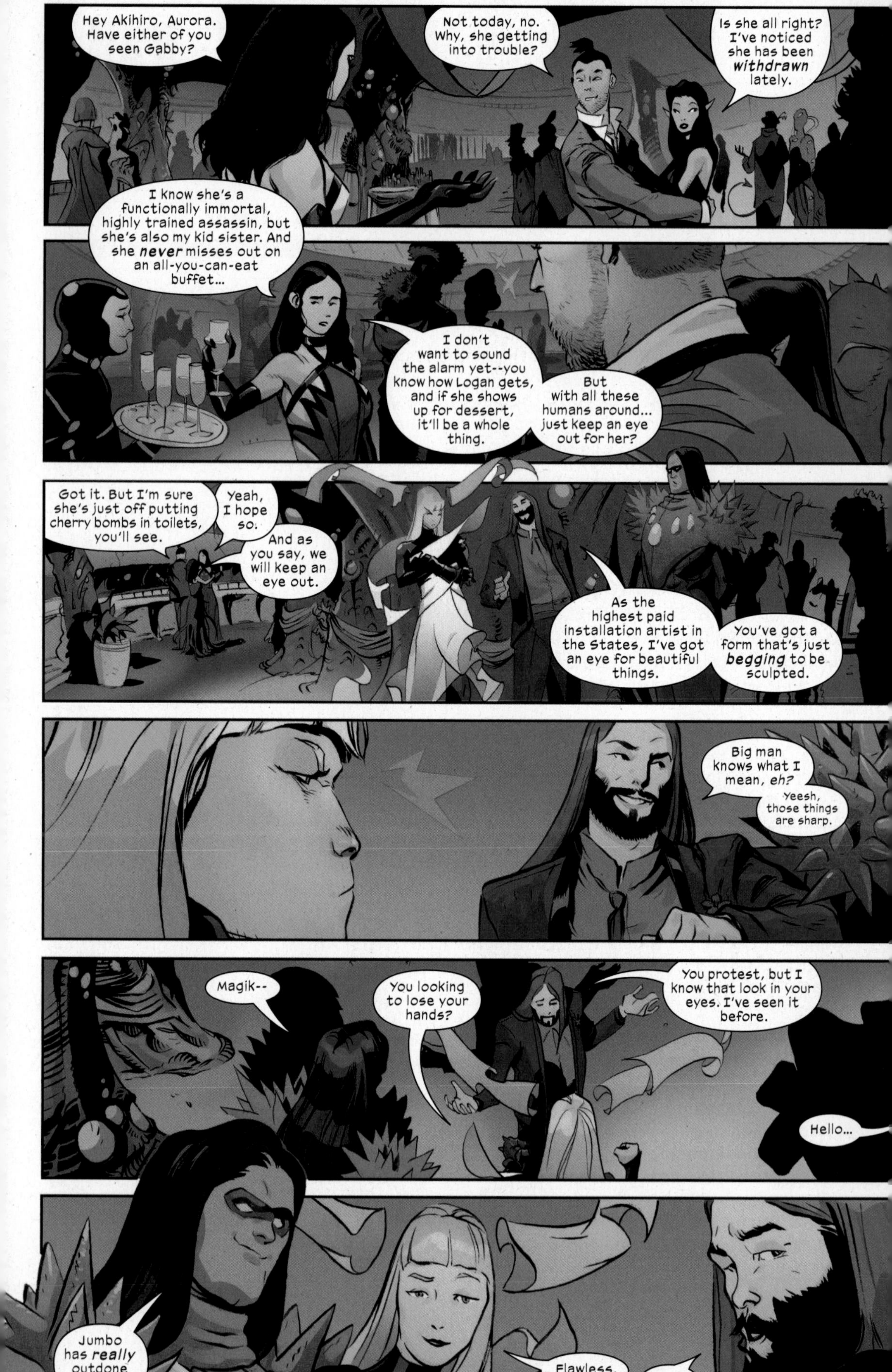
Hey Akihiro, Aurora. Have either of you seen Gabby?
Not today, no. Why, she getting into trouble?
Is she all right? I've noticed she has been ***withdrawn*** lately.
I know she's a functionally immortal, highly trained assassin, but she's also my kid sister. And she ***never*** misses out on an all-you-can-eat buffet...
I don't want to sound the alarm yet--you know how Logan gets, and if she shows up for dessert, it'll be a whole thing.
But with all these humans around... just keep an eye out for her?
Got it. But I'm sure she's just off putting cherry bombs in toilets, you'll see.
Yeah, I hope so.
And as you say, we will keep an eye out.
As the highest paid installation artist in the States, I've got an eye for beautiful things.
You've got a form that's just ***begging*** to be sculpted.
Big man knows what I mean, *eh?*
Yeesh, those things are sharp.
Magik--
You looking to lose your hands?
You protest, but I know that look in your eyes. I've seen it before.
Hello...
Jumbo has ***really*** outdone himself.
Flawless.
Gah!

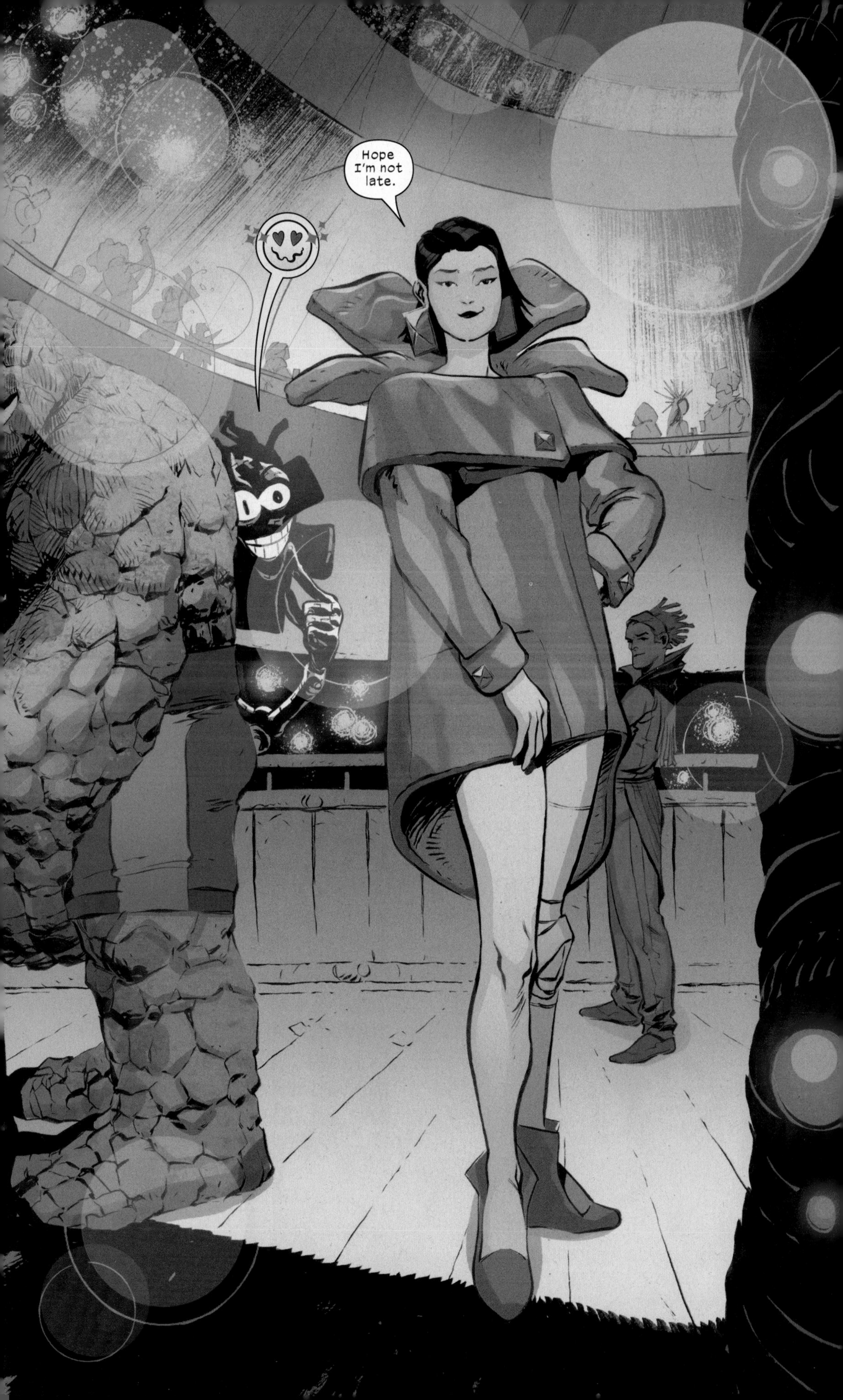
Hope I'm not late.

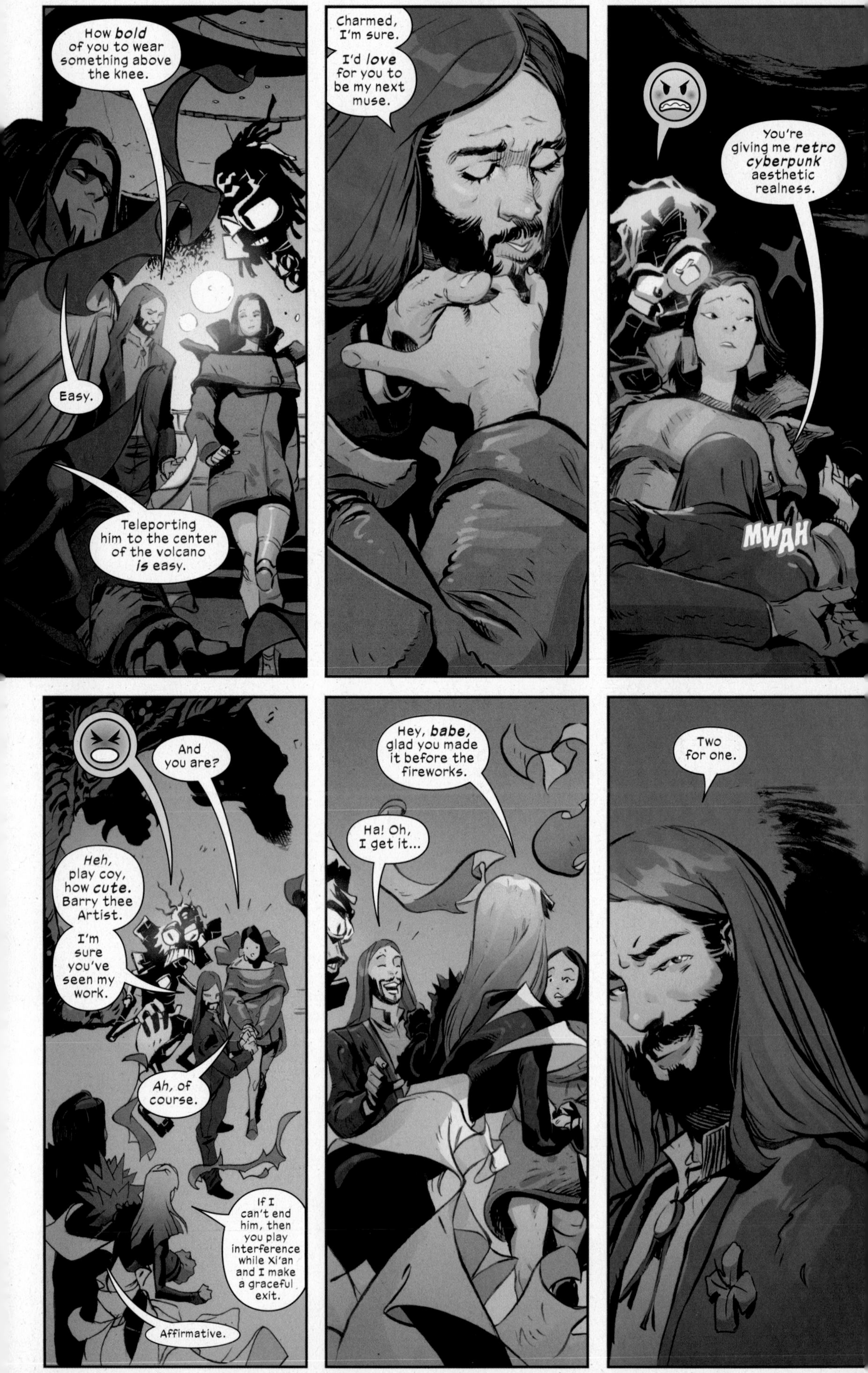
How *bold* of you to wear something above the knee.
Easy.
Teleporting him to the center of the volcano *is* easy.
Charmed, I'm sure.
I'd *love* for you to be my next muse.
You're giving me *retro cyberpunk* aesthetic realness.
MWAH
And you are?
Heh, play coy, how *cute.* Barry thee Artist.
I'm sure you've seen my work.
Ah, of course.
If I can't end him, then you play interference while Xi'an and I make a graceful exit.
Affirmative.
Hey, *babe,* glad you made it before the fireworks.
Ha! Oh, I get it...
Two for one.

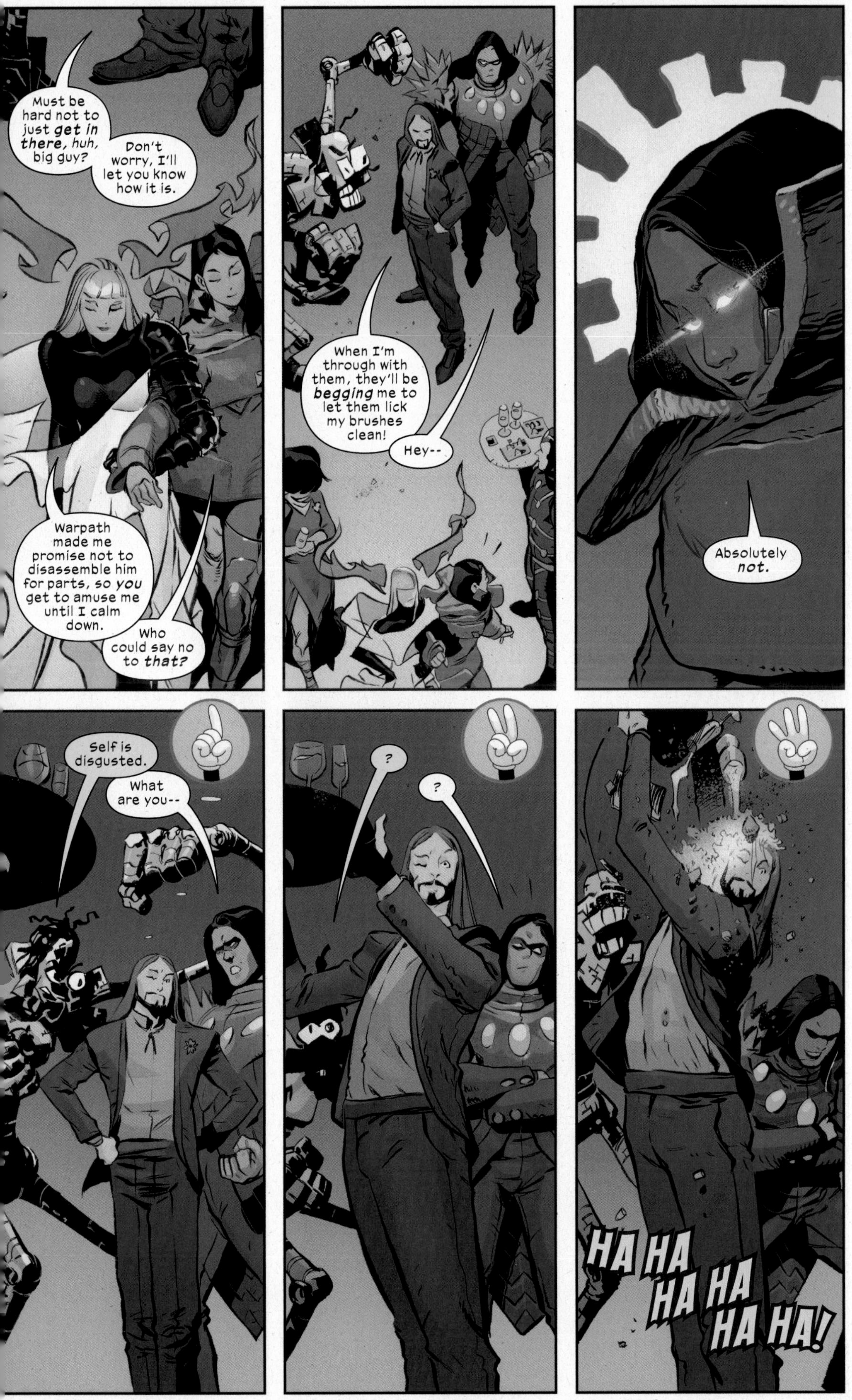

Must be hard not to just *get in there,* huh, big guy?
Don't worry, I'll let you know how it is.
Warpath made me promise not to disassemble him for parts, so *you* get to amuse me until I calm down.
Who could say no to *that?*
When I'm through with them, they'll be *begging* me to let them lick my brushes clean!
Hey--
Absolutely *not.*
Self is disgusted.
What are you--
?
?
HA HA HA HA HA HA!

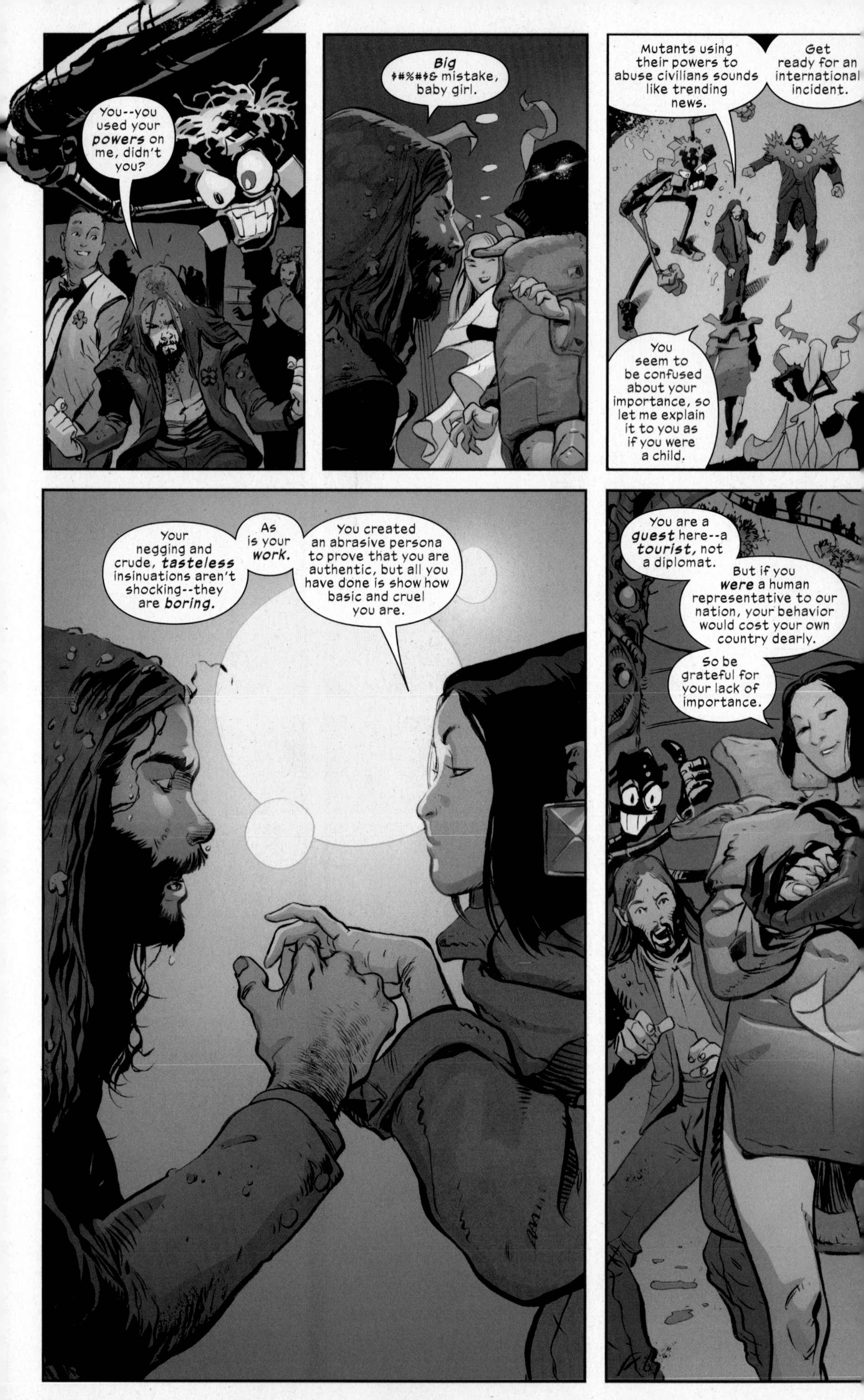
You--you used your *powers* on me, didn't you?
Big $#%#$& mistake, baby girl.
Mutants using their powers to abuse civilians sounds like trending news.
Get ready for an international incident.
You seem to be confused about your importance, so let me explain it to you as if you were a child.
Your negging and crude, *tasteless* insinuations aren't shocking--they are *boring.*
As is your *work.*
You created an abrasive persona to prove that you are authentic, but all you have done is show how basic and cruel you are.
You are a *guest* here--a *tourist,* not a diplomat.
But if you *were* a human representative to our nation, your behavior would cost your own country dearly.
So be grateful for your lack of importance.

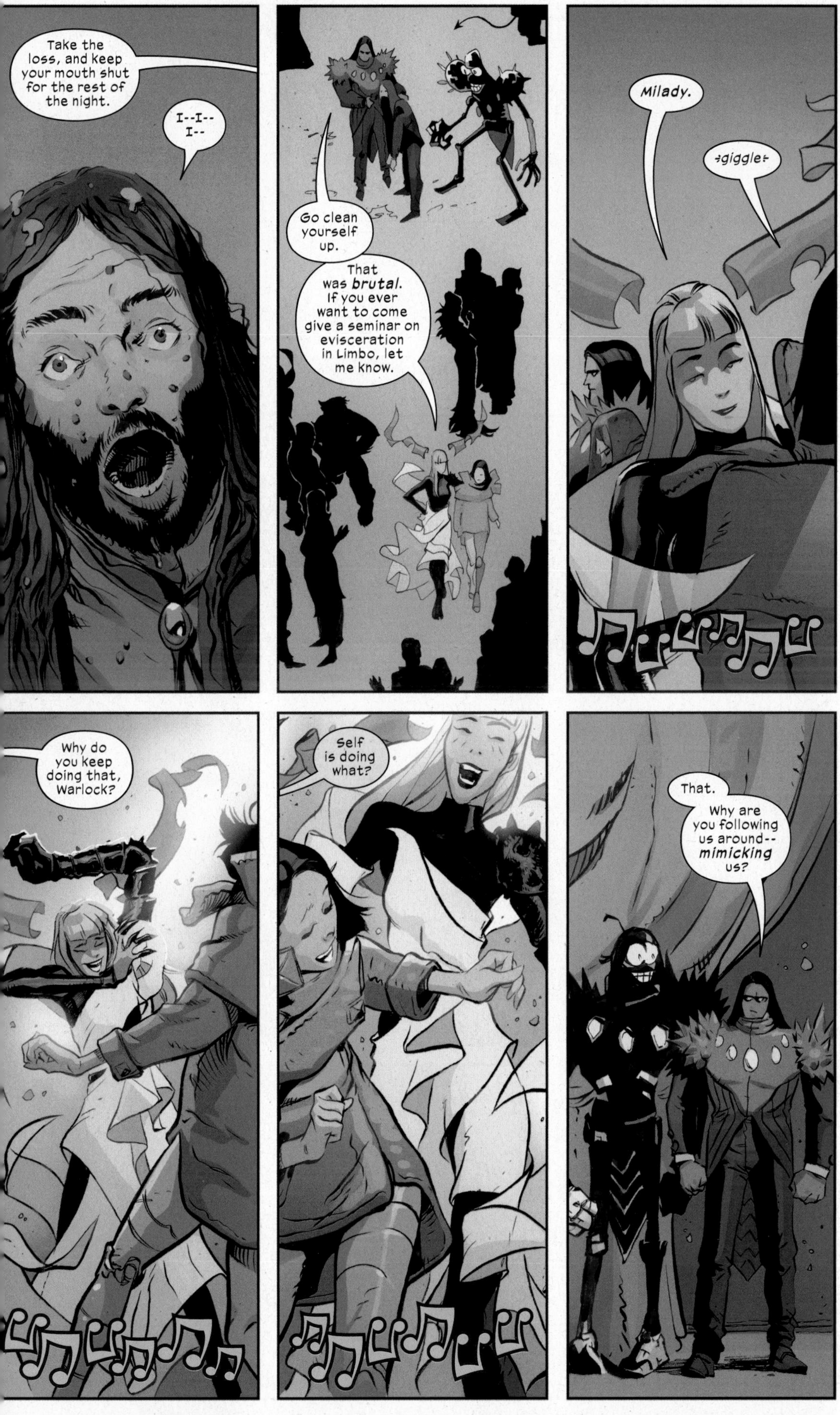
Take the loss, and keep your mouth shut for the rest of the night.
I--I-- I--
Go clean yourself up.
That was *brutal*. If you ever want to come give a seminar on evisceration in Limbo, let me know.
Milady.
giggle
Why do you keep doing that, Warlock?
Self is doing what?
That.
Why are you following us around-- *mimicking* us?

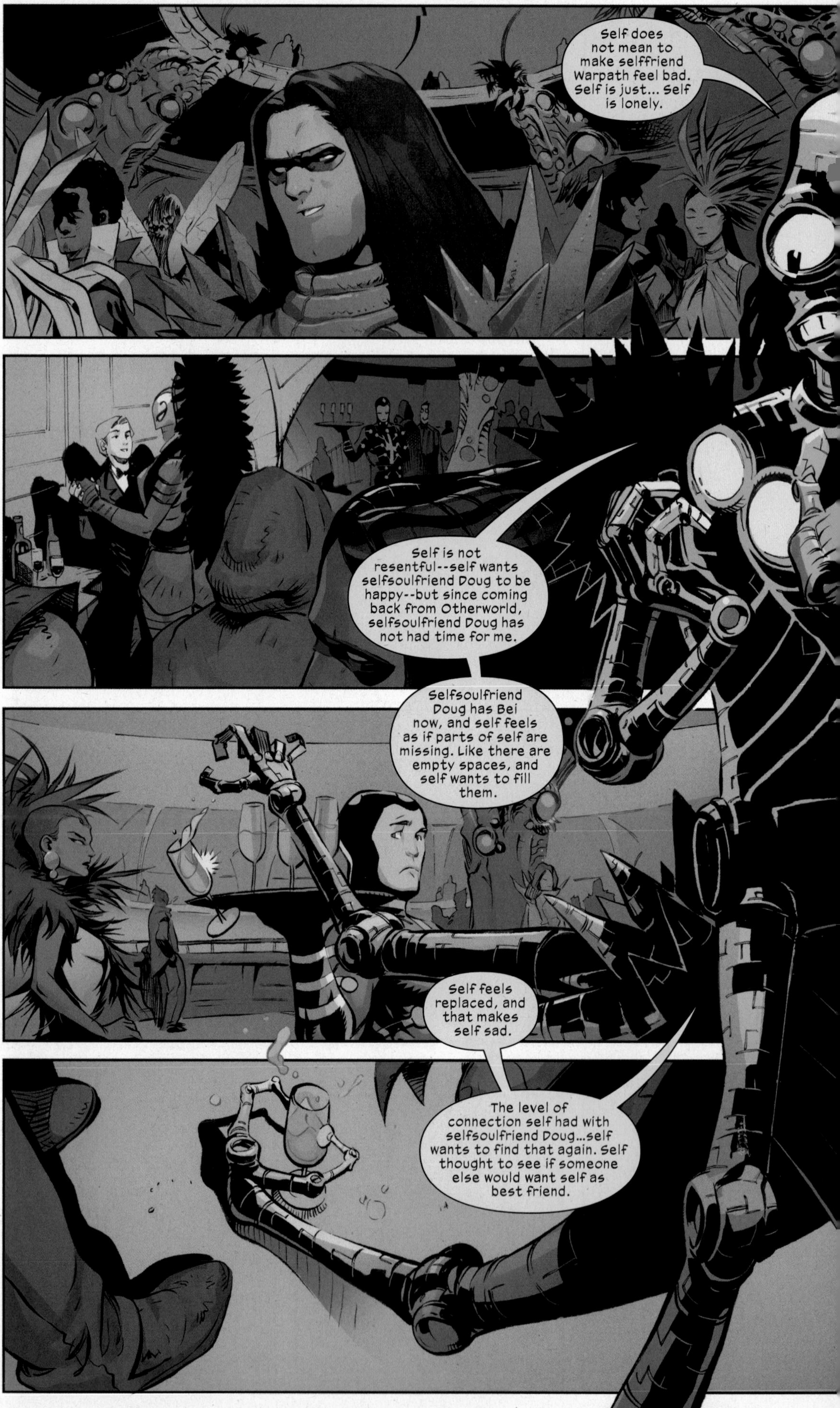

Self does not mean to make selffriend Warpath feel bad. Self is just... Self is lonely.
Self is not resentful--self wants selfsoulfriend Doug to be happy--but since coming back from Otherworld, selfsoulfriend Doug has not had time for me.
Selfsoulfriend Doug has Bei now, and self feels as if parts of self are missing. Like there are empty spaces, and self wants to fill them.
Self feels replaced, and that makes self sad.
The level of connection self had with selfsoulfriend Doug...self wants to find that again. Self thought to see if someone else would want self as best friend.

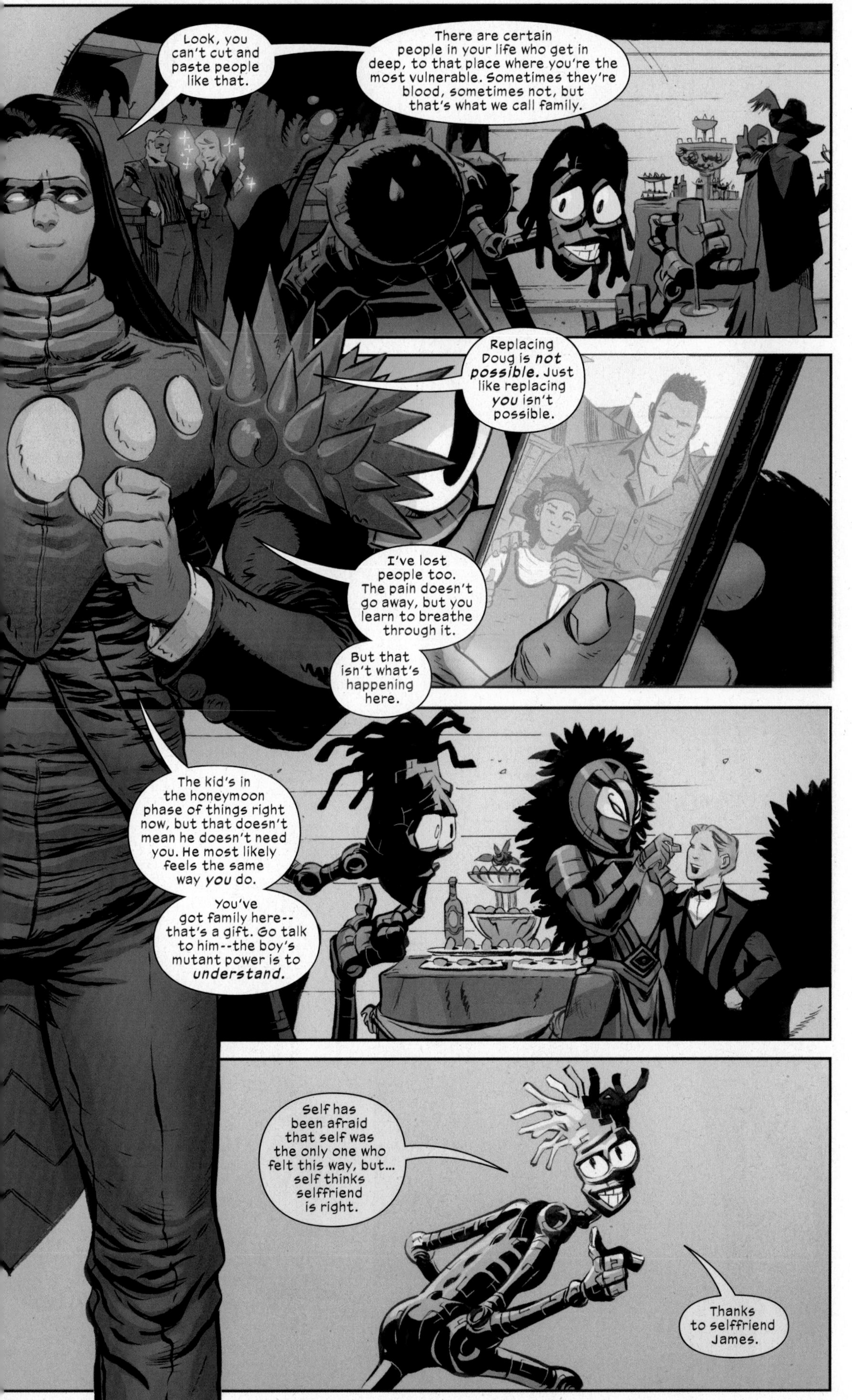
Look, you can't cut and paste people like that.
There are certain people in your life who get in deep, to that place where you're the most vulnerable. Sometimes they're blood, sometimes not, but that's what we call family.
Replacing Doug is *not possible.* Just like replacing *you* isn't possible.
I've lost people too. The pain doesn't go away, but you learn to breathe through it.
But that isn't what's happening here.
The kid's in the honeymoon phase of things right now, but that doesn't mean he doesn't need you. He most likely feels the same way *you* do.
You've got family here--that's a gift. Go talk to him--the boy's mutant power is to *understand.*
Self has been afraid that self was the only one who felt this way, but... self thinks selffriend is right.
Thanks to selffriend James.

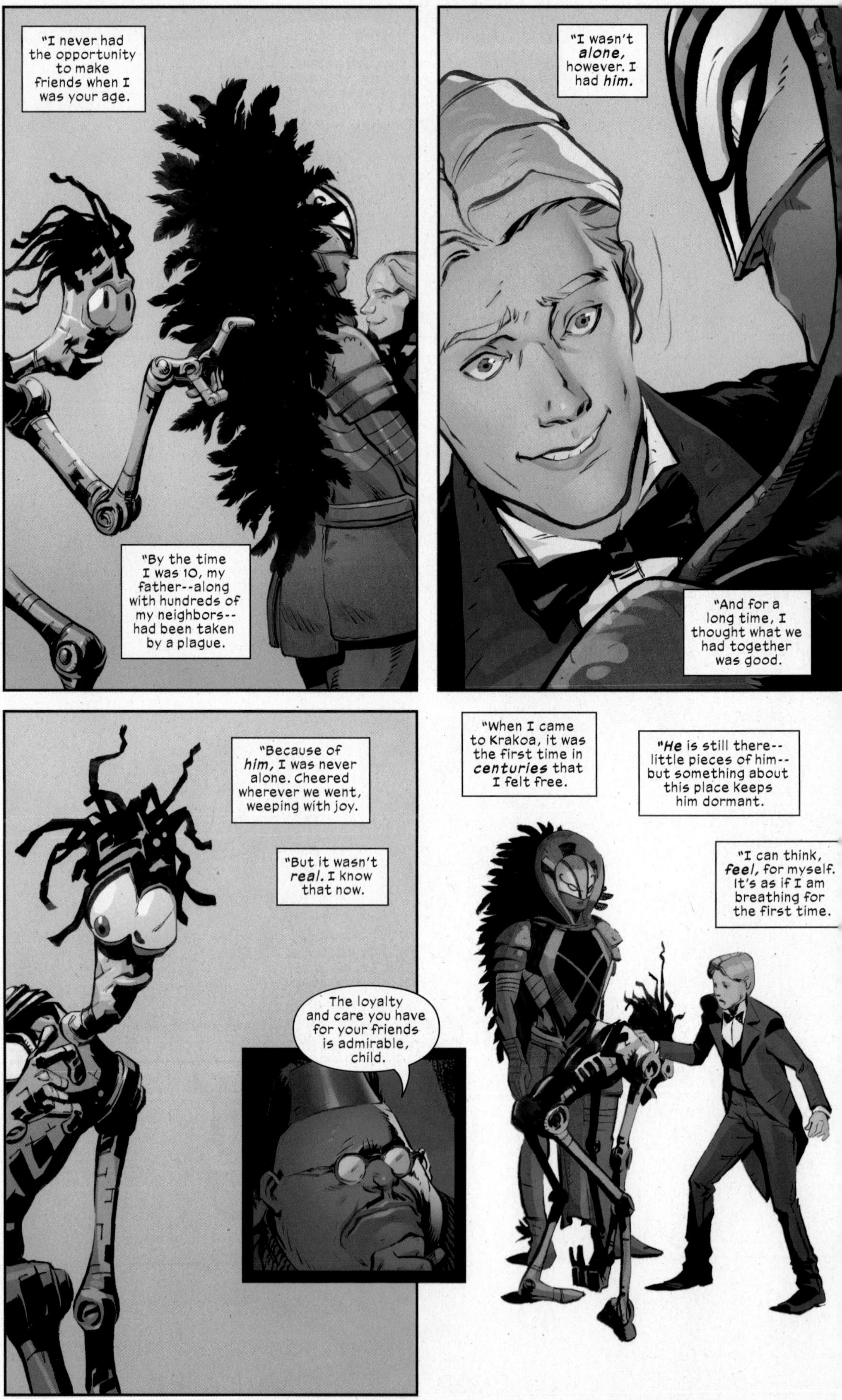
"I never had the opportunity to make friends when I was your age.
"By the time I was 10, my father--along with hundreds of my neighbors--had been taken by a plague.
"I wasn't *alone,* however. I had *him.*
"And for a long time, I thought what we had together was good.
"Because of *him,* I was never alone. Cheered wherever we went, weeping with joy.
"But it wasn't *real.* I know that now.
The loyalty and care you have for your friends is admirable, child.
"When I came to Krakoa, it was the first time in *centuries* that I felt free.
"*He* is still there--little pieces of him--but something about this place keeps him dormant.
"I can think, *feel,* for myself. It's as if I am breathing for the first time.

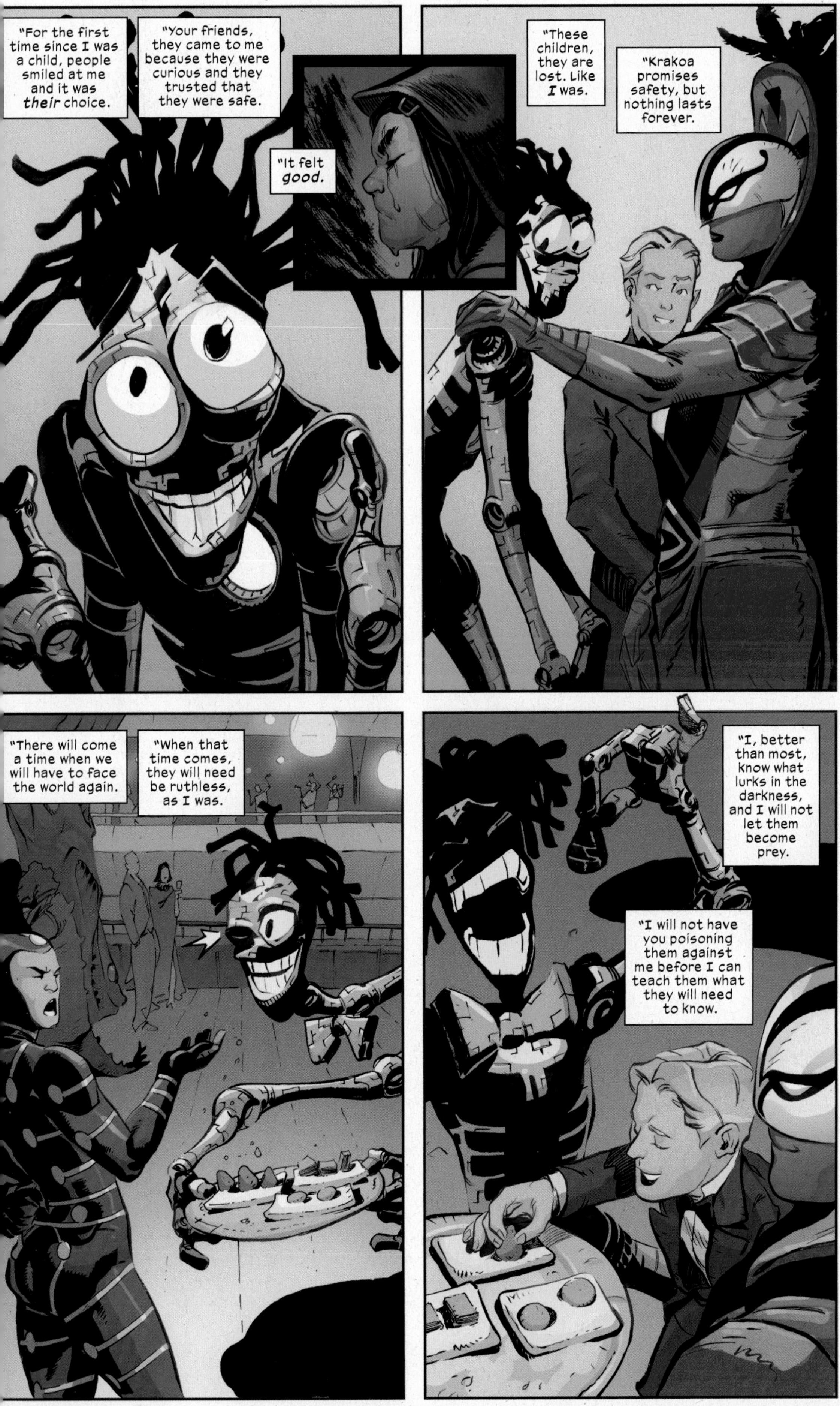
"For the first time since I was a child, people smiled at me and it was *their* choice.
"Your friends, they came to me because they were curious and they trusted that they were safe.
"It felt *good.*
"These children, they are lost. Like *I* was.
"Krakoa promises safety, but nothing lasts forever.
"There will come a time when we will have to face the world again.
"When that time comes, they will need be ruthless, as I was.
"I, better than most, know what lurks in the darkness, and I will not let them become prey.
"I will not have you poisoning them against me before I can teach them what they will need to know.

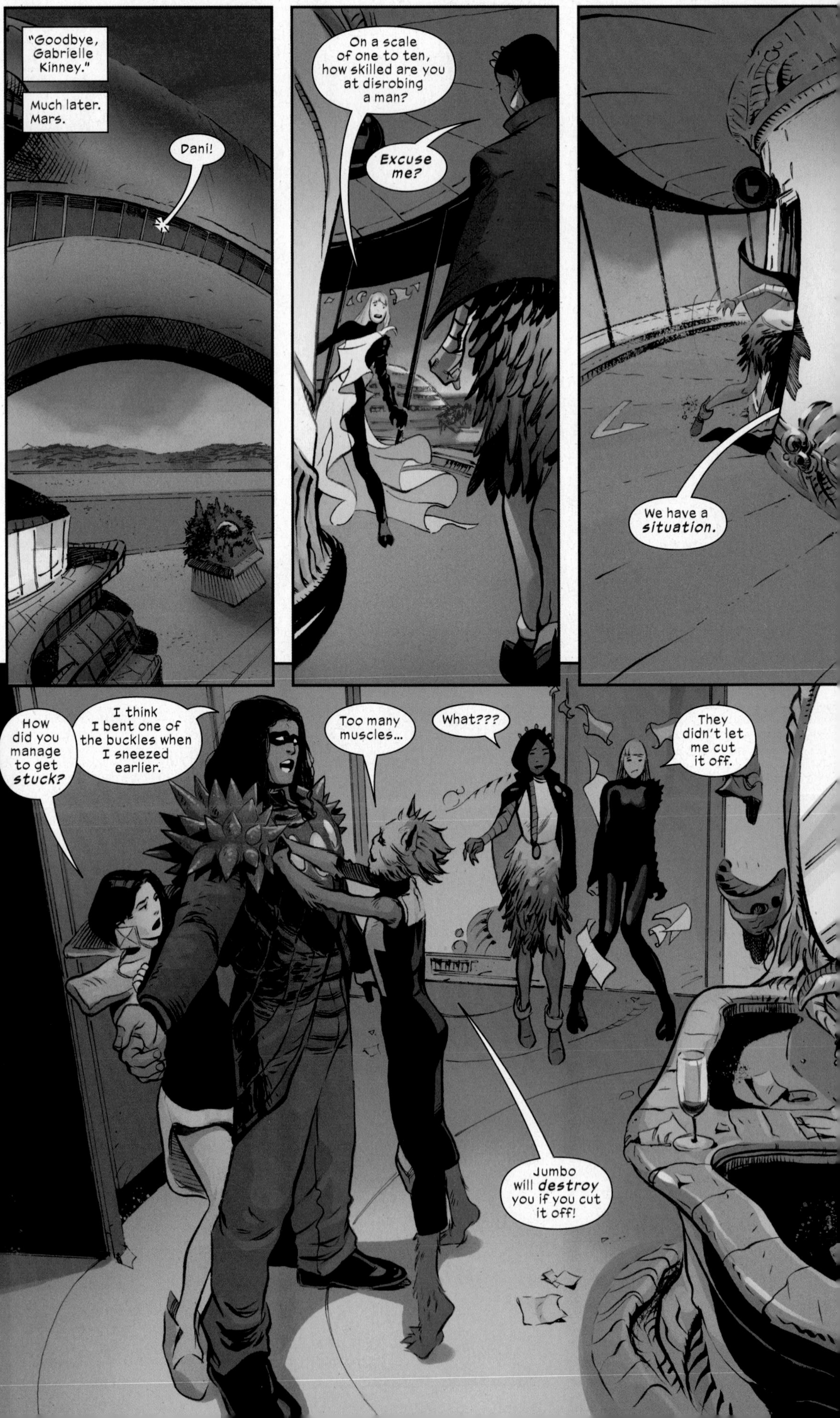
"Goodbye, Gabrielle Kinney."
Much later. Mars.
Dani!
On a scale of one to ten, how skilled are you at disrobing a man?
Excuse me?
We have a situation.
How did you manage to get stuck?
I think I bent one of the buckles when I sneezed earlier.
Too many muscles...
What???
They didn't let me cut it off.
Jumbo will destroy you if you cut it off!

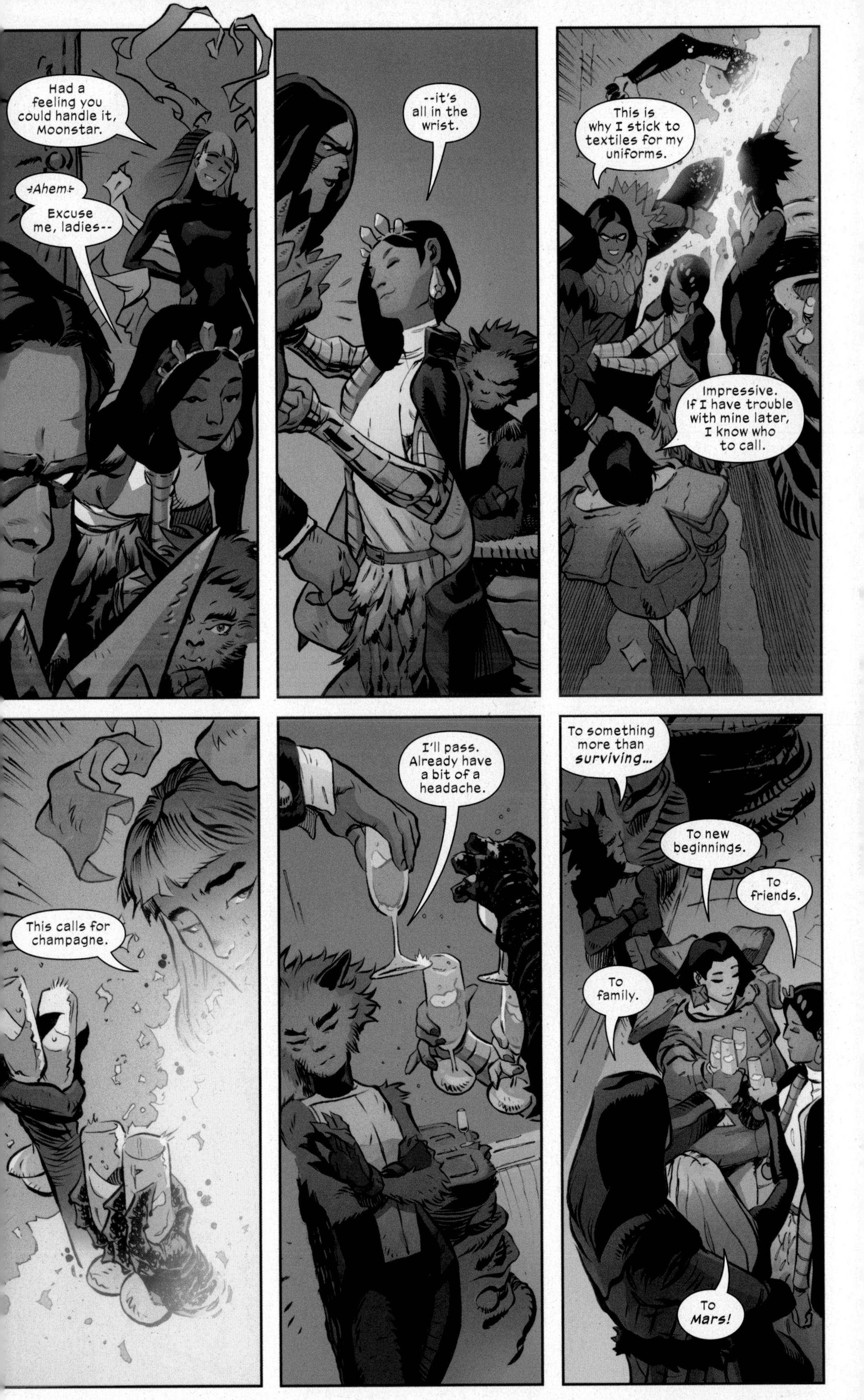

Had a feeling you could handle it, Moonstar.
=Ahem=
Excuse me, ladies--
--it's all in the wrist.
This is why I stick to textiles for my uniforms.
Impressive. If I have trouble with mine later, I know who to call.
This calls for champagne.
I'll pass. Already have a bit of a headache.
To something more than *surviving...*
To new beginnings.
To friends.
To family.
To *Mars!*

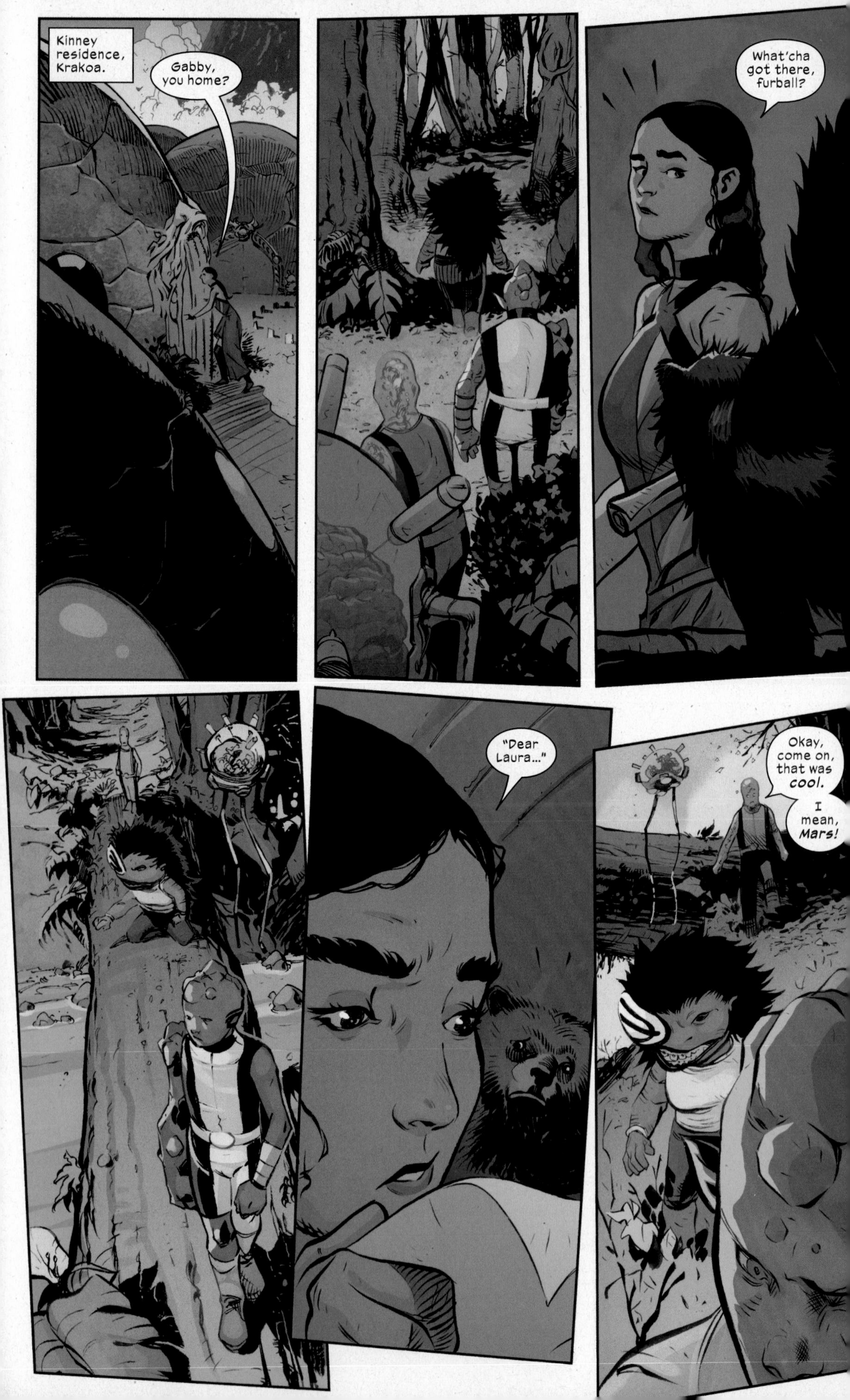
Kinney residence, Krakoa.
Gabby, you home?
What'cha got there, furball?
"Dear Laura..."
Okay, come on, that was cool.
I mean, Mars!

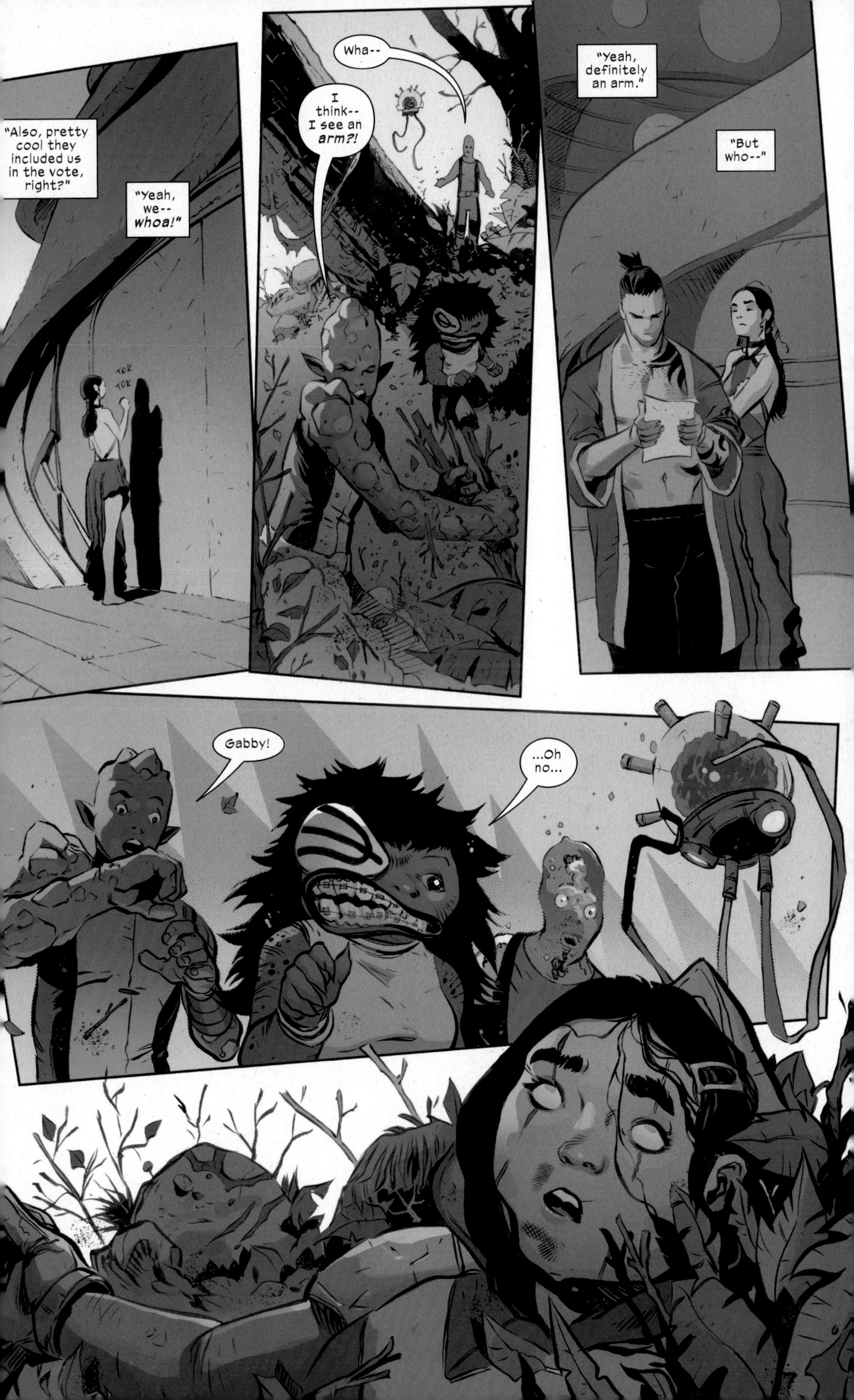
"Also, pretty cool they included us in the vote, right?"
"Yeah, we-- whoa!"
TOK TOK
Wha--
I think-- I see an arm?!
"Yeah, definitely an arm."
"But who--"
Gabby!
...Oh no...

DEAR LAURA

Dear Laura,

So I wanted to talk to you about this, but I feel like there is this gap between us right now, and I don't know how to cross it. Which I hate. It's NEVER been like that for us. I think we've both been feeling weird since you got back. Or maybe I feel weird that you don't feel weird? You don't remember being gone, but a lot of stuff happened when you were, and I don't really know how to talk about it yet... Yeah, I guess it's me. Sorry.

I hope writing all this out makes it easier to talk to you later.

Living on Krakoa is weird in ways that I don't really get. The rules are always shifting (except the Big Three, I guess), and it feels like if you don't already know what you should be doing, who you are here, then you're out of luck. I hate that. I don't want to go back to what my life was before I met you, but I miss knowing who I was and what I was expected to do.

It feels like I'm not really supposed to be here?

BUT, I made more friends while you were away, so I'm trying! And I really like them -- they're kinda lost too, but they aren't as stressed out about it, which makes me less stressed.

Except, now there is this thing that's kind of making it hard to connect with them. They're spending time with someone who makes me feel bad -- reminds me of the people who made me. Nothing, like, against "The Rules" has happened yet, and I know Krakoa is all about "second chances" (which, as a former assassin, uh, I appreciate) but this feels different -- wrong.

I've tried to stay out of it, but I really care about my friends. So I'm going to try and convince them one last time to stop whatever is happening. I can't make them, but I want to tell what I went through (we went through), what it's like to be used. Then maybe they'll see?

Either way, I'm hoping you read this before the gala and we can be less weird. I want to party with my sister. Jumbo even made me a cool outfit -- it has a hood!!! He said he gave us a similar pattern so we looked like we belonged to together, which made me happy.

I want to belong with you. You're my sister. You make me feel like a real person who matters. I missed you.

Let's eat all the fancy food together and take lots of pictures.

Love,
Gabby <3

[reign_of_x]

[kra_]
[koa_]

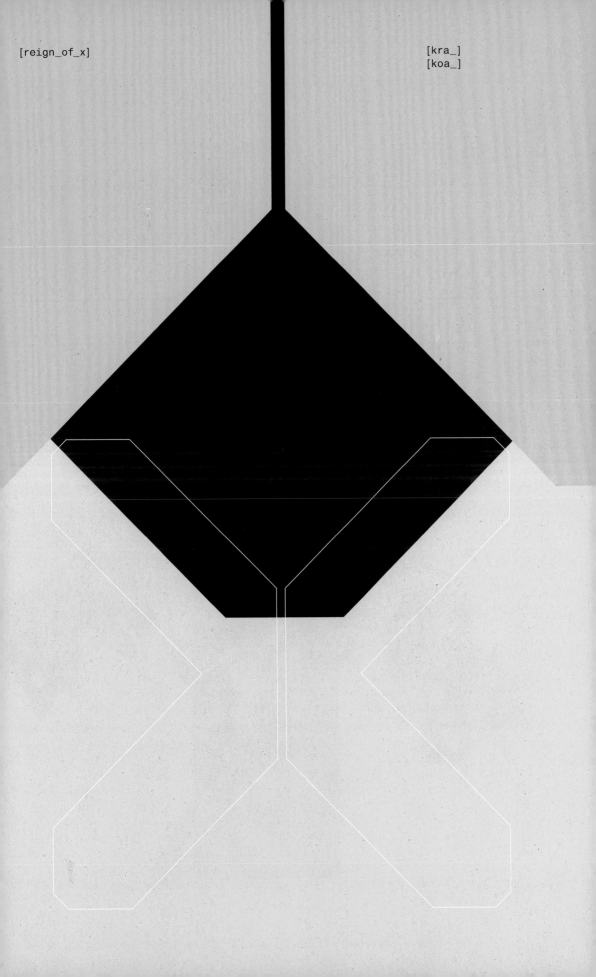

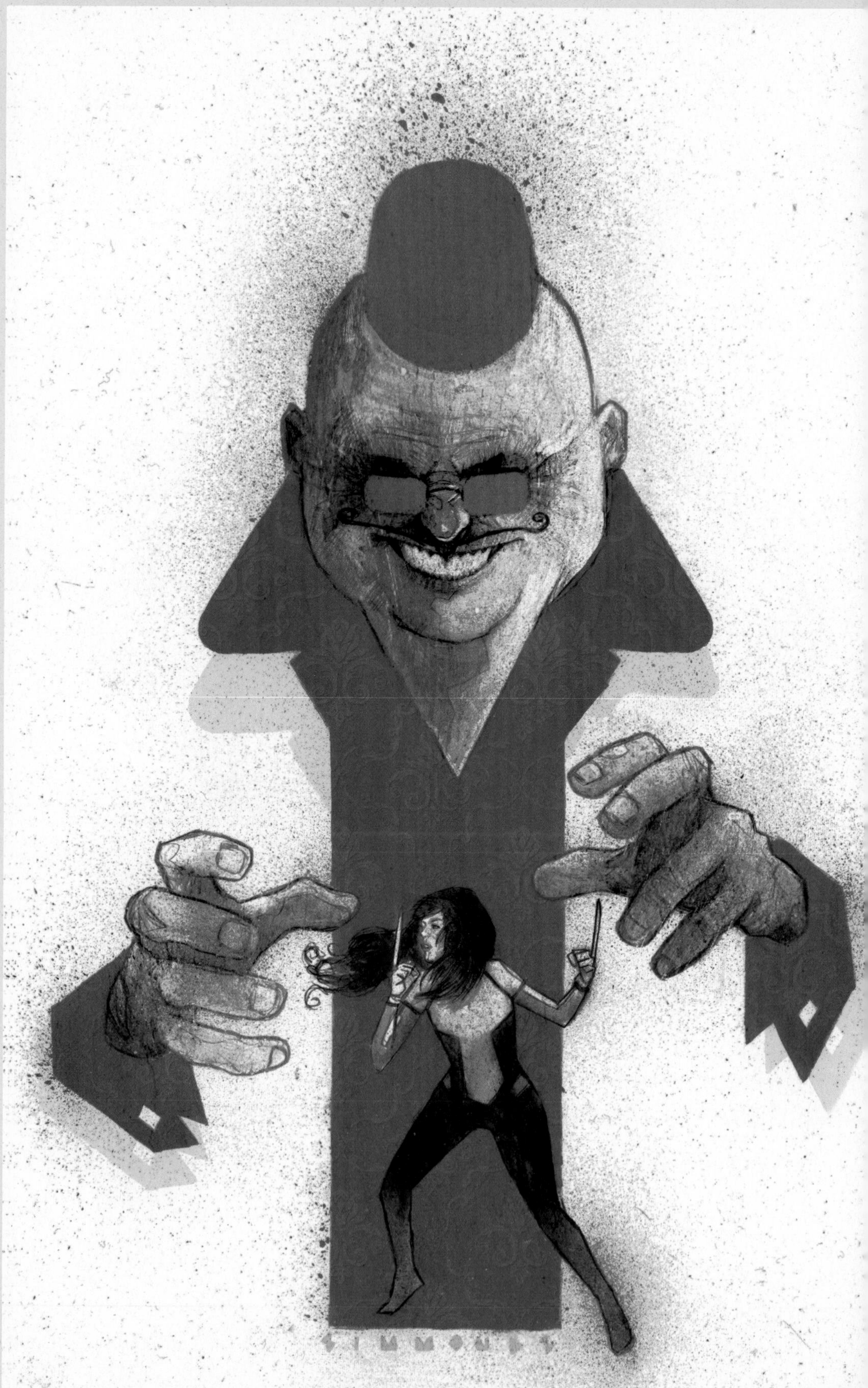

Secrets and Lies

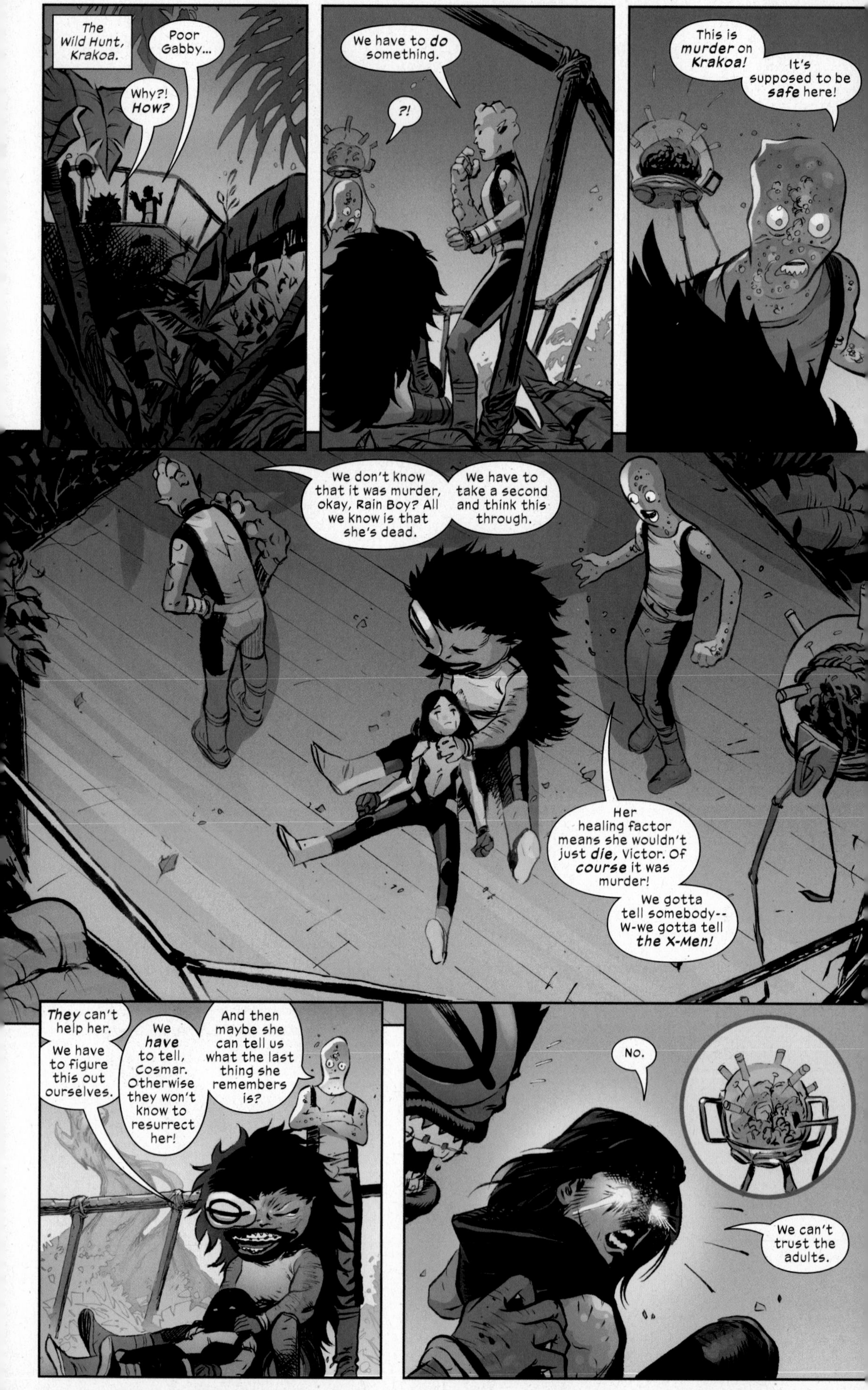
The Wild Hunt, Krakoa.
Poor Gabby...
Why?! HOW?
We have to do something.
?!
This is murder on Krakoa!
It's supposed to be safe here!
We don't know that it was murder, okay, Rain Boy? All we know is that she's dead.
We have to take a second and think this through.
Her healing factor means she wouldn't just die, Victor. Of course it was murder!
We gotta tell somebody-- W-we gotta tell the X-Men!
They can't help her.
We have to figure this out ourselves.
We have to tell, Cosmar. Otherwise they won't know to resurrect her!
And then maybe she can tell us what the last thing she remembers is?
No.
We can't trust the adults.

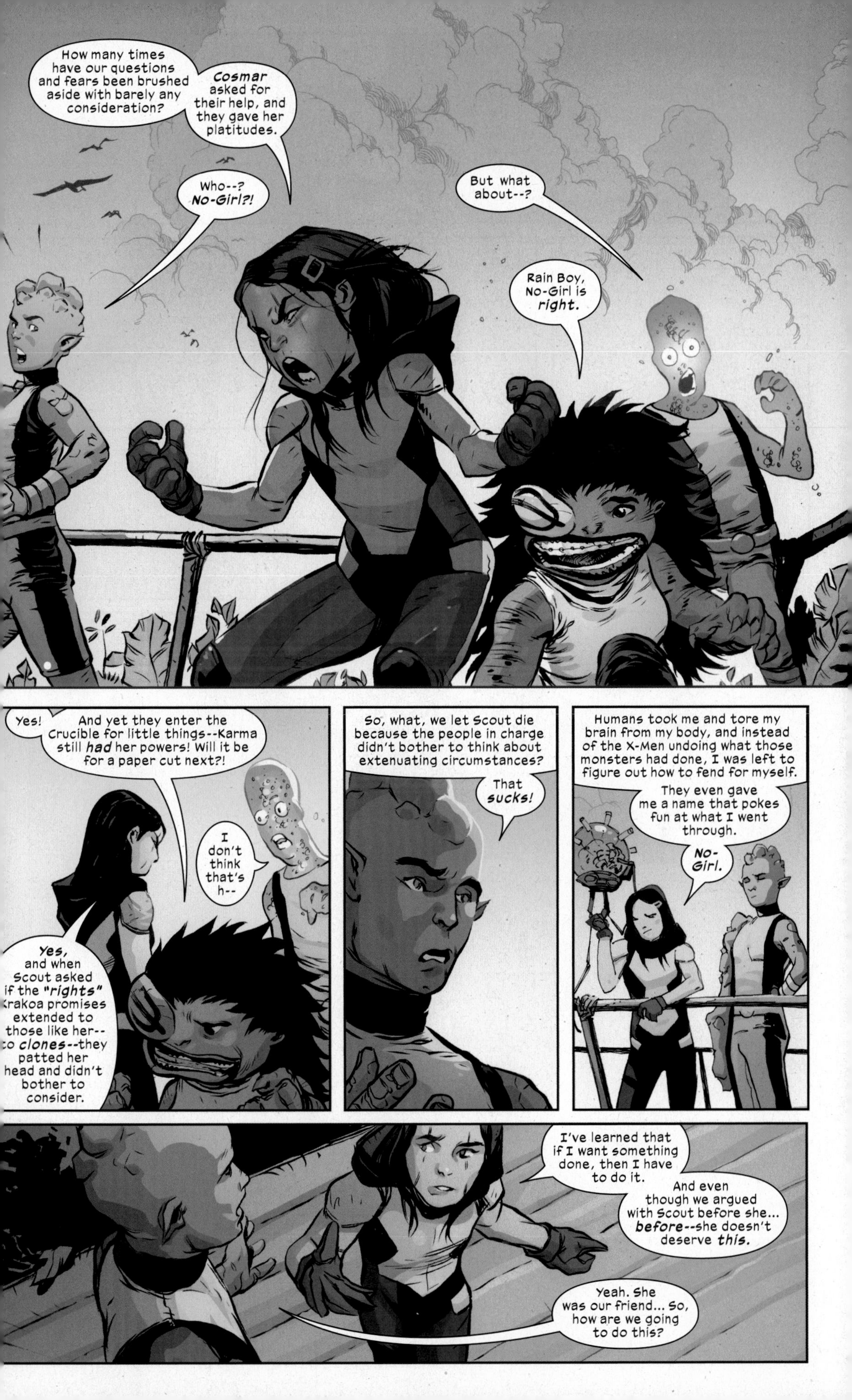
How many times have our questions and fears been brushed aside with barely any consideration?
Cosmar asked for their help, and they gave her platitudes.
Who--? No-Girl?!
But what about--?
Rain Boy, No-Girl is right.
Yes!
And yet they enter the Crucible for little things--Karma still had her powers! Will it be for a paper cut next?!
I don't think that's h--
Yes, and when Scout asked if the "rights" Krakoa promises extended to those like her--to clones--they patted her head and didn't bother to consider.
So, what, we let Scout die because the people in charge didn't bother to think about extenuating circumstances?
That sucks!
Humans took me and tore my brain from my body, and instead of the X-Men undoing what those monsters had done, I was left to figure out how to fend for myself.
They even gave me a name that pokes fun at what I went through.
No-Girl.
I've learned that if I want something done, then I have to do it.
And even though we argued with Scout before she... before--she doesn't deserve this.
Yeah. She was our friend... So, how are we going to do this?

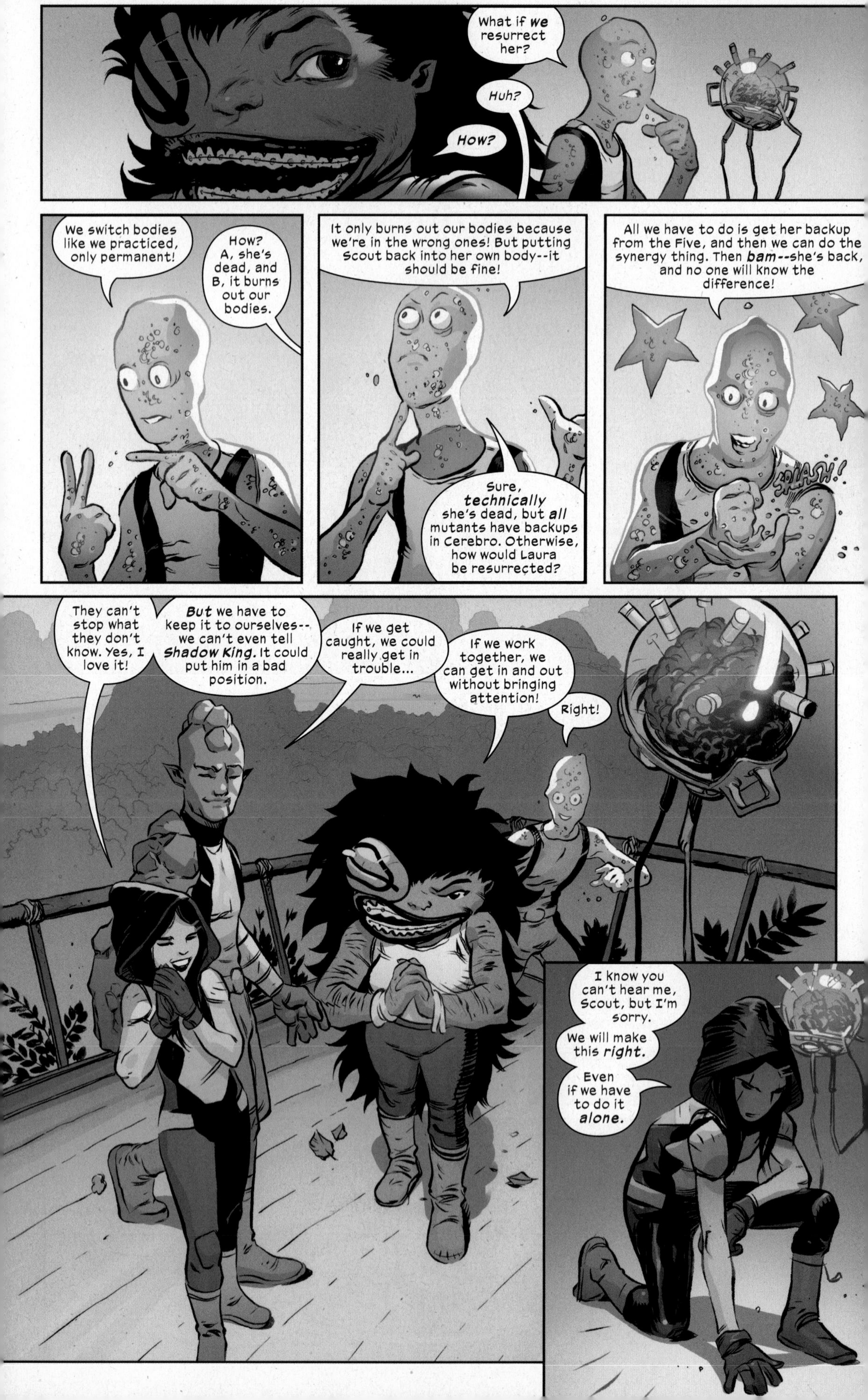
What if *we* resurrect her?
Huh?
How?
We switch bodies like we practiced, only permanent!
How? A, she's dead, and B, it burns out our bodies.
It only burns out our bodies because we're in the wrong ones! But putting Scout back into her own body--it should be fine!
Sure, *technically* she's dead, but *all* mutants have backups in Cerebro. Otherwise, how would Laura be resurrected?
All we have to do is get her backup from the Five, and then we can do the synergy thing. Then *bam*--she's back, and no one will know the difference!
SPLASH!
They can't stop what they don't know. Yes, I love it!
But we have to keep it to ourselves--we can't even tell *Shadow King*. It could put him in a bad position.
If we get caught, we could really get in trouble...
If we work together, we can get in and out without bringing attention!
Right!
I know you can't hear me, Scout, but I'm sorry.
We will make this *right.*
Even if we have to do it *alone.*

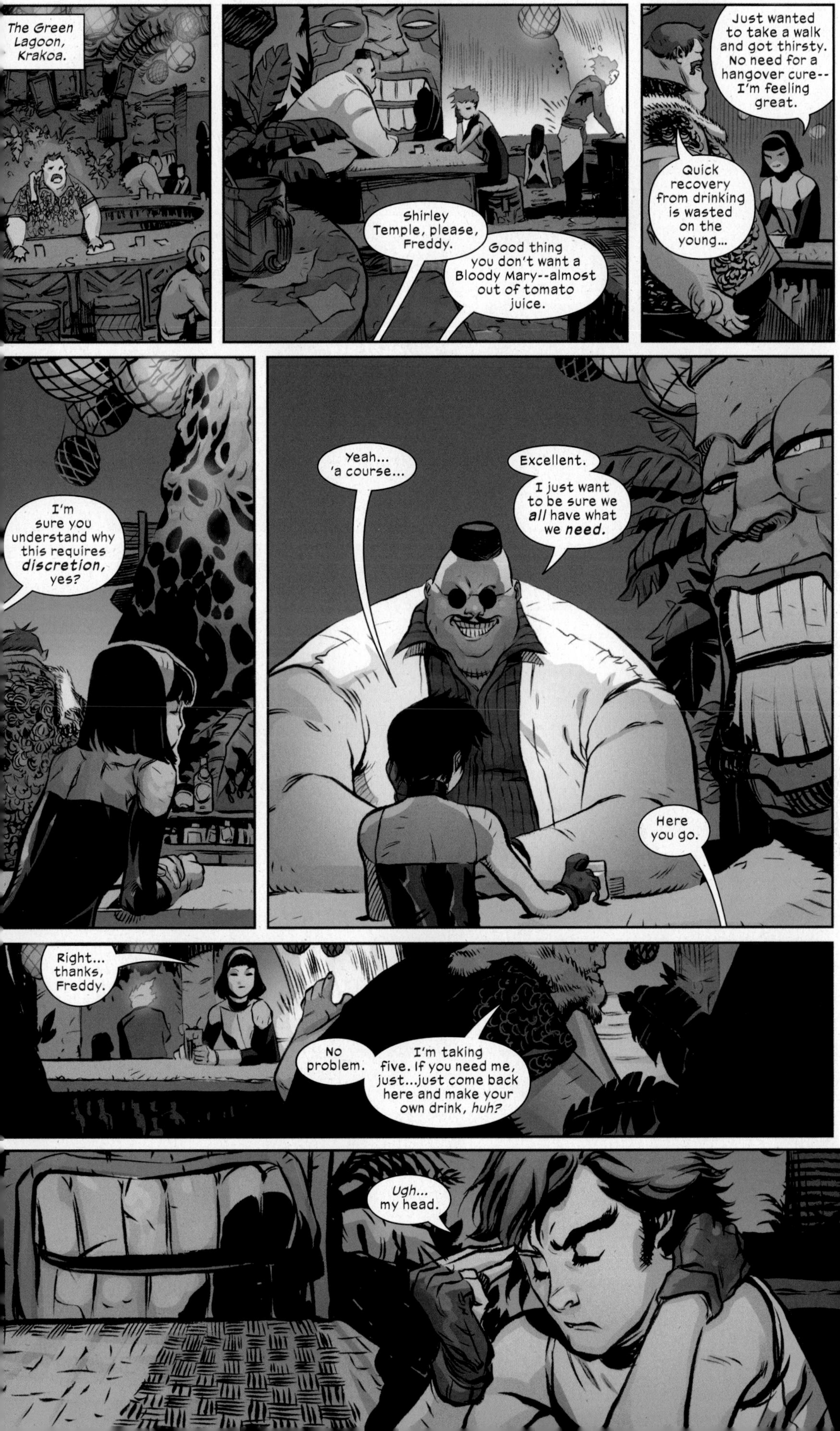
The Green Lagoon, Krakoa.
Shirley Temple, please, Freddy.
Good thing you don't want a Bloody Mary--almost out of tomato juice.
Just wanted to take a walk and got thirsty. No need for a hangover cure-- I'm feeling great.
Quick recovery from drinking is wasted on the young...
I'm sure you understand why this requires *discretion,* yes?
Yeah... 'a course...
Excellent.
I just want to be sure we *all* have what we *need.*
Here you go.
Right... thanks, Freddy.
No problem.
I'm taking five. If you need me, just...just come back here and make your own drink, *huh?*
Ugh... my head.

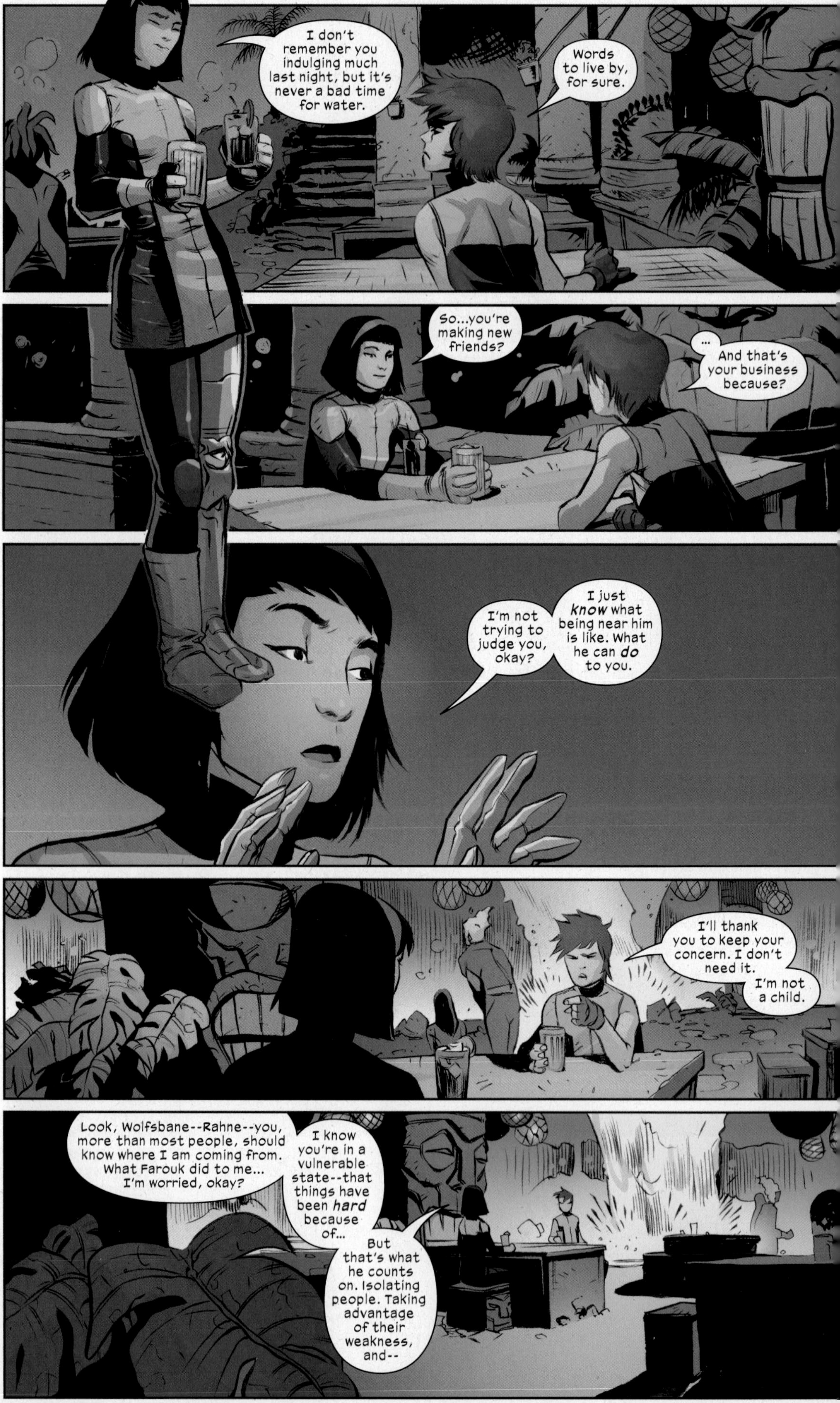

I don't remember you indulging much last night, but it's never a bad time for water.
Words to live by, for sure.
So...you're making new friends?
... And that's your business because?
I'm not trying to judge you, okay?
I just *know* what being near him is like. What he can *do* to you.
I'll thank you to keep your concern. I don't need it.
I'm not a child.
Look, Wolfsbane--Rahne--you, more than most people, should know where I am coming from. What Farouk did to me... I'm worried, okay?
I know you're in a vulnerable state--that things have been *hard* because of...
But that's what he counts on. Isolating people. Taking advantage of their weakness, and--

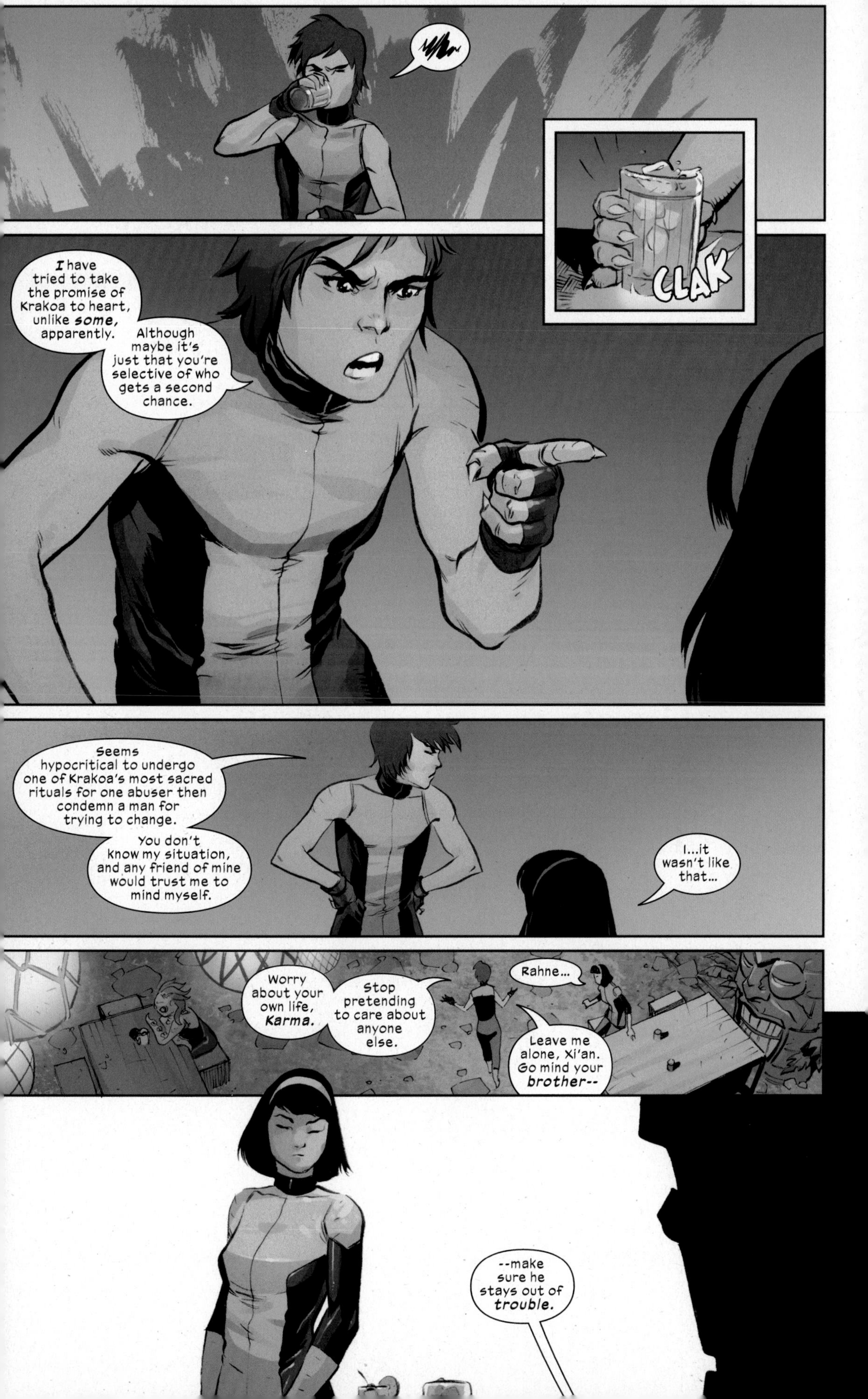
CLAK
I have tried to take the promise of Krakoa to heart, unlike some, apparently.
Although maybe it's just that you're selective of who gets a second chance.
Seems hypocritical to undergo one of Krakoa's most sacred rituals for one abuser then condemn a man for trying to change.
You don't know my situation, and any friend of mine would trust me to mind myself.
I...it wasn't like that...
Worry about your own life, Karma.
Stop pretending to care about anyone else.
Rahne...
Leave me alone, Xi'an. Go mind your brother--
--make sure he stays out of trouble.

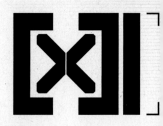

MISSION BRIEF: TRISTAN DA CUNHA, BRITISH OVERSEAS TERRITORY

Location: Tristan da Cunha, British Overseas Territory

Primary Objective: Locate and recover newly manifested mutant

Secondary Objective: Damage control/assistance for seismic event

Priority/Threat Level: Medium/low -- suggest sending noncombatants

Brief: Approximately an hour ago, Cerebro detected the manifestation of a new mutant on the island of Tristan da Cunha. A massive seismic event was detected at the same time -- our assumption is that they are related.

Massive damage to the man-made structures on the island has been detected through satellite imaging, and fires continue to burn. The closest standard human aid is over 24 hours away, and as of this brief, no communications with groups like the Avengers have been detected.

There is no indication that the locals are anti-mutant, and offering assistance may ingratiate them to us and make recovering the newly manifested mutant smoother.

I think we should give this one to Magik and Warpath to head -- they've been pushing to train their students in the field, under noncombat situations, and a search and rescue seems like a good opportunity.

-- Sage

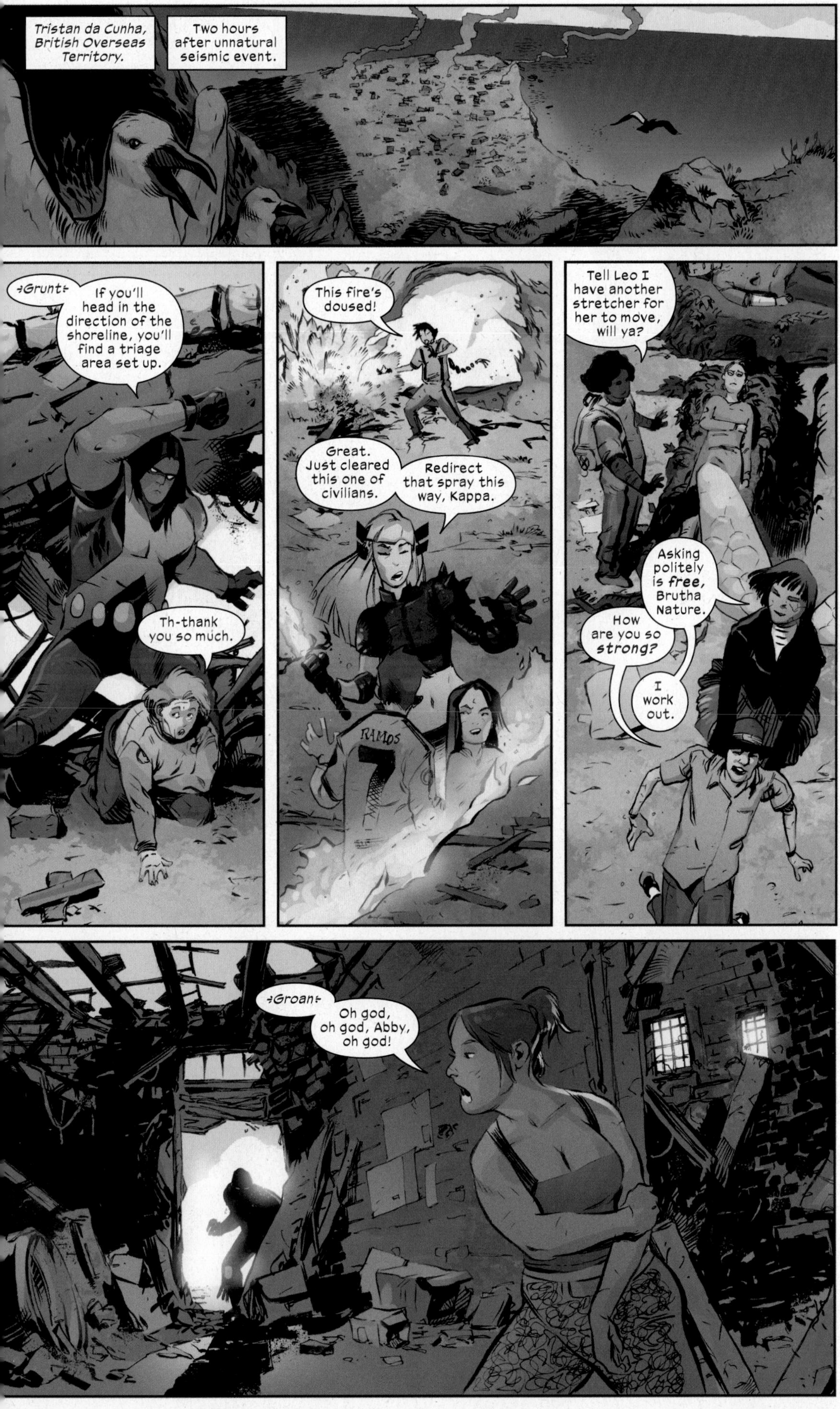
Tristan da Cunha, British Overseas Territory.
Two hours after unnatural seismic event.
=Grunt=
If you'll head in the direction of the shoreline, you'll find a triage area set up.
Th-thank you so much.
This fire's doused!
Great. Just cleared this one of civilians.
Redirect that spray this way, Kappa.
RAMOS
7
Tell Leo I have another stretcher for her to move, will ya?
Asking politely is *free,* Brutha Nature.
How are you so *strong?*
I work out.
=Groan=
Oh god, oh god, Abby, oh god!

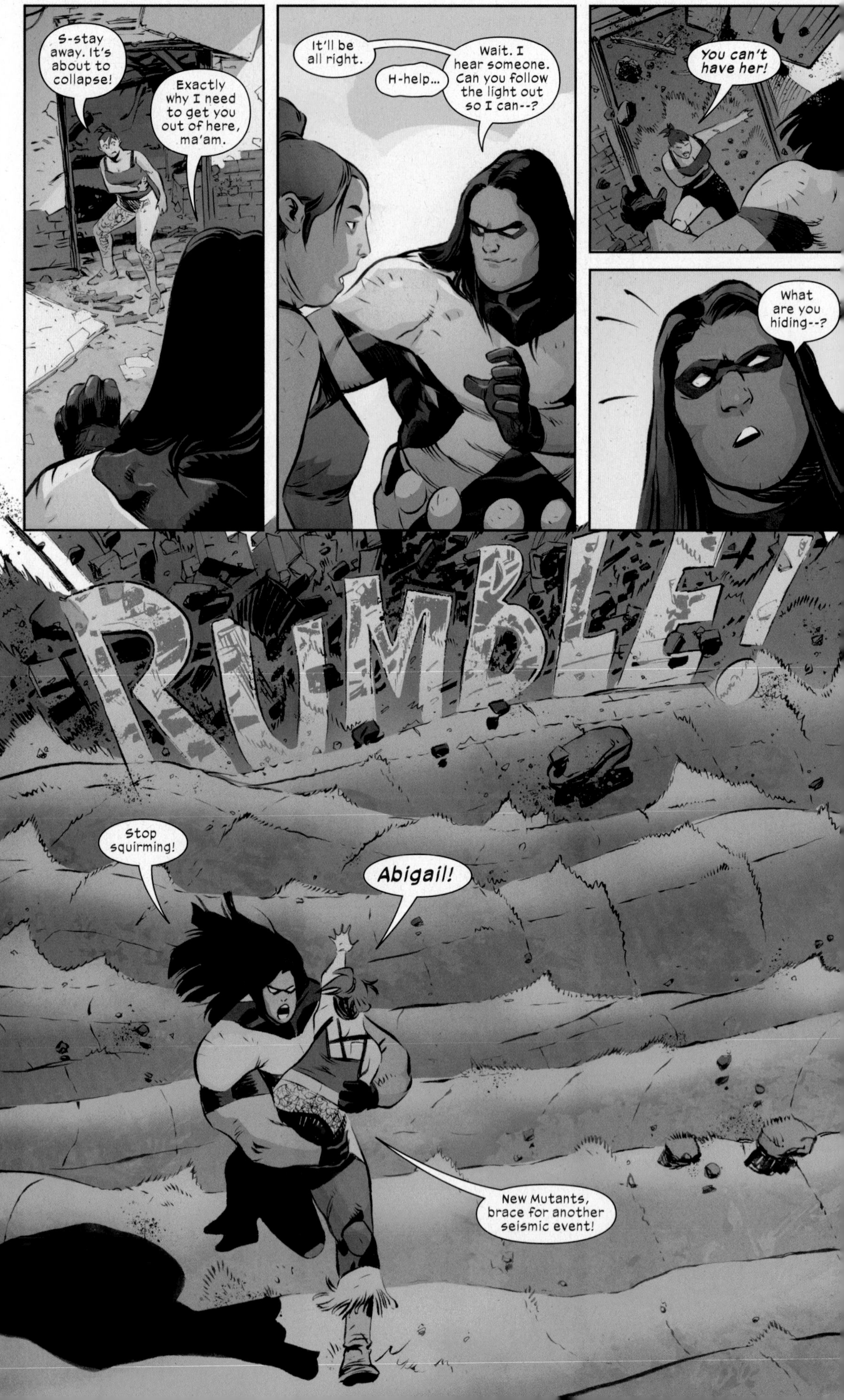
S-stay away. It's about to collapse!
Exactly why I need to get you out of here, ma'am.
It'll be all right.
H-help...
Wait. I hear someone. Can you follow the light out so I can--?
You can't have her!
What are you hiding--?
RUMBLE!
Stop squirming!
Abigail!
New Mutants, brace for another seismic event!

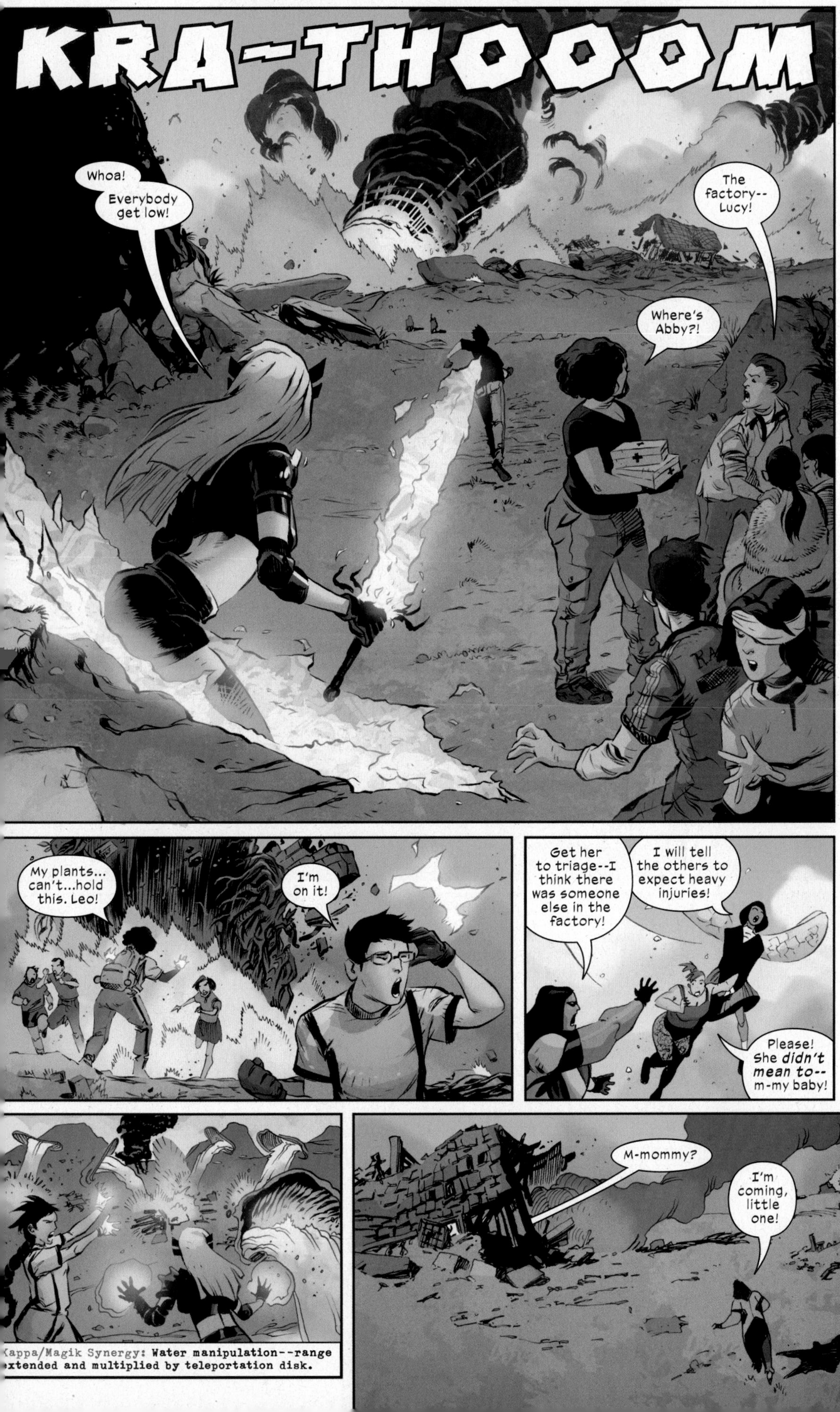
KRA-THOOOOM
Whoa! Everybody get low!
The factory-- Lucy!
Where's Abby?!
My plants... can't...hold this. Leo!
I'm on it!
Get her to triage--I think there was someone else in the factory!
I will tell the others to expect heavy injuries!
Please! She *didn't mean to*-- m-my baby!
Kappa/Magik Synergy: Water manipulation--range extended and multiplied by teleportation disk.
M-mommy?
I'm coming, little one!

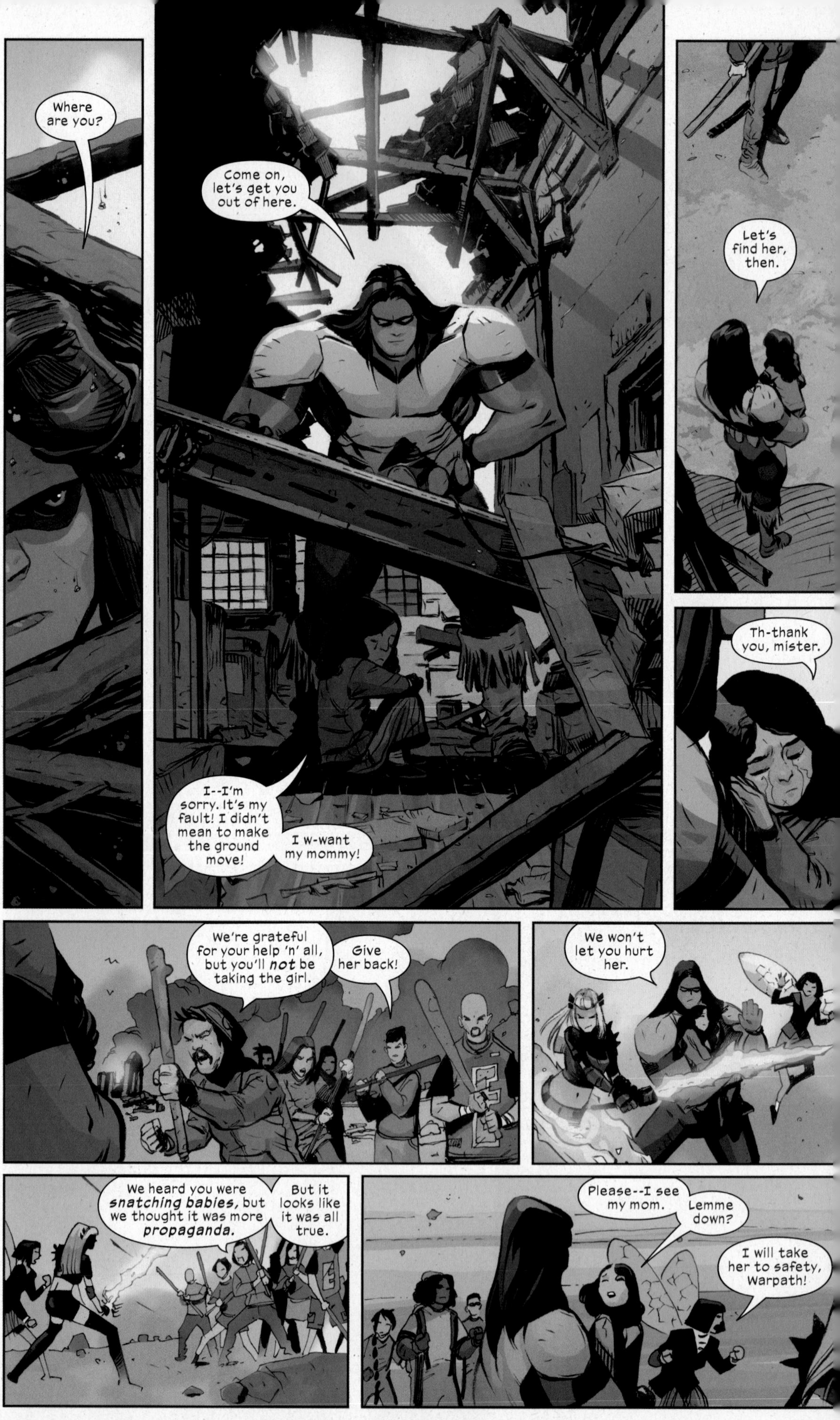
Where are you?
Come on, let's get you out of here.
I--I'm sorry. It's my fault! I didn't mean to make the ground move!
I w-want my mommy!
Let's find her, then.
Th-thank you, mister.
We're grateful for your help 'n' all, but you'll *not* be taking the girl.
Give her back!
We won't let you hurt her.
We heard you were *snatching babies*, but we thought it was more *propaganda.*
But it looks like it was all true.
Please--I see my mom.
Lemme down?
I will take her to safety, Warpath!

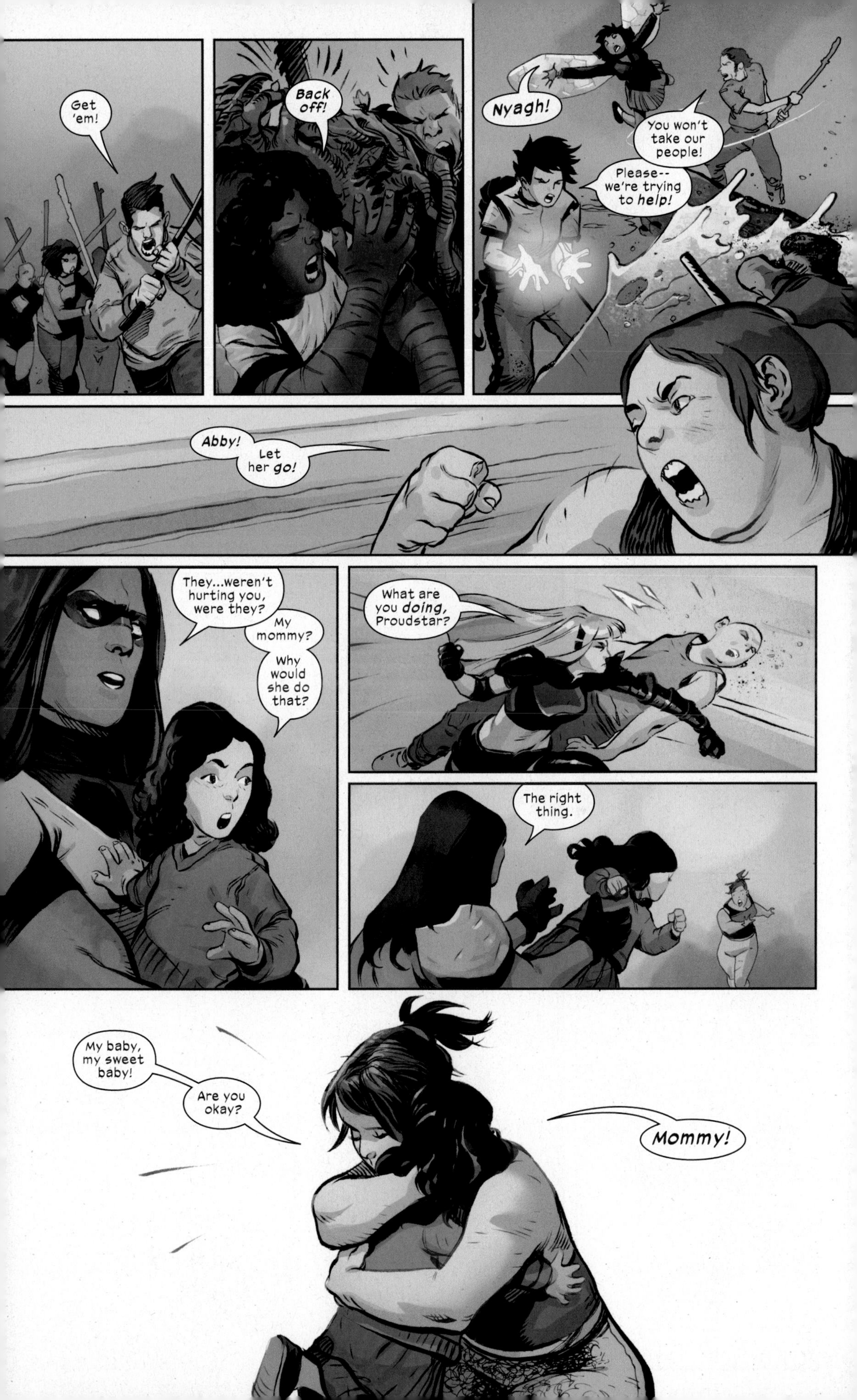
Get 'em!
Back off!
Nyagh!
You won't take our people!
Please-- we're trying to *help!*
Abby!
Let her *go!*
They...weren't hurting you, were they?
My mommy?
Why would she do that?
What are you *doing,* Proudstar?
The right thing.
My baby, my sweet baby!
Are you okay?
Mommy!

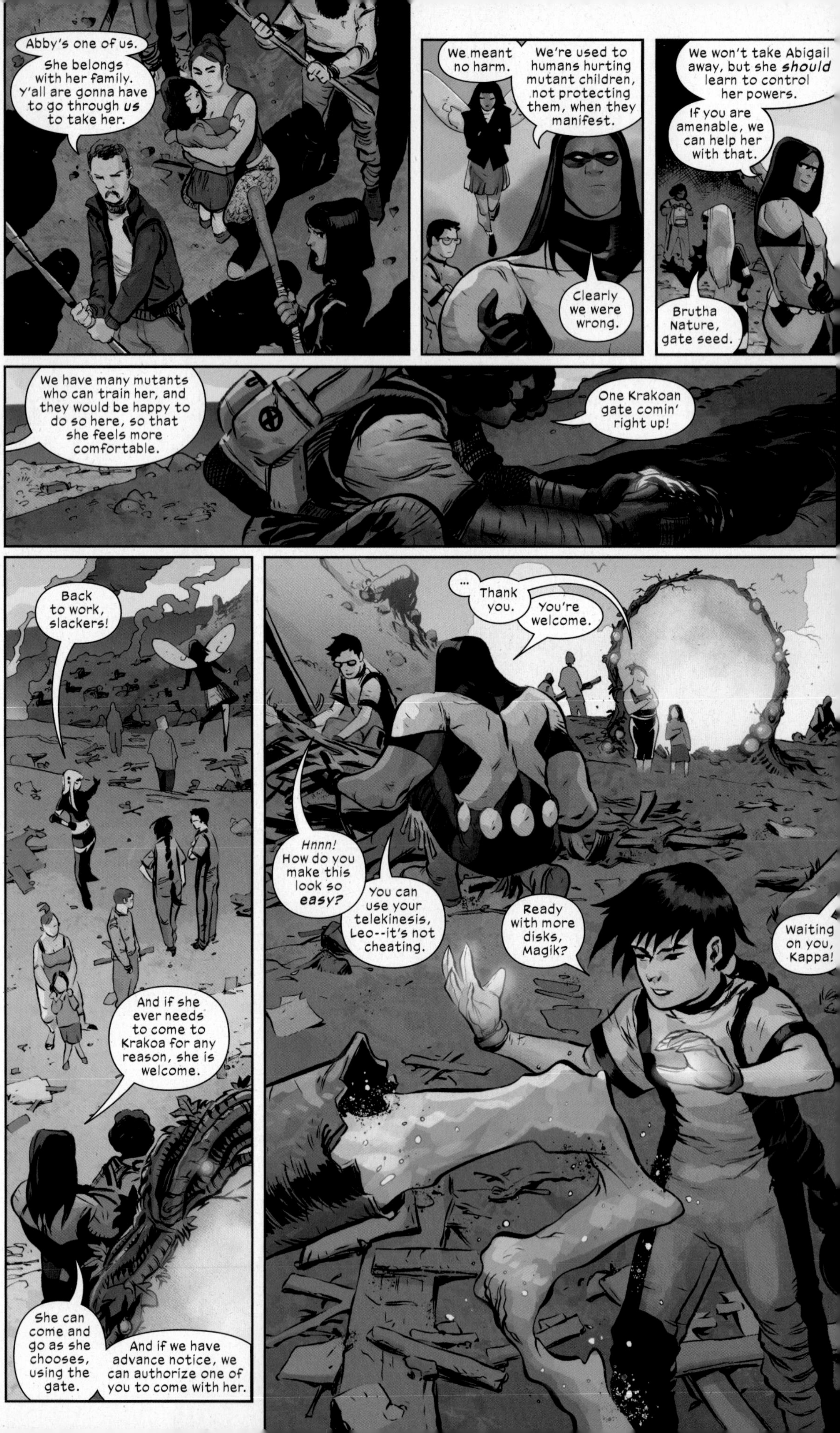
Abby's one of us.
She belongs with her family. Y'all are gonna have to go through *us* to take her.
We meant no harm.
We're used to humans hurting mutant children, not protecting them, when they manifest.
Clearly we were wrong.
We won't take Abigail away, but she *should* learn to control her powers.
If you are amenable, we can help her with that.
Brutha Nature, gate seed.
We have many mutants who can train her, and they would be happy to do so here, so that she feels more comfortable.
One Krakoan gate comin' right up!
Back to work, slackers!
And if she ever needs to come to Krakoa for any reason, she is welcome.
She can come and go as she chooses, using the gate.
And if we have advance notice, we can authorize one of you to come with her.
...
Thank you.
You're welcome.
Hnnn! How do you make this look so *easy?*
You can use your telekinesis, Leo--it's not cheating.
Ready with more disks, Magik?
Waiting on you, Kappa!

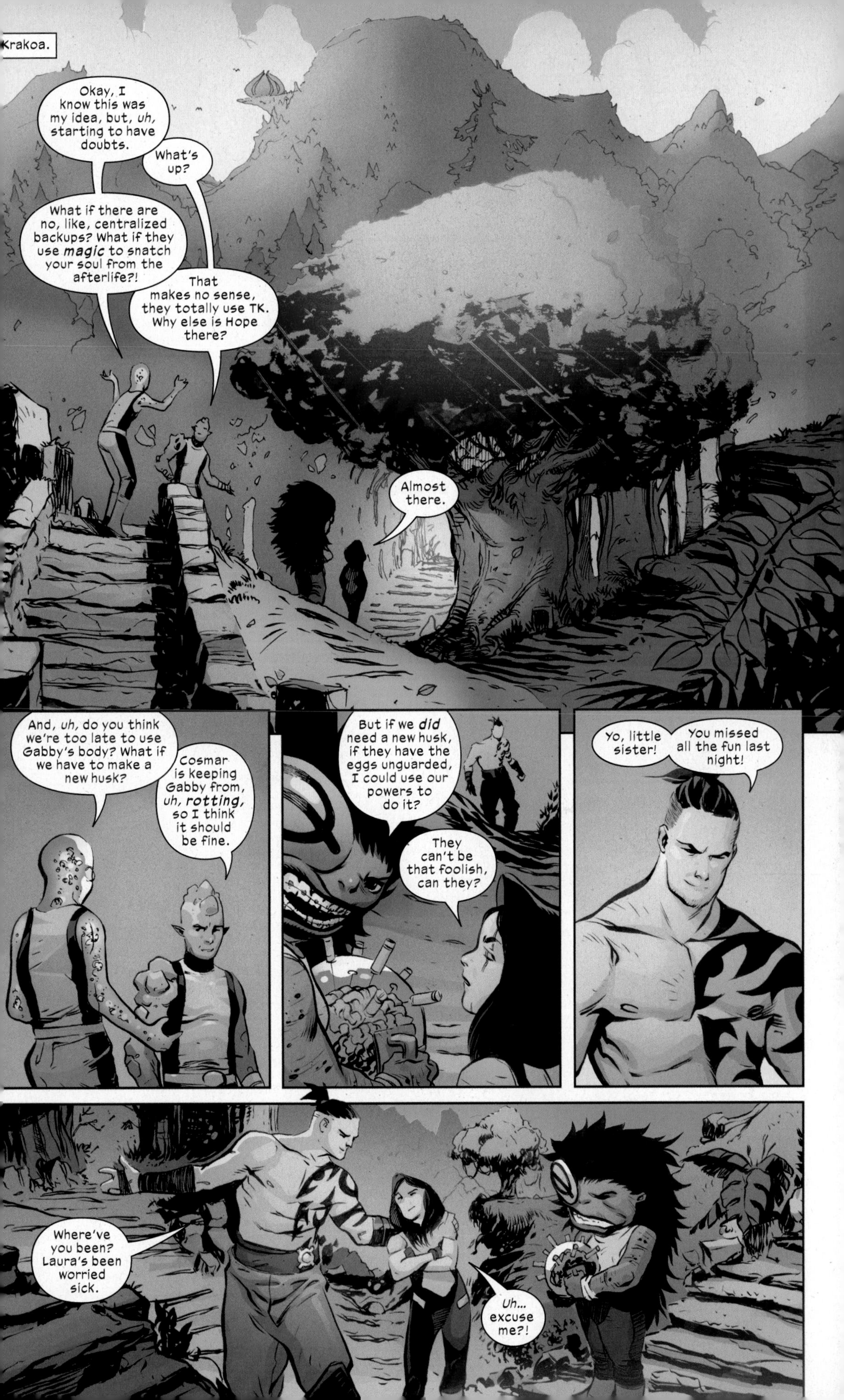
Krakoa.
Okay, I know this was my idea, but, *uh*, starting to have doubts.
What's up?
What if there are no, like, centralized backups? What if they use ***magic*** to snatch your soul from the afterlife?!
That makes no sense, they totally use TK. Why else is Hope there?
Almost there.
And, *uh*, do you think we're too late to use Gabby's body? What if we have to make a new husk?
Cosmar is keeping Gabby from, *uh*, ***rotting***, so I think it should be fine.
But if we ***did*** need a new husk, if they have the eggs unguarded, I could use our powers to do it?
They can't be that foolish, can they?
Yo, little sister!
You missed all the fun last night!
Where've you been? Laura's been worried sick.
Uh... excuse me?!

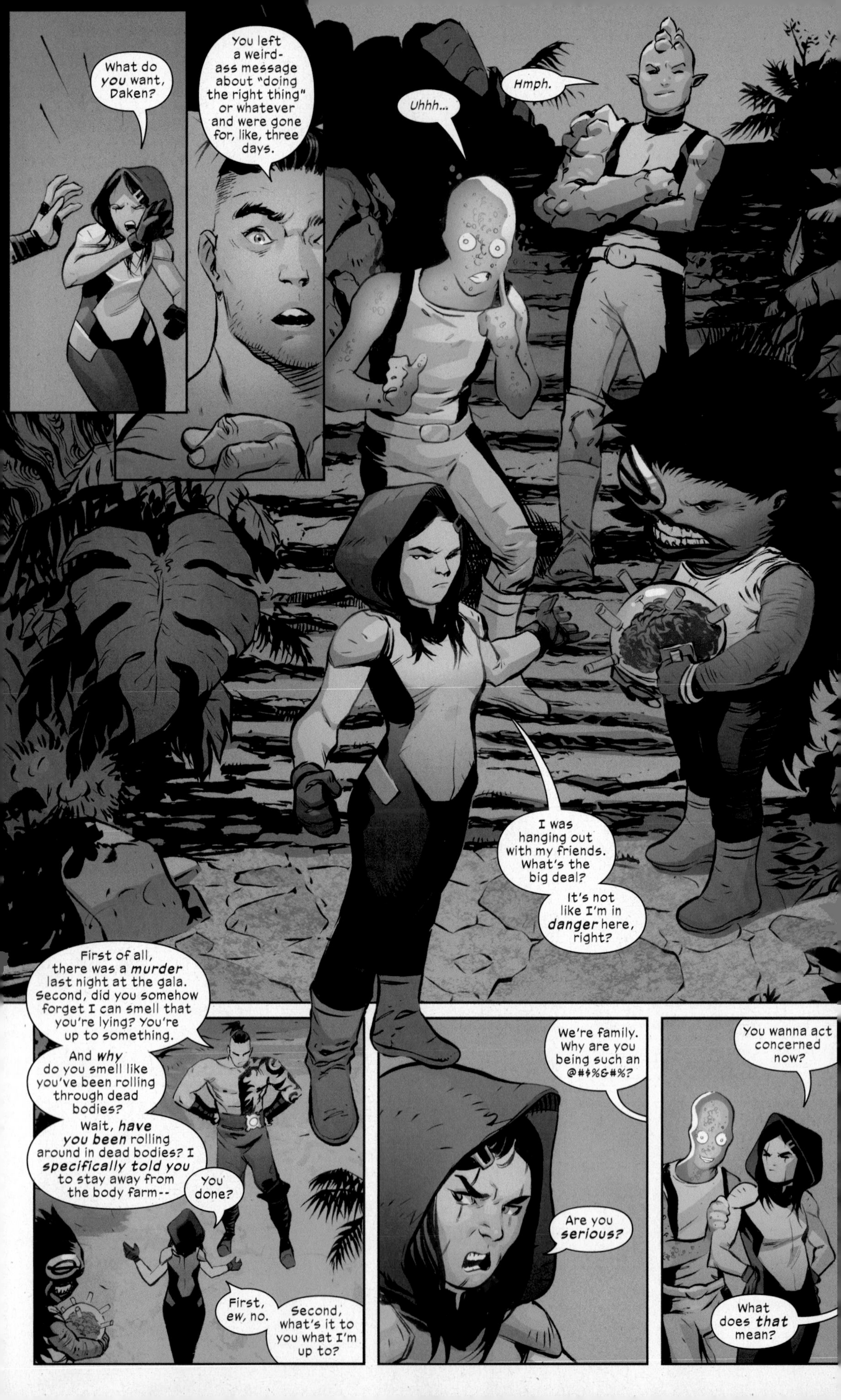

What do you want, Daken?
You left a weird-ass message about "doing the right thing" or whatever and were gone for, like, three days.
Uhhh...
Hmph.
I was hanging out with my friends. What's the big deal?
It's not like I'm in danger here, right?
First of all, there was a murder last night at the gala. Second, did you somehow forget I can smell that you're lying? You're up to something.
And why do you smell like you've been rolling through dead bodies?
Wait, have you been rolling around in dead bodies? I specifically told you to stay away from the body farm--
You done?
First, ew, no.
Second, what's it to you what I'm up to?
We're family. Why are you being such an @#$%&#%?
Are you serious?
You wanna act concerned now?
What does that mean?

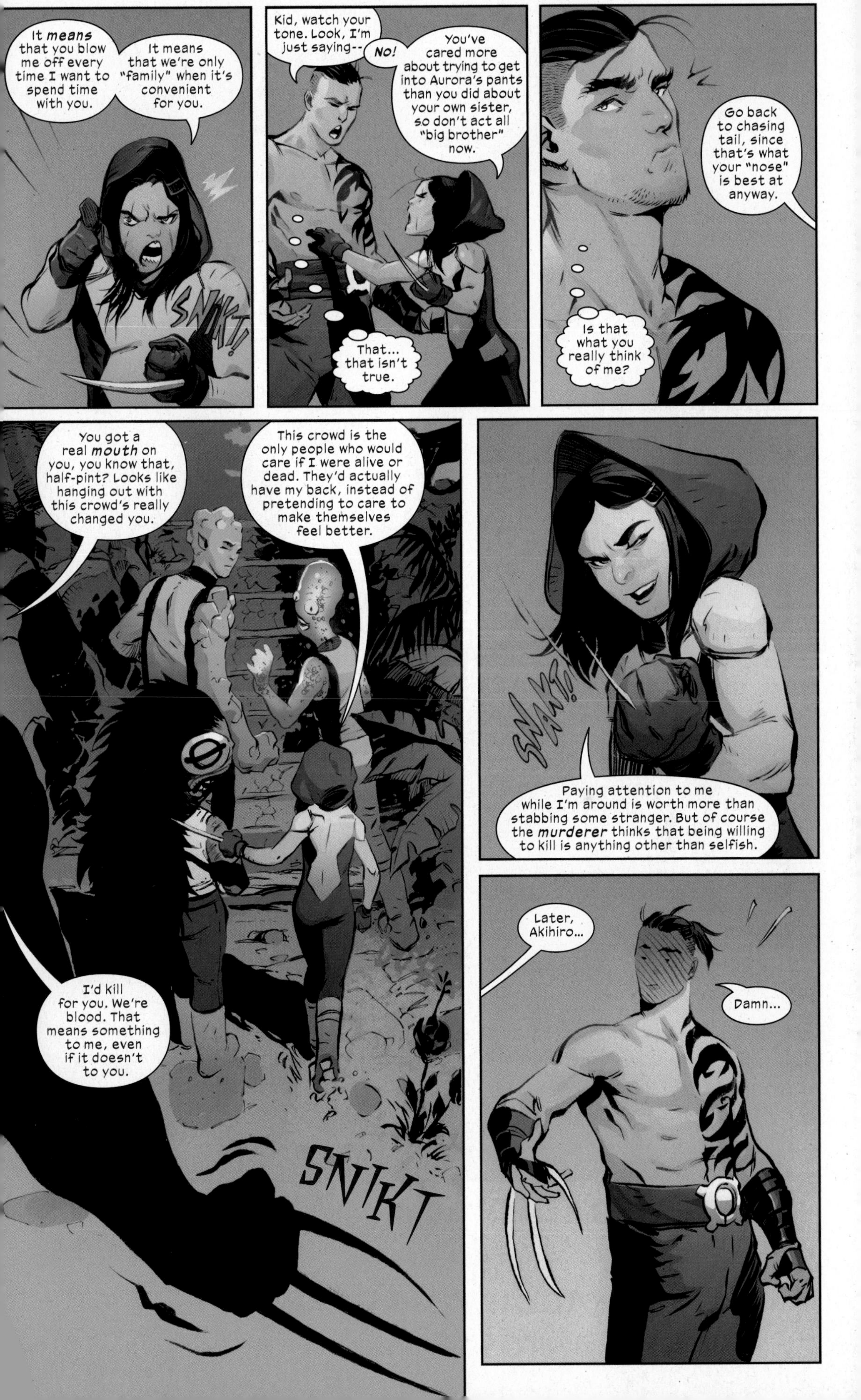

It means that you blow me off every time I want to spend time with you.
It means that we're only "family" when it's convenient for you.
SNIKT!
Kid, watch your tone. Look, I'm just saying--
No!
You've cared more about trying to get into Aurora's pants than you did about your own sister, so don't act all "big brother" now.
That... that isn't true.
Go back to chasing tail, since that's what your "nose" is best at anyway.
Is that what you really think of me?
You got a real mouth on you, you know that, half-pint? Looks like hanging out with this crowd's really changed you.
This crowd is the only people who would care if I were alive or dead. They'd actually have my back, instead of pretending to care to make themselves feel better.
I'd kill for you. We're blood. That means something to me, even if it doesn't to you.
SNIKT
SNAKT!
Paying attention to me while I'm around is worth more than stabbing some stranger. But of course the murderer thinks that being willing to kill is anything other than selfish.
Later, Akihiro...
Damn...

LOST CLUB'S *UPDATED* MAP OF KRAKOA

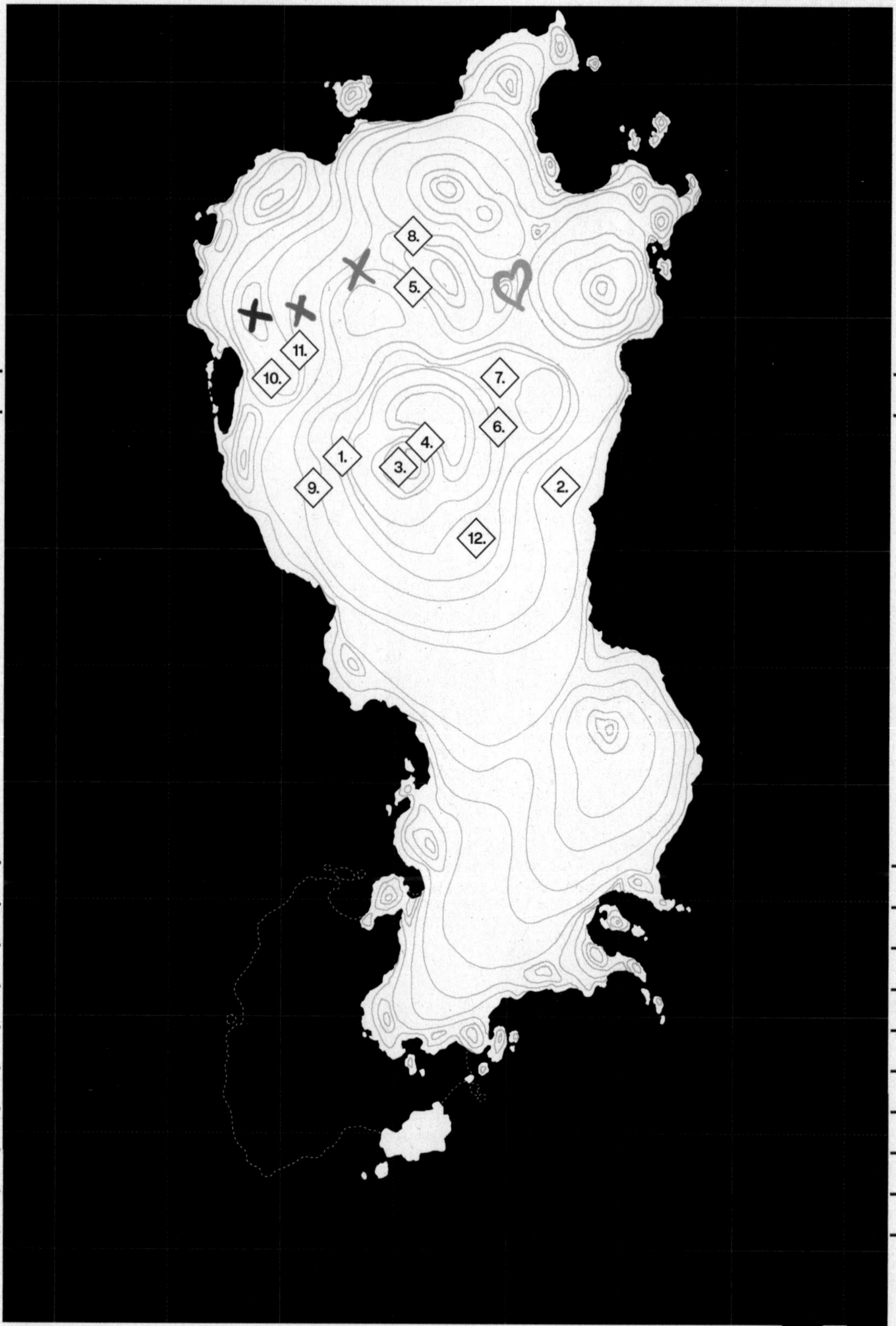
8.
5.
11.
10.
7.
6.
4.
1.
3.
9.
2.
12.

[00.08]
[00.15]

THE FORT
THE CROW'S NEST
SHADOW KING'S CAVE
SANTOS

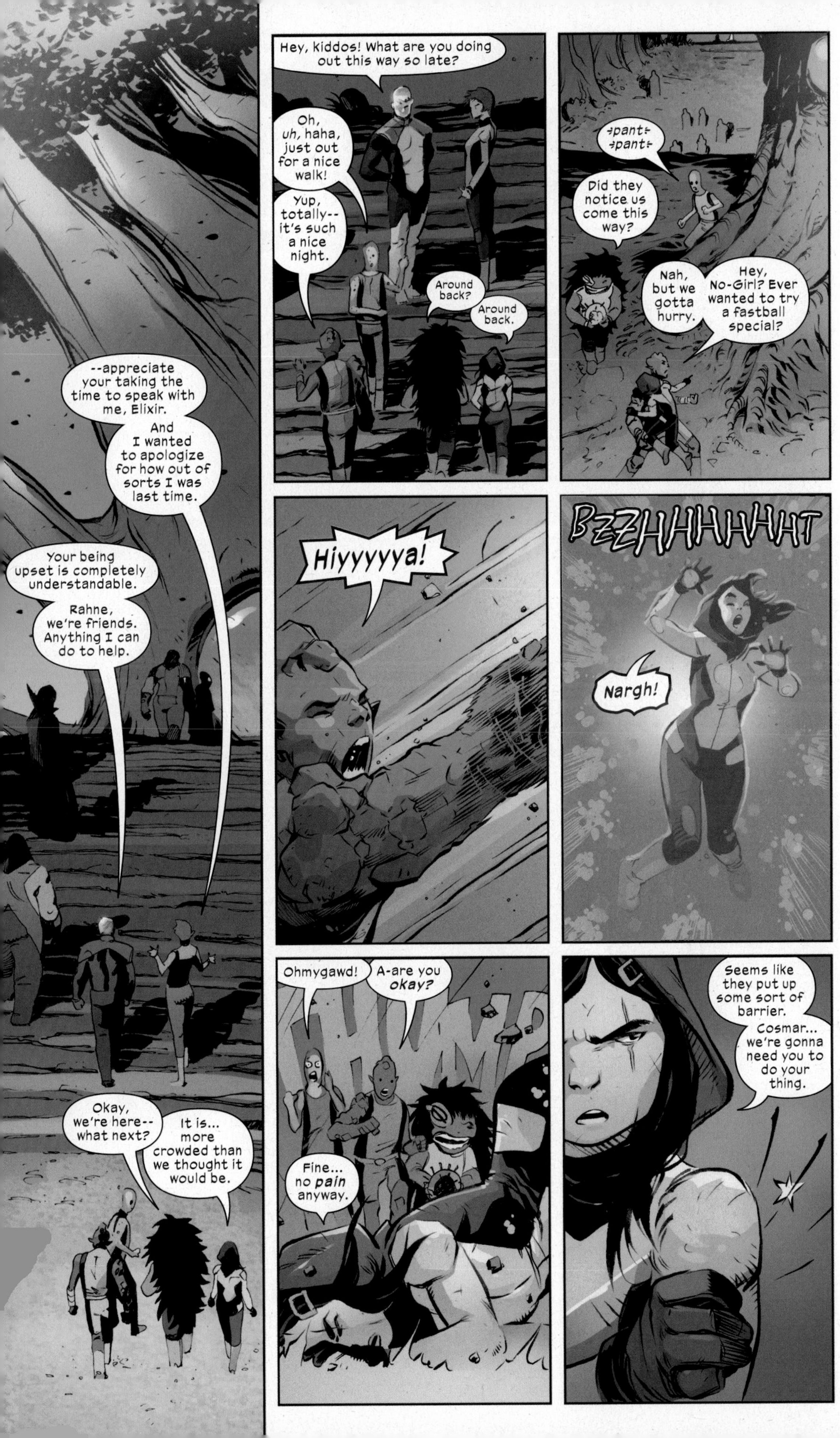

--appreciate your taking the time to speak with me, Elixir.
And I wanted to apologize for how out of sorts I was last time.
Your being upset is completely understandable.
Rahne, we're friends. Anything I can do to help.
Okay, we're here-- what next?
It is... more crowded than we thought it would be.
Hey, kiddos! What are you doing out this way so late?
Oh, uh, haha, just out for a nice walk!
Yup, totally-- it's such a nice night.
Around back?
Around back.
pant *pant*
Did they notice us come this way?
Nah, but we gotta hurry.
Hey, No-Girl? Ever wanted to try a fastball special?
Hiyyyyya!
BZZHHHHHHT
Nargh!
Ohmygawd!
A-are you okay?
Fine... no pain anyway.
Seems like they put up some sort of barrier.
Cosmar... we're gonna need you to do your thing.

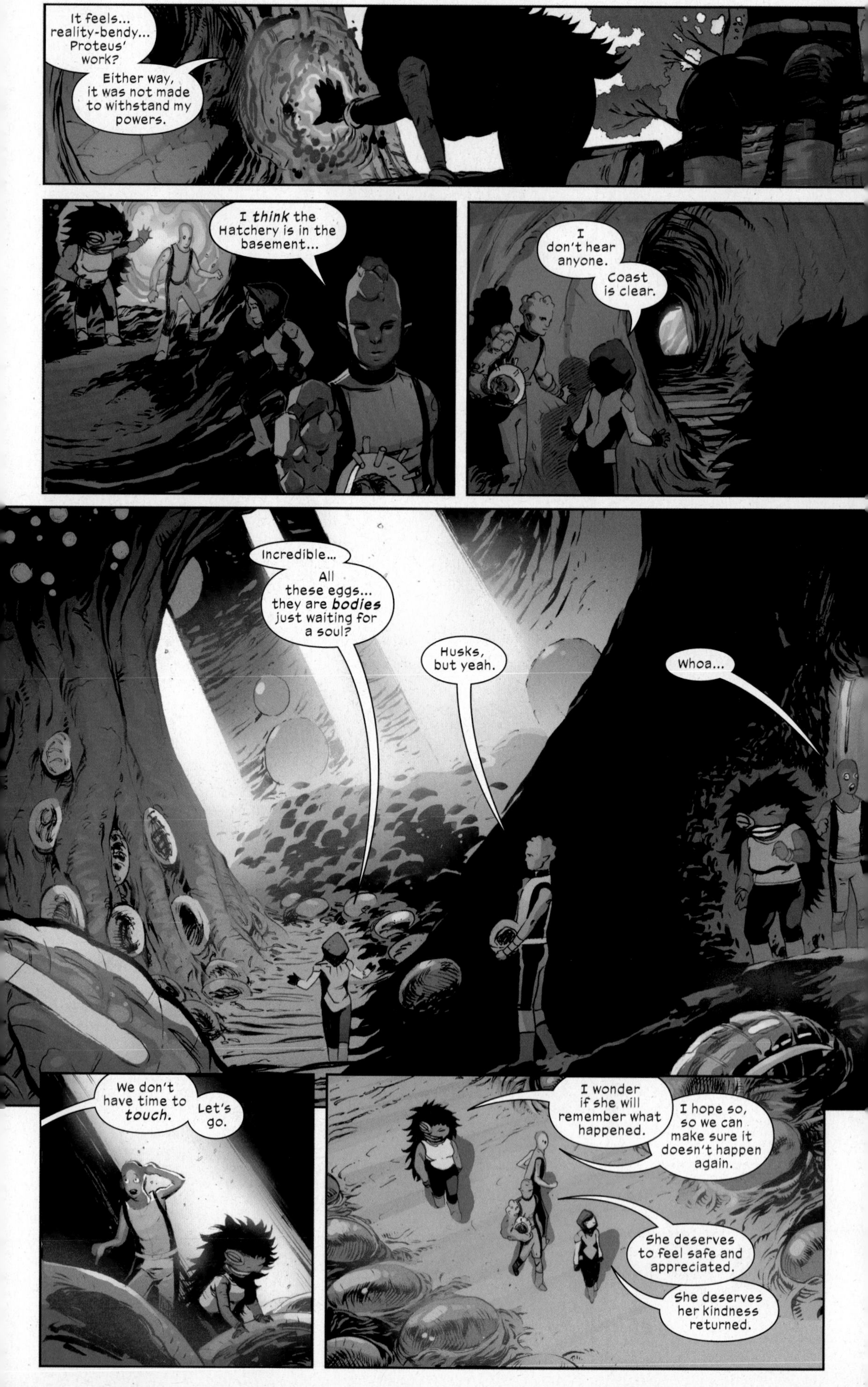
It feels... reality-bendy... Proteus' work?
Either way, it was not made to withstand my powers.
I *think* the Hatchery is in the basement...
I don't hear anyone.
Coast is clear.
Incredible...
All these eggs... they are *bodies* just waiting for a soul?
Husks, but yeah.
Whoa...
We don't have time to *touch.*
Let's go.
I wonder if she will remember what happened.
I hope so, so we can make sure it doesn't happen again.
She deserves to feel safe and appreciated.
She deserves her kindness returned.

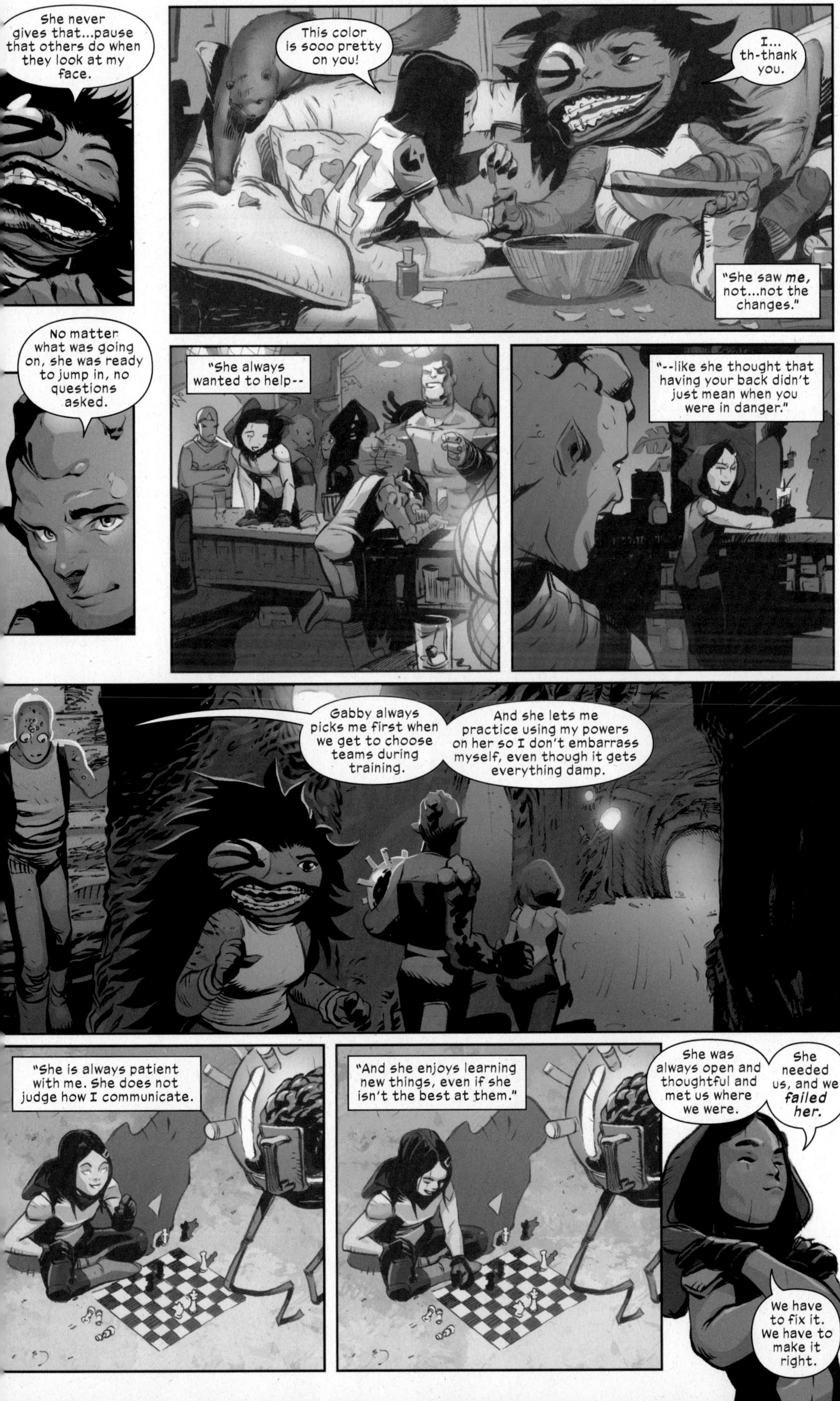
She never gives that...pause that others do when they look at my face.
This color is sooo pretty on you!
I... th-thank you.
"She saw me, not...not the changes."
No matter what was going on, she was ready to jump in, no questions asked.
"She always wanted to help--
"--like she thought that having your back didn't just mean when you were in danger."
Gabby always picks me first when we get to choose teams during training.
And she lets me practice using my powers on her so I don't embarrass myself, even though it gets everything damp.
"She is always patient with me. She does not judge how I communicate.
"And she enjoys learning new things, even if she isn't the best at them."
She was always open and thoughtful and met us where we were.
She needed us, and we failed her.
We have to fix it. We have to make it right.

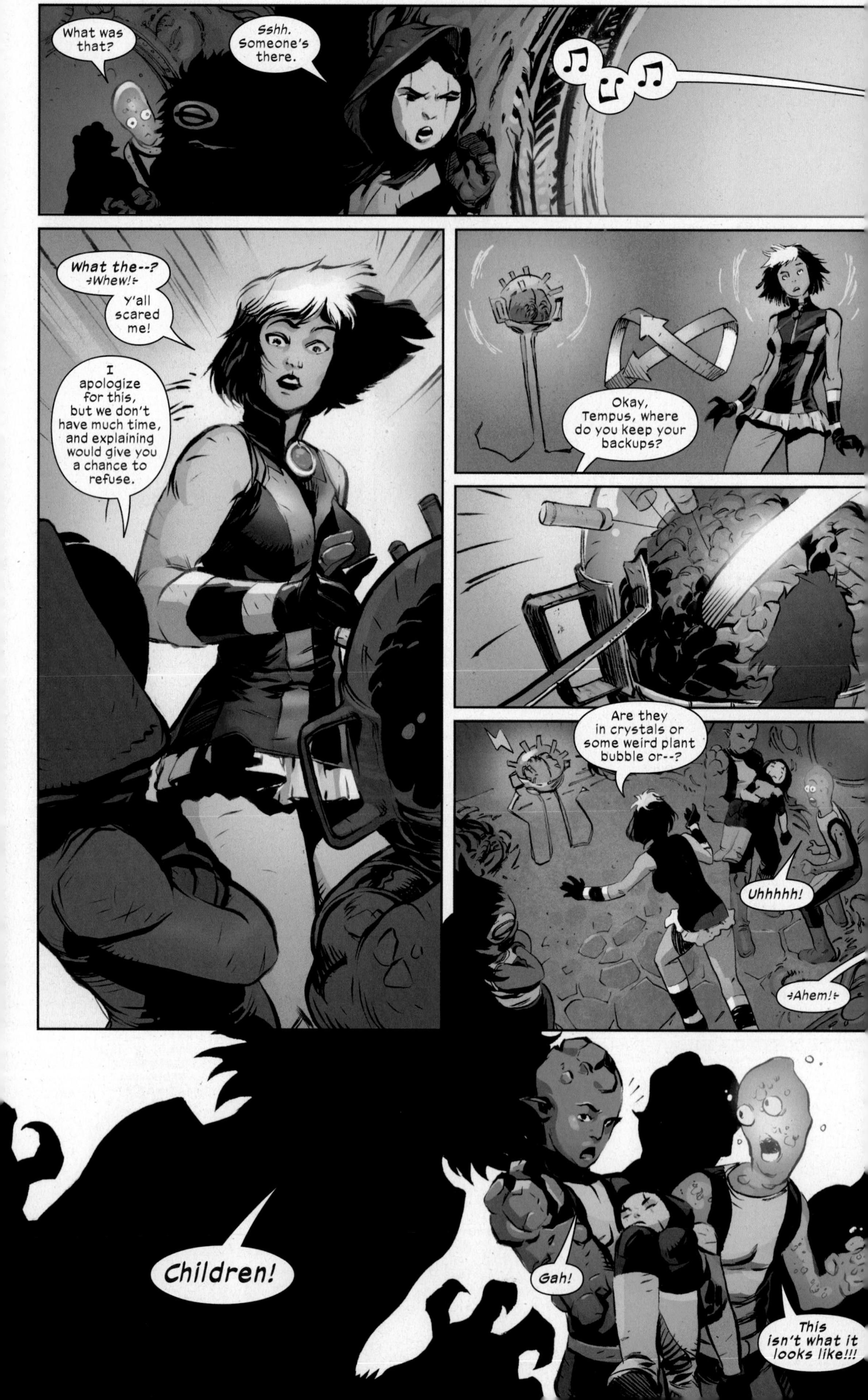
What was that?
Sshh. Someone's there.
What the--? ≠Whew!≠
Y'all scared me!
I apologize for this, but we don't have much time, and explaining would give you a chance to refuse.
Okay, Tempus, where do you keep your backups?
Are they in crystals or some weird plant bubble or--?
Uhhhhh!
≠Ahem!≠
Children!
Gah!
This isn't what it looks like!!!

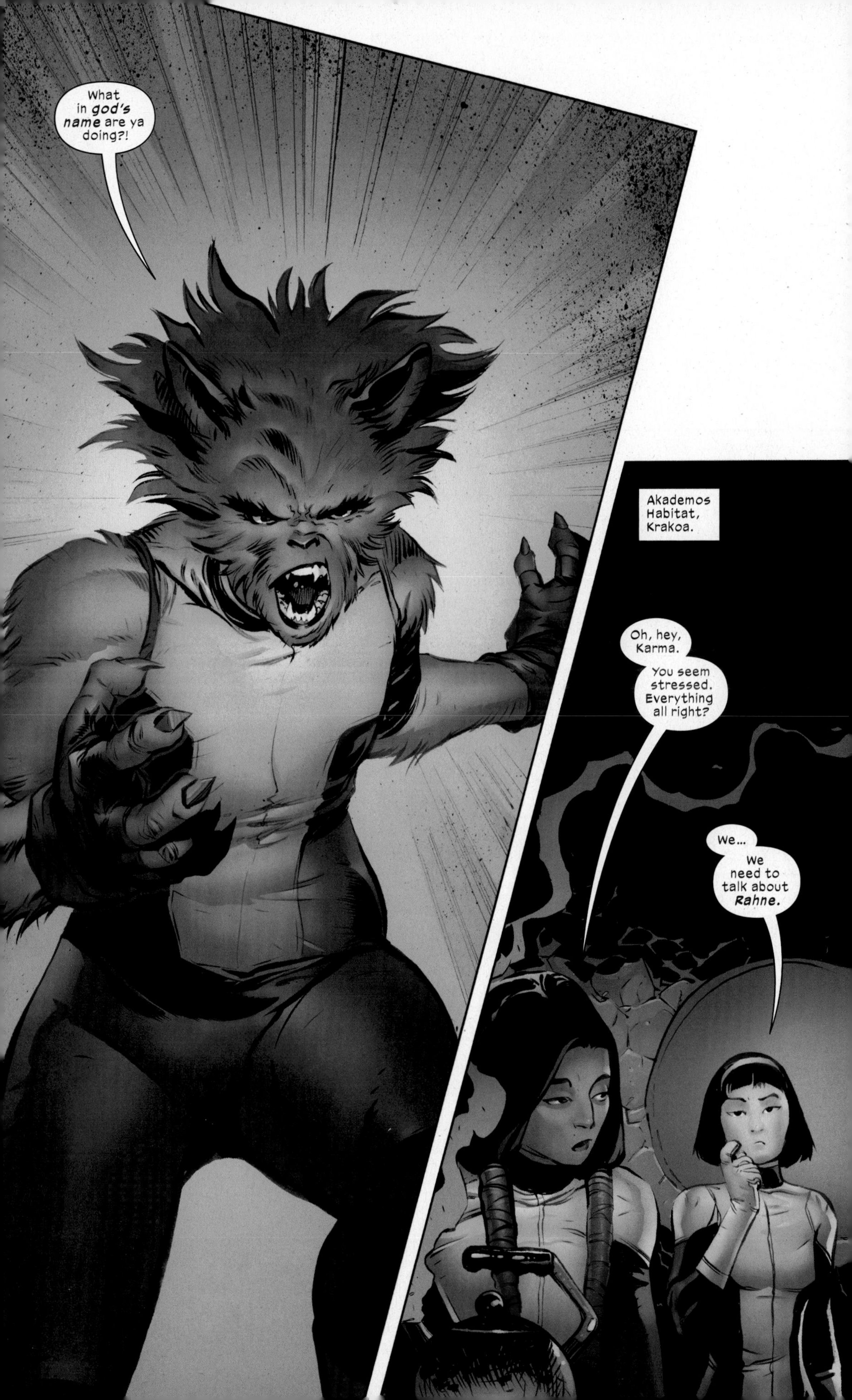
What in god's name are ya doing?!
Akademos Habitat, Krakoa.
Oh, hey, Karma.
You seem stressed. Everything all right?
We...
We need to talk about Rahne.

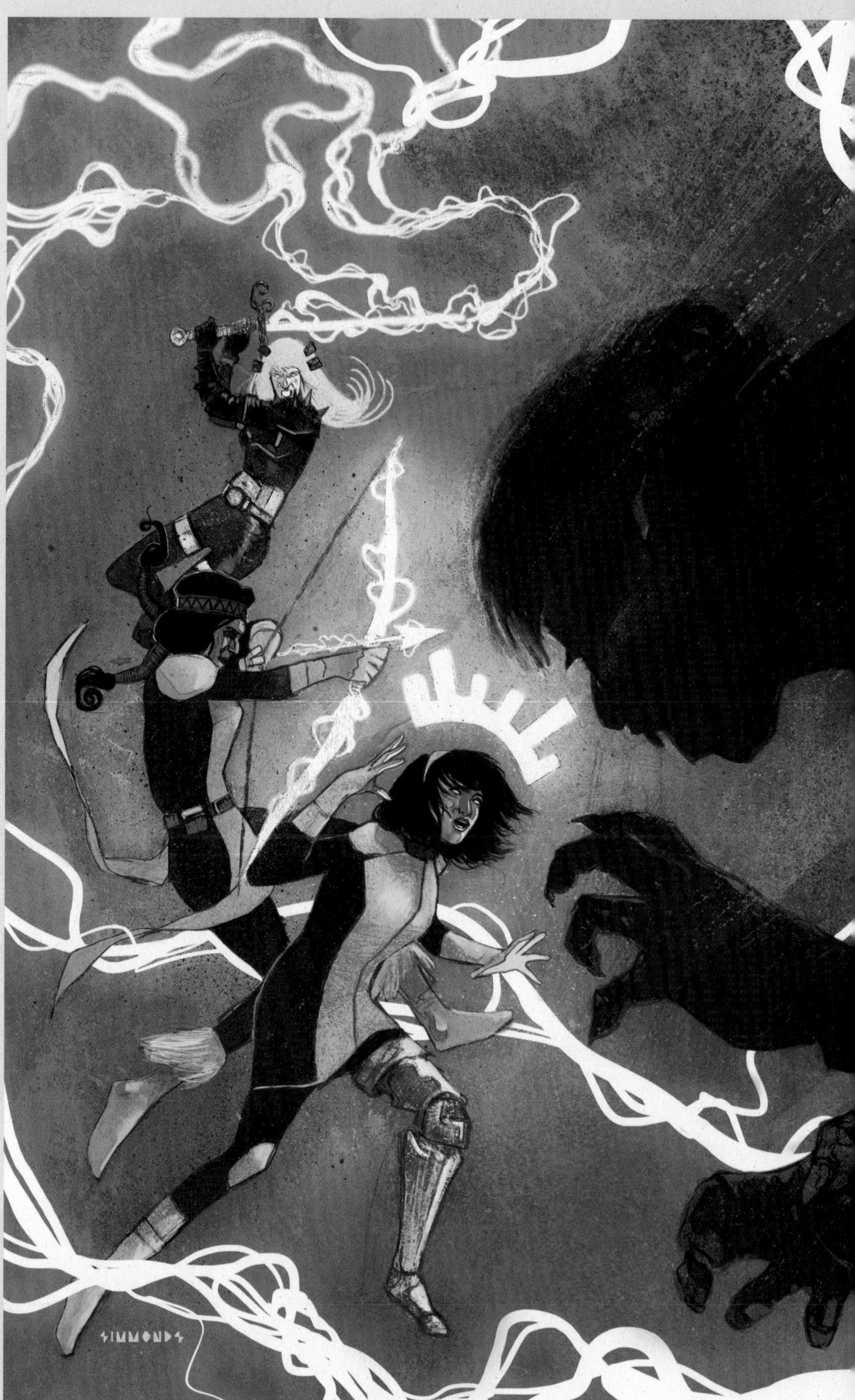
SIMMONDS

Krakoa Welcomes Gabby Kinney

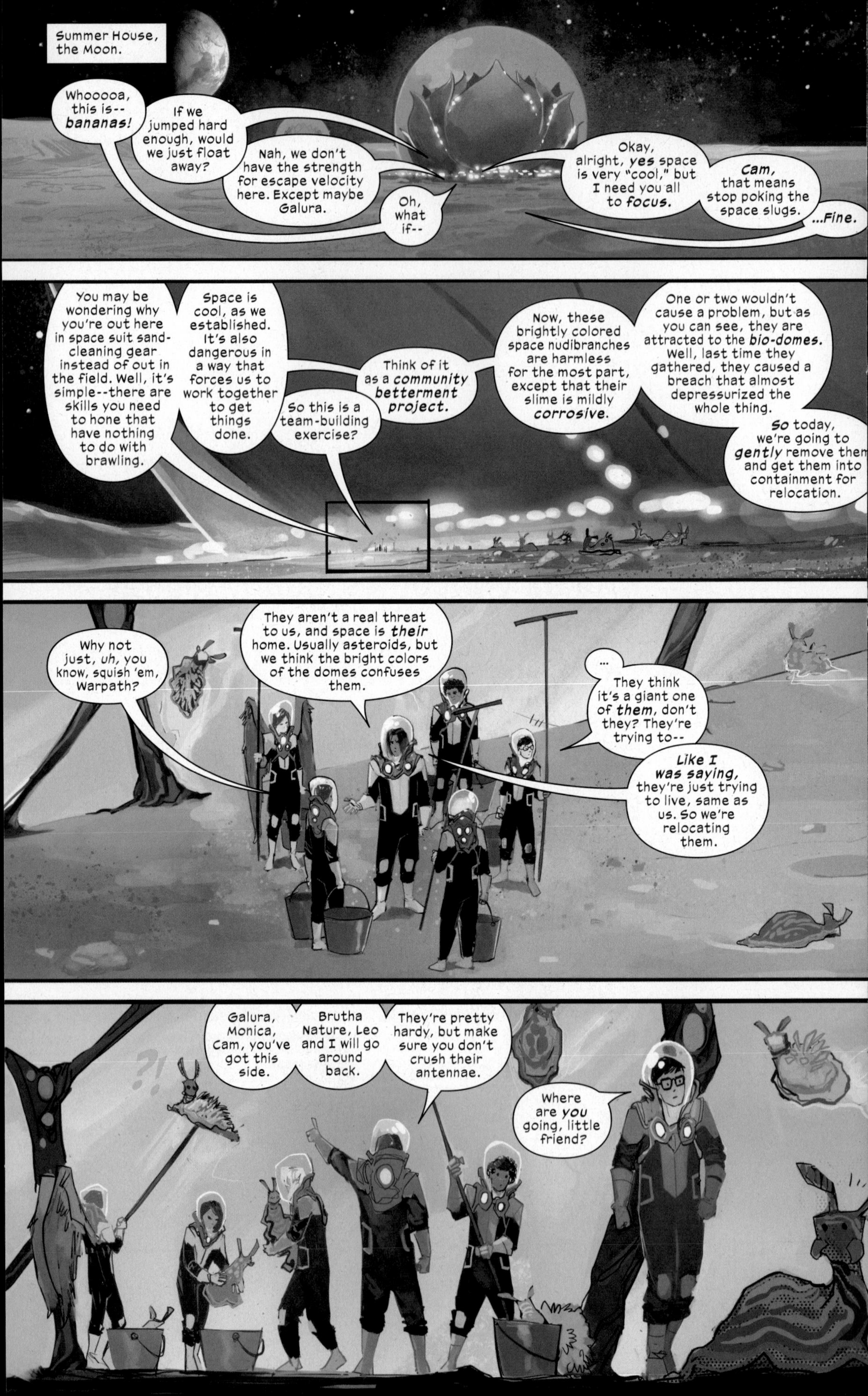

Summer House, the Moon.
Whoooa, this is-- bananas!
If we jumped hard enough, would we just float away?
Nah, we don't have the strength for escape velocity here. Except maybe Galura.
Oh, what if--
Okay, alright, yes space is very "cool," but I need you all to focus.
Cam, that means stop poking the space slugs.
...Fine.
You may be wondering why you're out here in space suit sand-cleaning gear instead of out in the field. Well, it's simple--there are skills you need to hone that have nothing to do with brawling.
Space is cool, as we established. It's also dangerous in a way that forces us to work together to get things done.
So this is a team-building exercise?
Think of it as a community betterment project.
Now, these brightly colored space nudibranches are harmless for the most part, except that their slime is mildly corrosive.
One or two wouldn't cause a problem, but as you can see, they are attracted to the bio-domes. Well, last time they gathered, they caused a breach that almost depressurized the whole thing.
So today, we're going to gently remove them and get them into containment for relocation.
Why not just, uh, you know, squish 'em, Warpath?
They aren't a real threat to us, and space is their home. Usually asteroids, but we think the bright colors of the domes confuses them.
...
They think it's a giant one of them, don't they? They're trying to--
Like I was saying, they're just trying to live, same as us. So we're relocating them.
?!
Galura, Monica, Cam, you've got this side.
Brutha Nature, Leo and I will go around back.
They're pretty hardy, but make sure you don't crush their antennae.
Where are you going, little friend?

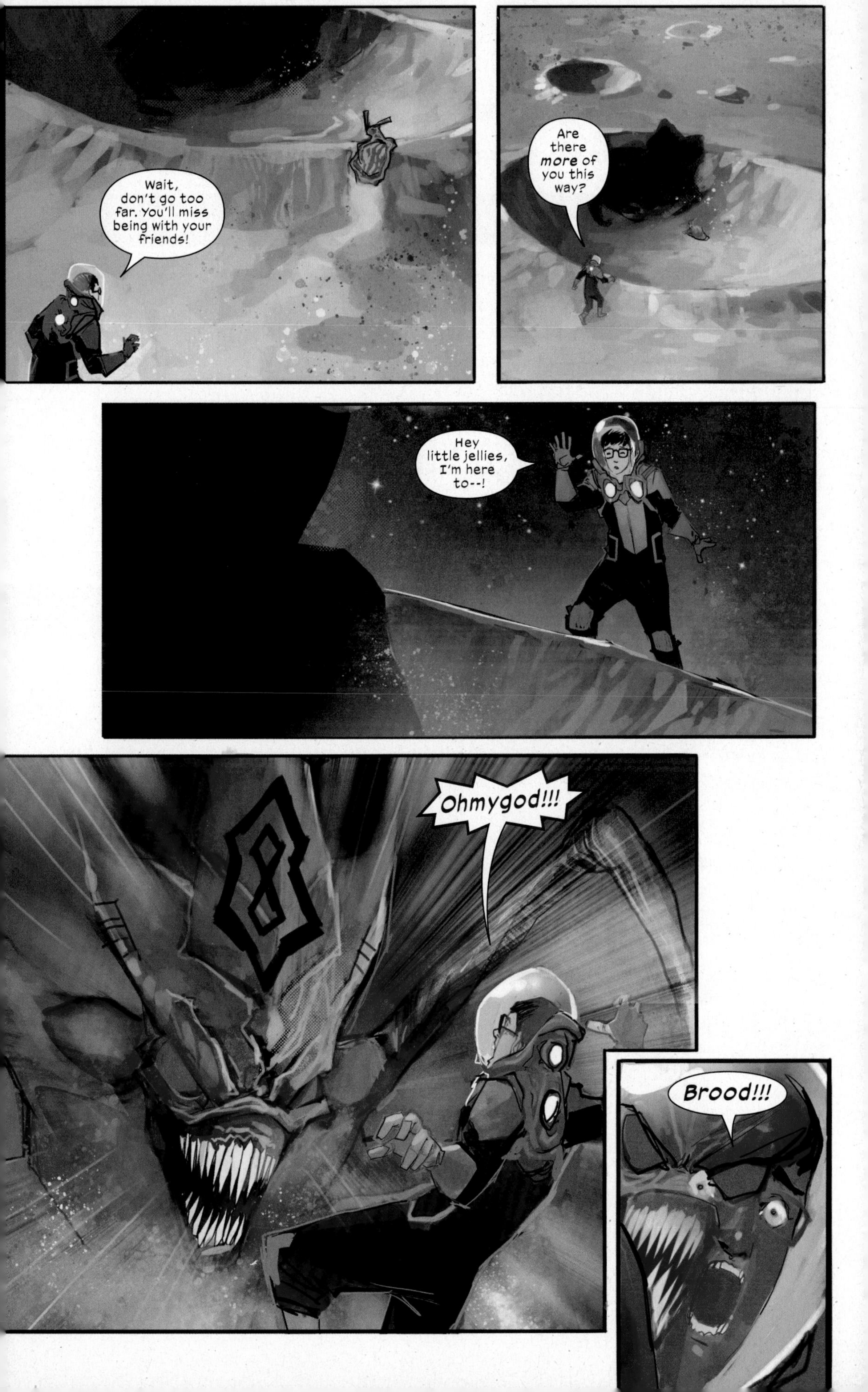
Wait, don't go too far. You'll miss being with your friends!
Are there *more* of you this way?
Hey little jellies, I'm here to--!
Ohmygod!!!
Brood!!!

WARPATH JOURNAL, ENTRY 005

Write about an incredibly difficult choice you've had to make in your life.

The choice to live. There has never been a harder choice than to continue in this world without...without some of the people I loved most. While resurrection has changed some of what that means, it hasn't erased the pain or loneliness that comes from turning to share words with someone and they aren't there.

I work hard not to dwell on things I cannot change, but it would be a lie of omission not to say that sometimes I see faces in my dreams, and my heart grieves because I can't remember the voices that go with them.

But I do not regret staying to fight for a world where mutant children will feel more joy than sadness.

What are some silver linings in hard lessons that you've learned?

There is always someone relying on you. I think many people would not think that this is a silver lining, but it has often been the only reason I have been able to endure some of the worst times. The misunderstanding that those people have is that being someone others rely upon is a position solely of giving, but they are wrong.

No matter how terribly you stumble, if you are committed to your people then you have not failed, and they will continue to trust and support you. I give my strength, and receive strength in return. I give my blood and tears, and I receive the effort and vulnerability of my people in return.

I can't fathom something more important or sacred than this.

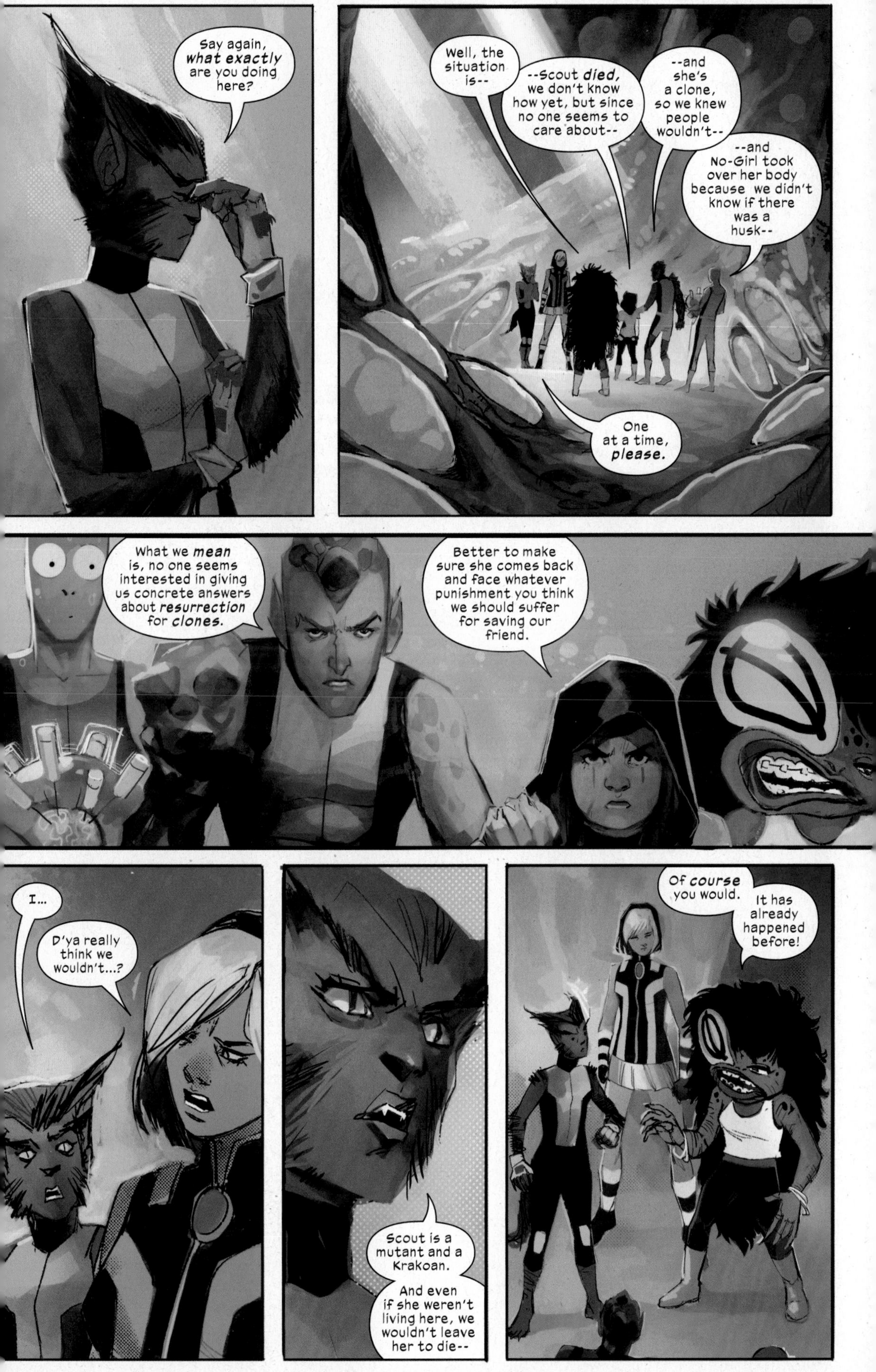
Say again, *what exactly* are you doing here?
Well, the situation is--
--Scout *died,* we don't know how yet, but since no one seems to care about--
--and she's a clone, so we knew people wouldn't--
--and No-Girl took over her body because we didn't know if there was a husk--
One at a time, *please.*
What we *mean* is, no one seems interested in giving us concrete answers about *resurrection* for *clones.*
Better to make sure she comes back and face whatever punishment you think we should suffer for saving our friend.
I...
D'ya really think we wouldn't...?
Scout is a mutant and a Krakoan.
And even if she weren't living here, we wouldn't leave her to die--
Of *course* you would.
It has already happened before!

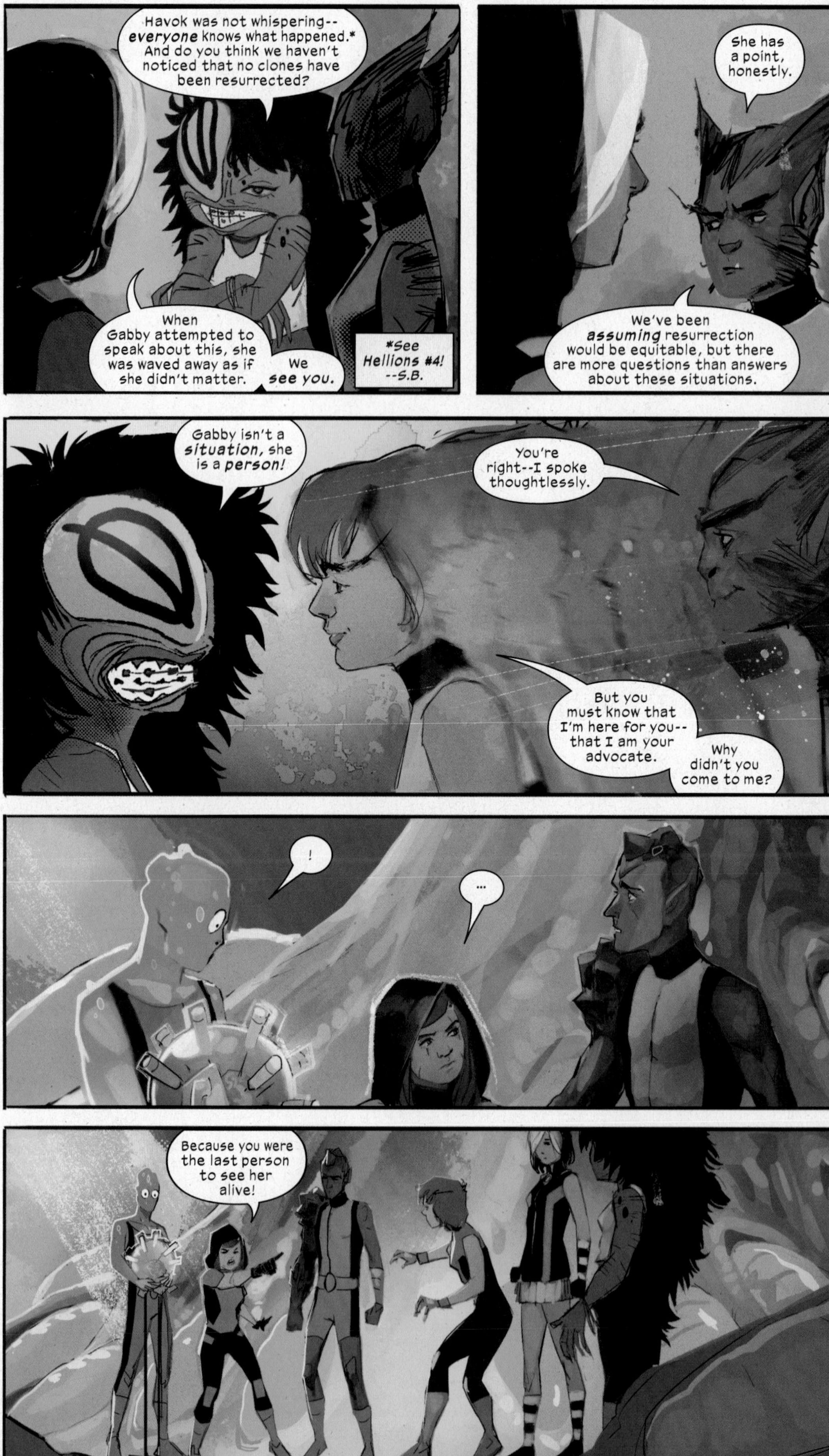

Havok was not whispering-- everyone knows what happened.* And do you think we haven't noticed that no clones have been resurrected?
When Gabby attempted to speak about this, she was waved away as if she didn't matter.
We see you.
*See Hellions #4! --S.B.
She has a point, honestly.
We've been assuming resurrection would be equitable, but there are more questions than answers about these situations.
Gabby isn't a situation, she is a person!
You're right--I spoke thoughtlessly.
But you must know that I'm here for you-- that I am your advocate.
Why didn't you come to me?
!
...
Because you were the last person to see her alive!

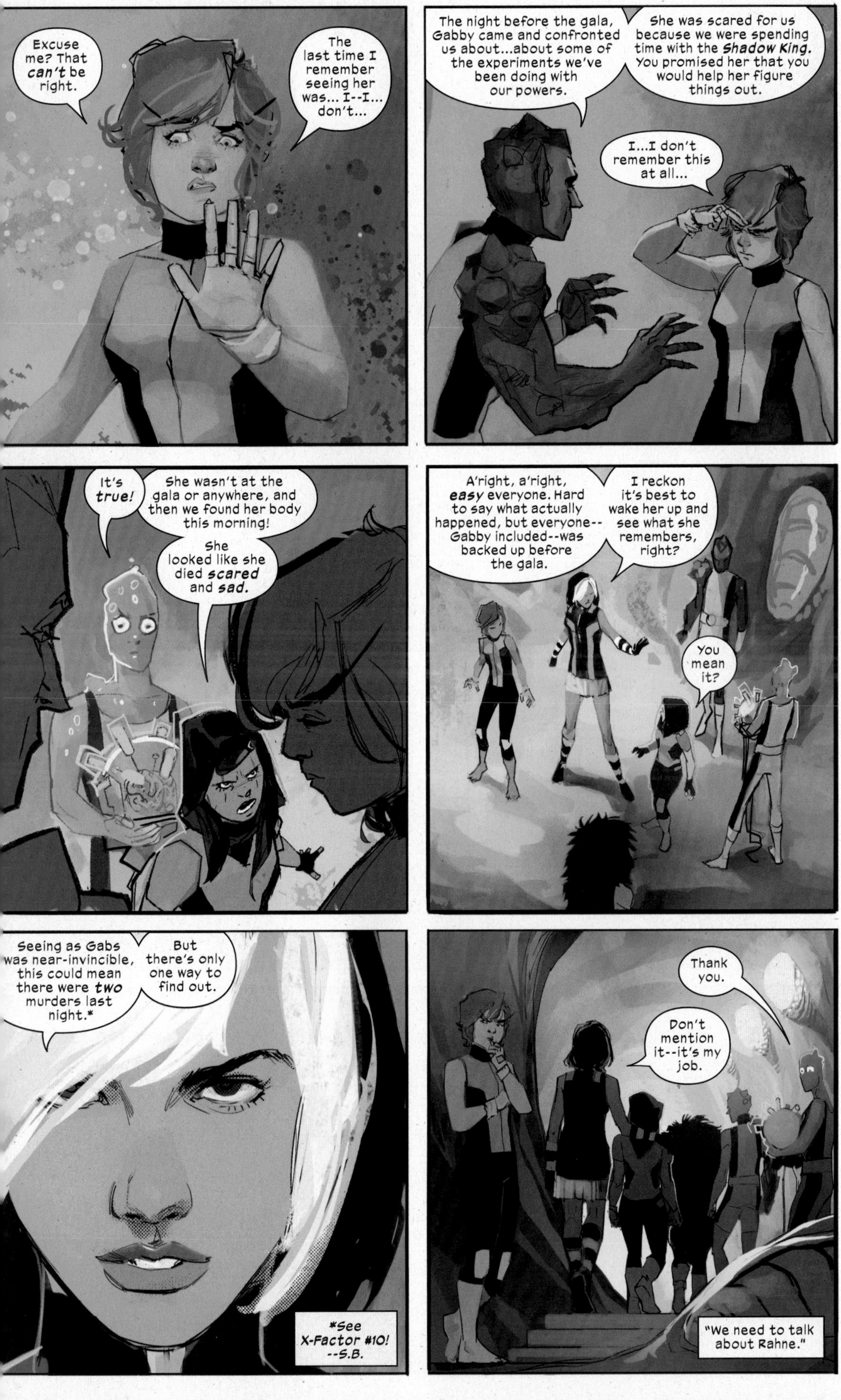
Excuse me? That *can't* be right.
The last time I remember seeing her was... I--I... don't...
The night before the gala, Gabby came and confronted us about...about some of the experiments we've been doing with our powers.
She was scared for us because we were spending time with the *Shadow King.* You promised her that you would help her figure things out.
I...I don't remember this at all...
It's *true!*
She wasn't at the gala or anywhere, and then we found her body this morning!
She looked like she died *scared* and *sad.*
A'right, a'right, *easy* everyone. Hard to say what actually happened, but everyone--Gabby included--was backed up before the gala.
I reckon it's best to wake her up and see what she remembers, right?
You mean it?
Seeing as Gabs was near-invincible, this could mean there were *two* murders last night.*
But there's only one way to find out.
*See X-Factor #10! --S.B.
Thank you.
Don't mention it--it's my job.
"We need to talk about Rahne."

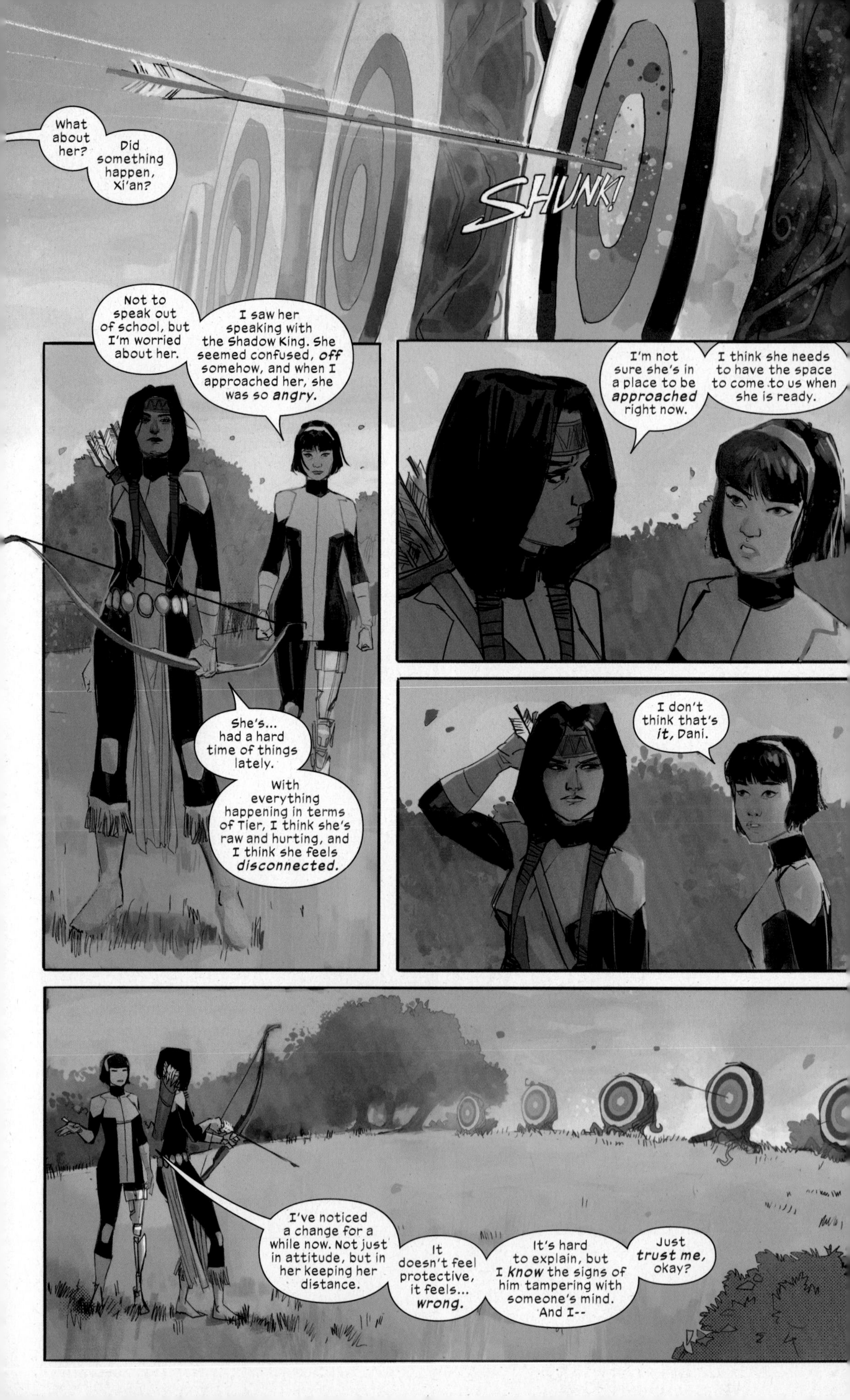
What about her?
Did something happen, Xi'an?
SHUNK!
Not to speak out of school, but I'm worried about her.
I saw her speaking with the Shadow King. She seemed confused, *off* somehow, and when I approached her, she was so *angry.*
I'm not sure she's in a place to be *approached* right now.
I think she needs to have the space to come to us when she is ready.
She's... had a hard time of things lately.
With everything happening in terms of Tier, I think she's raw and hurting, and I think she feels *disconnected.*
I don't think that's *it,* Dani.
I've noticed a change for a while now. Not just in attitude, but in her keeping her distance.
It doesn't feel protective, it feels... *wrong.*
It's hard to explain, but I *know* the signs of him tampering with someone's mind. And I--
Just *trust me,* okay?

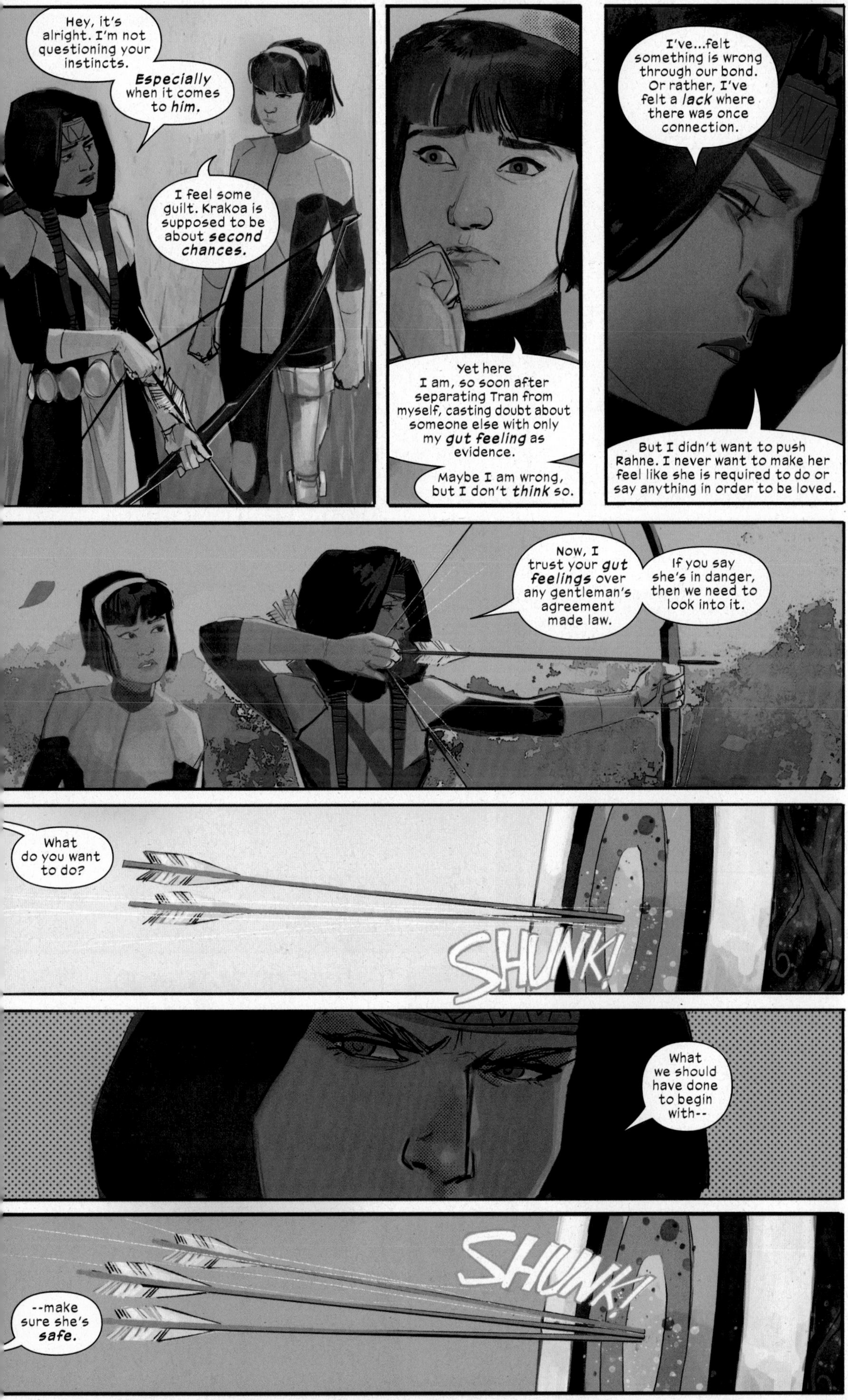
Hey, it's alright. I'm not questioning your instincts.
Especially when it comes to him.
I feel some guilt. Krakoa is supposed to be about second chances.
Yet here I am, so soon after separating Tran from myself, casting doubt about someone else with only my gut feeling as evidence.
Maybe I am wrong, but I don't think so.
I've...felt something is wrong through our bond. Or rather, I've felt a lack where there was once connection.
But I didn't want to push Rahne. I never want to make her feel like she is required to do or say anything in order to be loved.
Now, I trust your gut feelings over any gentleman's agreement made law.
If you say she's in danger, then we need to look into it.
What do you want to do?
SHUNK!
What we should have done to begin with--
SHUNK!
--make sure she's safe.

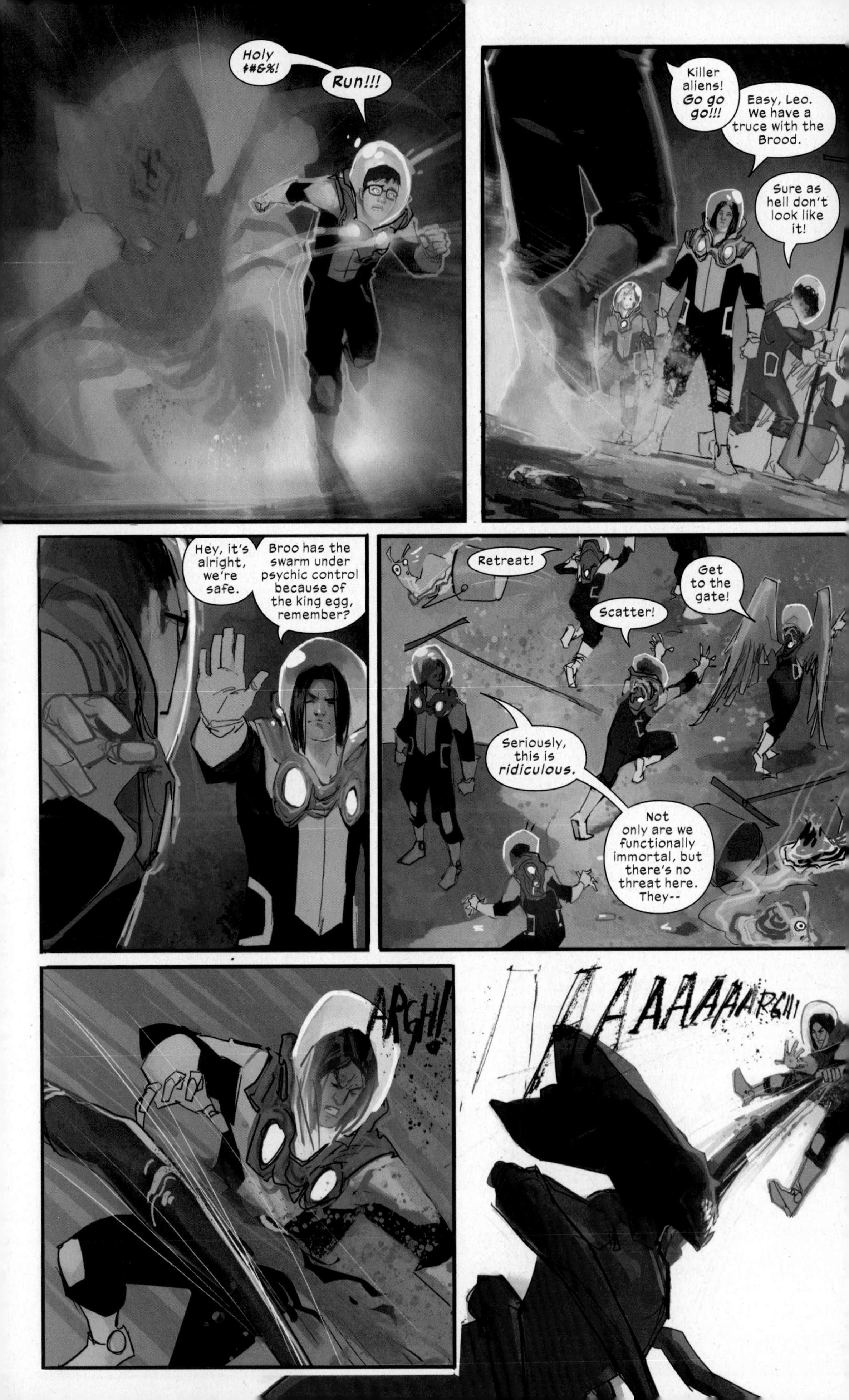
Holy $#&%!
Run!!!
Killer aliens! Go go go!!!
Easy, Leo. We have a truce with the Brood.
Sure as hell don't look like it!
Hey, it's alright, we're safe.
Broo has the swarm under psychic control because of the king egg, remember?
Retreat!
Scatter!
Get to the gate!
Seriously, this is ridiculous.
Not only are we functionally immortal, but there's no threat here. They--
ARGH!
AAAAAARGH!

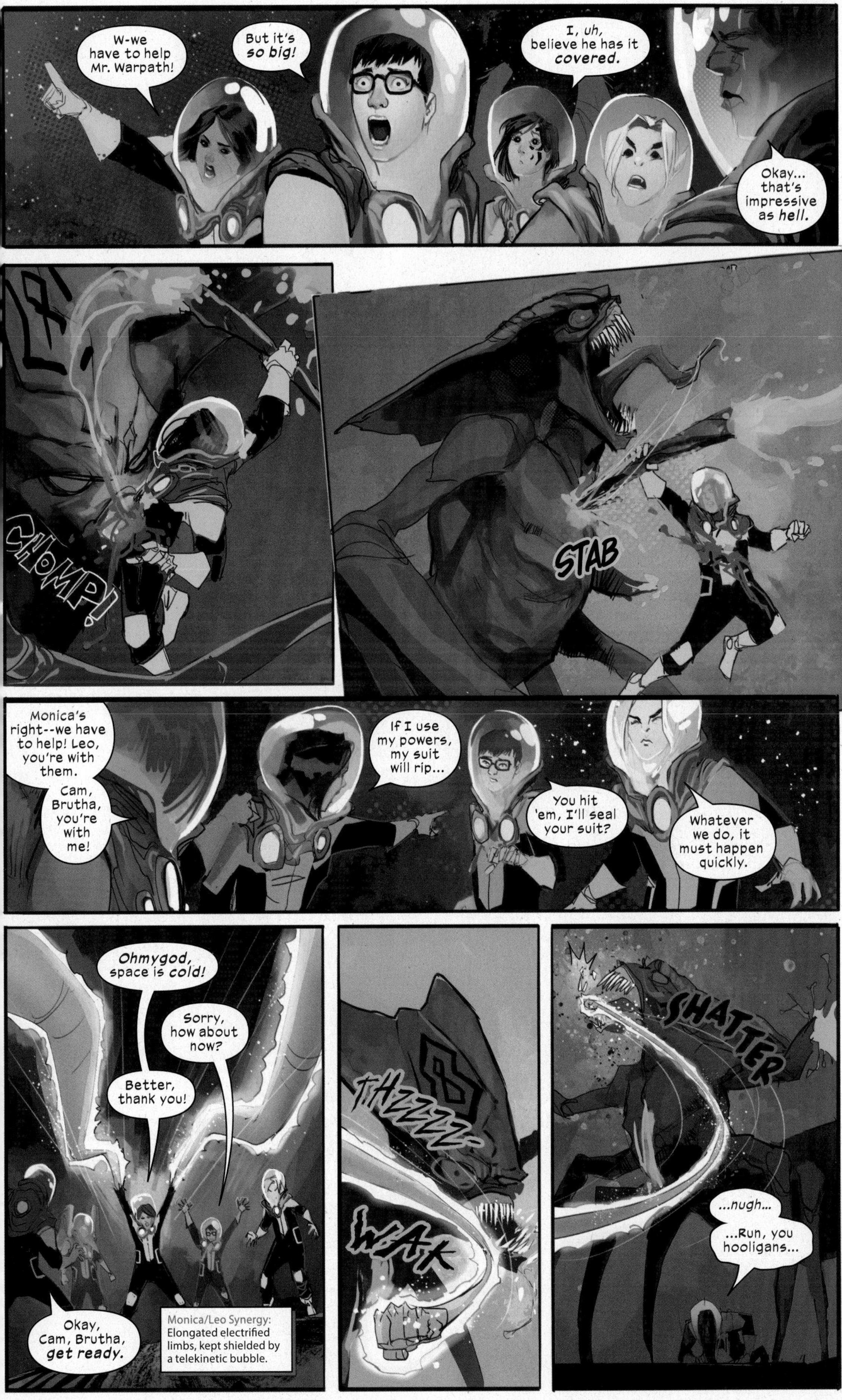
W-we have to help Mr. Warpath!
But it's *so big!*
I, uh, believe he has it ***covered.***
Okay... that's impressive as ***hell.***
CHOMP!
STAB
Monica's right--we have to help! Leo, you're with them.
Cam, Brutha, you're with me!
If I use my powers, my suit will rip...
You hit 'em, I'll seal your suit?
Whatever we do, it must happen quickly.
Ohmygod, space is *cold!*
Sorry, how about now?
Better, thank you!
Okay, Cam, Brutha, ***get ready.***
Monica/Leo Synergy: Elongated electrified limbs, kept shielded by a telekinetic bubble.
THZZZZ-
WAK
SHATTER
...nugh...
...Run, you hooligans...

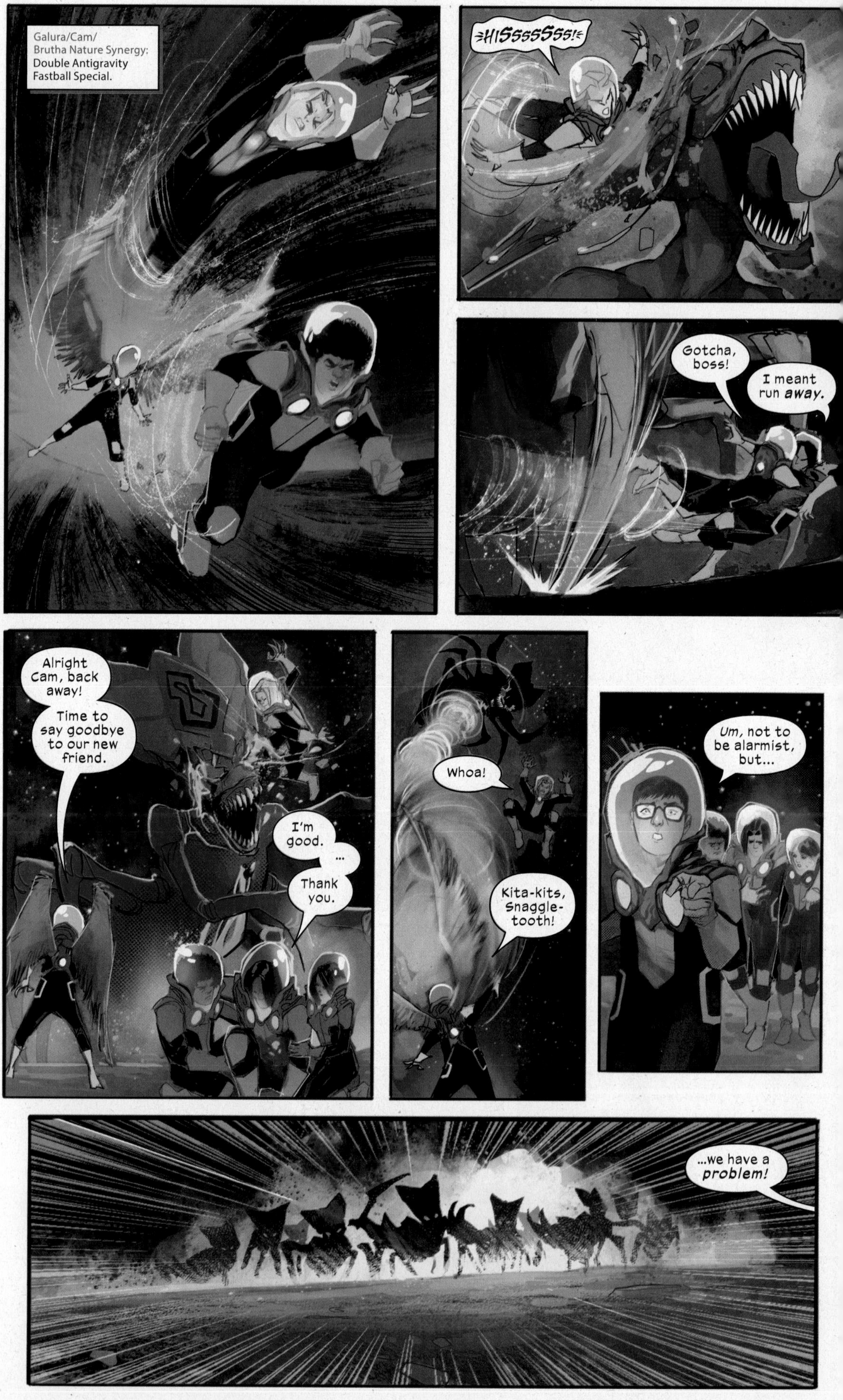

Galura/Cam/
Brutha Nature Synergy:
Double Antigravity
Fastball Special.
HISSSSSSS!
Gotcha, boss!
I meant run *away.*
Alright Cam, back away!
Time to say goodbye to our new friend.
I'm good.
...
Thank you.
Whoa!
Kita-kits, Snaggle-tooth!
Um, not to be alarmist, but...
...we have a *problem!*

RESURRECTION STATUS QUO

RE: The resurrection of "dupes"

It was our understanding that the purpose of "no copies" was to avoid making duplicates of individuals who are still active. However, we believe that there has been a misunderstanding of what it means to be an individual.

Genetically derivative or even genetically identical individuals are not necessarily "dupes" (identical twins exist even among humans). Mutants such as Gabby Kinney, Madelyne Pryor and Evan Sabahnur (and others in situations like theirs) are their own people, regardless of genetics.

Cerebro only recognizes individuals, not "dupes," and all of the above are registered and stored in the system as individuals.

We formally request that you update the understanding of personhood accordingly as the narrow definition is counter to the point of our work.

-- THE FIVE

Hope   *Proteus*

Elixir

Tempus   *Egg*

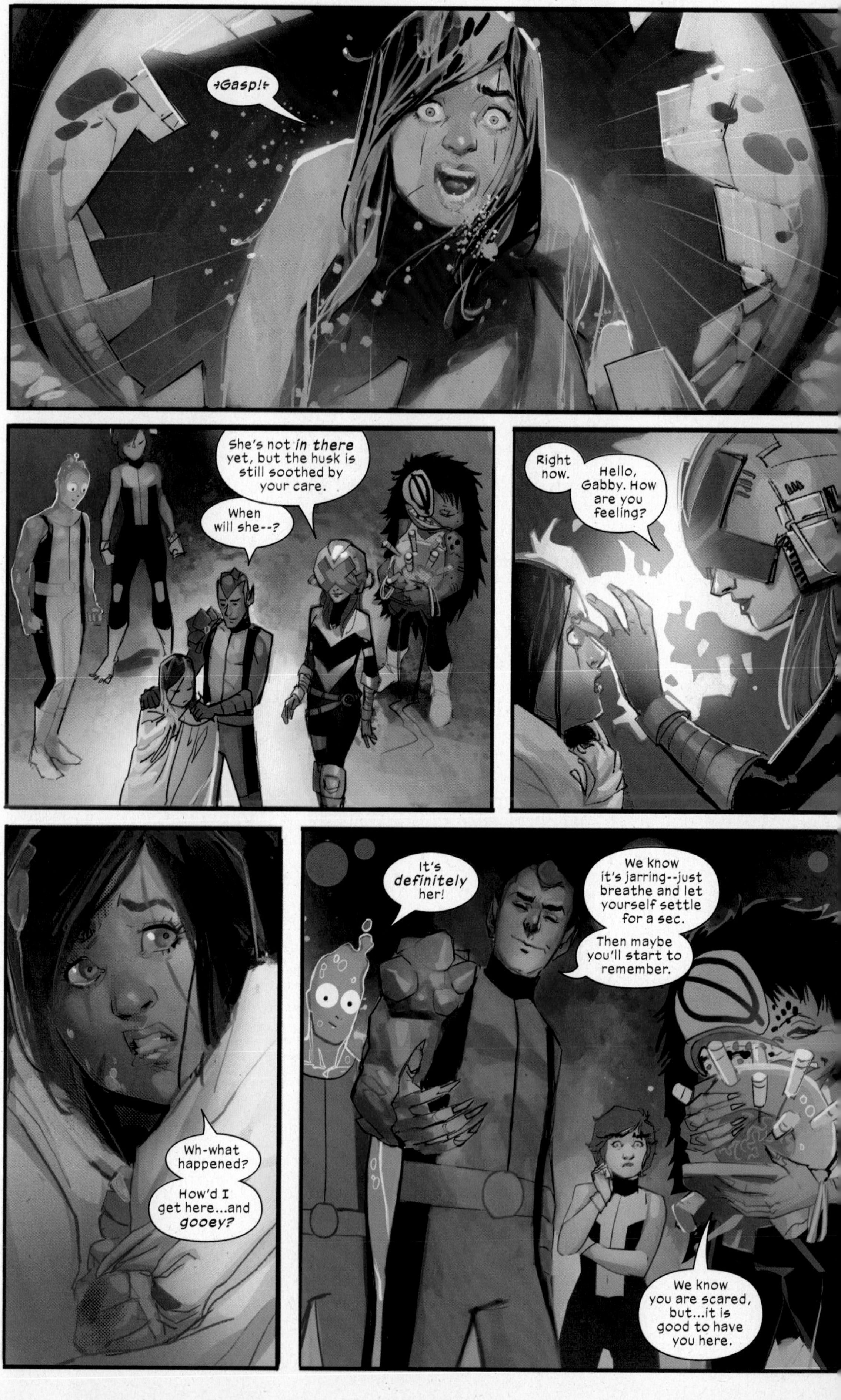

+Gasp!+
She's not in there yet, but the husk is still soothed by your care.
When will she--?
Right now.
Hello, Gabby. How are you feeling?
Wh-what happened?
How'd I get here...and gooey?
It's definitely her!
We know it's jarring--just breathe and let yourself settle for a sec.
Then maybe you'll start to remember.
We know you are scared, but...it is good to have you here.

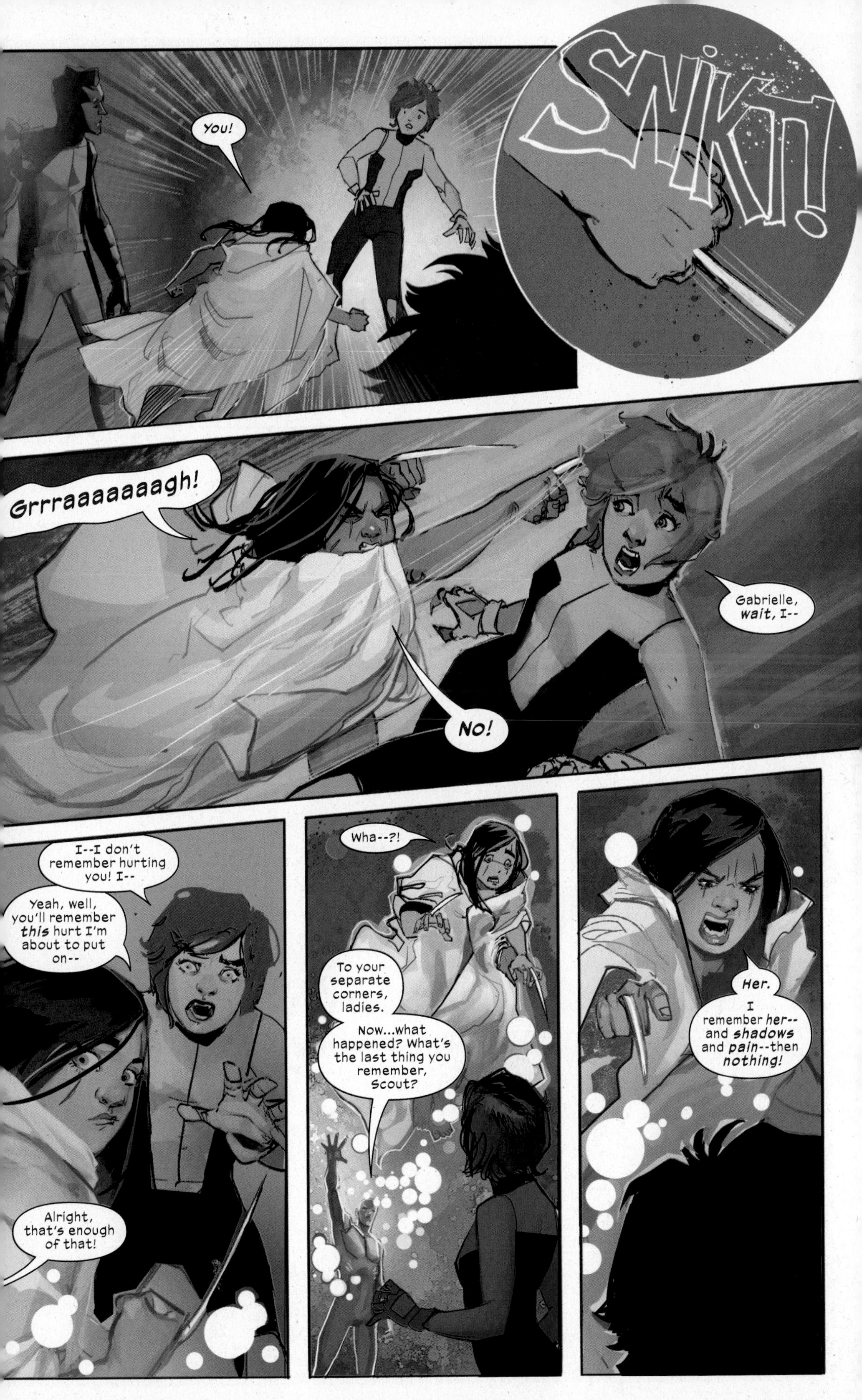
You!
SNIKT!
Grrraaaaaaagh!
Gabrielle, wait, I--
No!
I--I don't remember hurting you! I--
Yeah, well, you'll remember this hurt I'm about to put on--
Alright, that's enough of that!
Wha--?!
To your separate corners, ladies.
Now...what happened? What's the last thing you remember, Scout?
Her.
I remember her--and shadows and pain--then nothing!

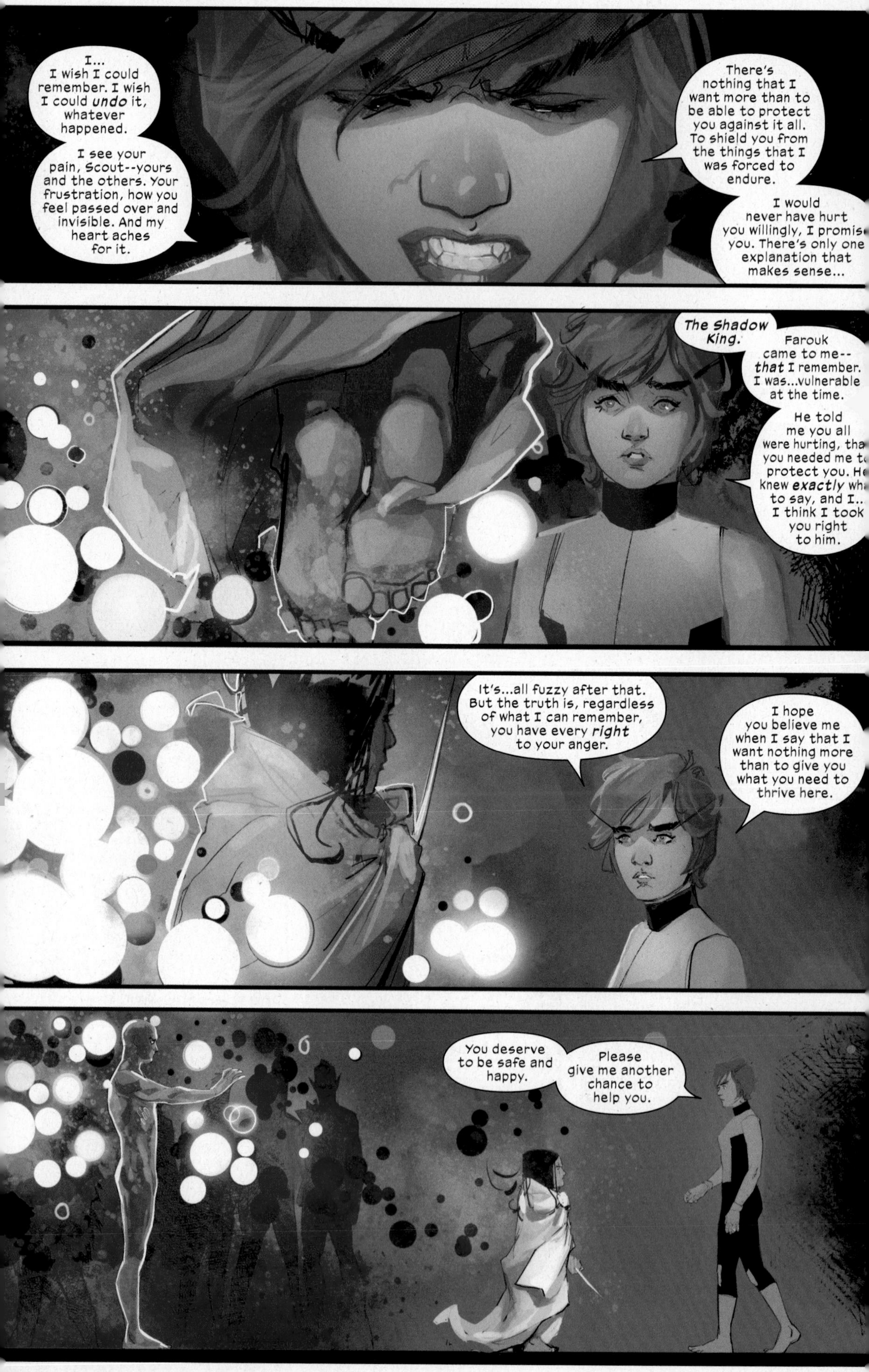

I... I wish I could remember. I wish I could *undo* it, whatever happened.
I see your pain, Scout--yours and the others. Your frustration, how you feel passed over and invisible. And my heart aches for it.
There's nothing that I want more than to be able to protect you against it all. To shield you from the things that I was forced to endure.
I would never have hurt you willingly, I promise you. There's only one explanation that makes sense...
The Shadow King.
Farouk came to me-- *that* I remember. I was...vulnerable at the time.
He told me you all were hurting, that you needed me to protect you. He knew *exactly* what to say, and I... I think I took you right to him.
It's...all fuzzy after that. But the truth is, regardless of what I can remember, you have every *right* to your anger.
I hope you believe me when I say that I want nothing more than to give you what you need to thrive here.
You deserve to be safe and happy.
Please give me another chance to help you.

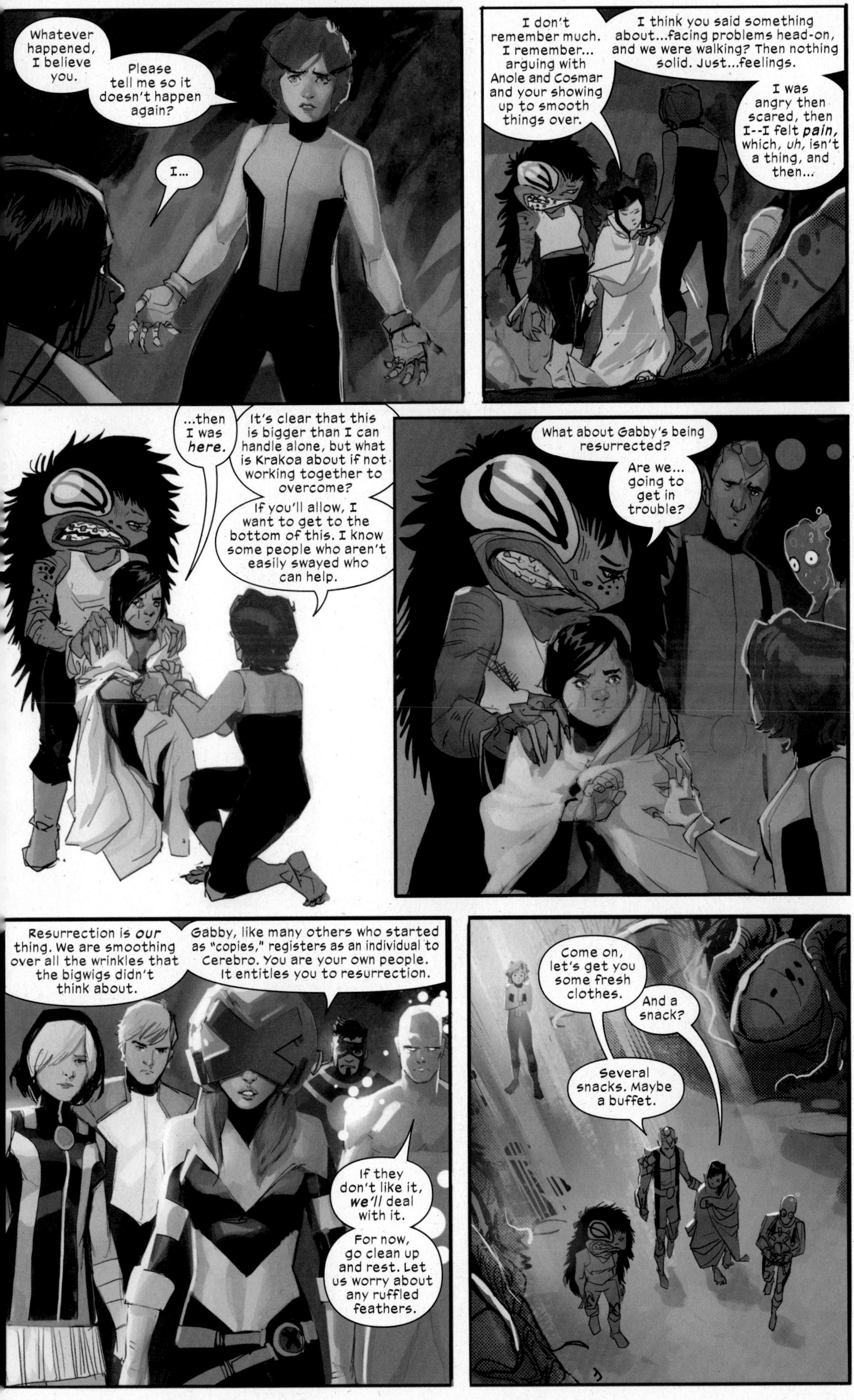
Whatever happened, I believe you.
Please tell me so it doesn't happen again?
I...
I don't remember much. I remember... arguing with Anole and Cosmar and your showing up to smooth things over.
I think you said something about...facing problems head-on, and we were walking? Then nothing solid. Just...feelings.
I was angry then scared, then I--I felt *pain,* which, *uh,* isn't a thing, and then...
...then I was *here.*
It's clear that this is bigger than I can handle alone, but what is Krakoa about if not working together to overcome?
If you'll allow, I want to get to the bottom of this. I know some people who aren't easily swayed who can help.
What about Gabby's being resurrected?
Are we... going to get in trouble?
Resurrection is *our* thing. We are smoothing over all the wrinkles that the bigwigs didn't think about.
Gabby, like many others who started as "copies," registers as an individual to Cerebro. You are your own people. It entitles you to resurrection.
If they don't like it, *we'll* deal with it.
For now, go clean up and rest. Let us worry about any ruffled feathers.
Come on, let's get you some fresh clothes.
And a snack?
Several snacks. Maybe a buffet.

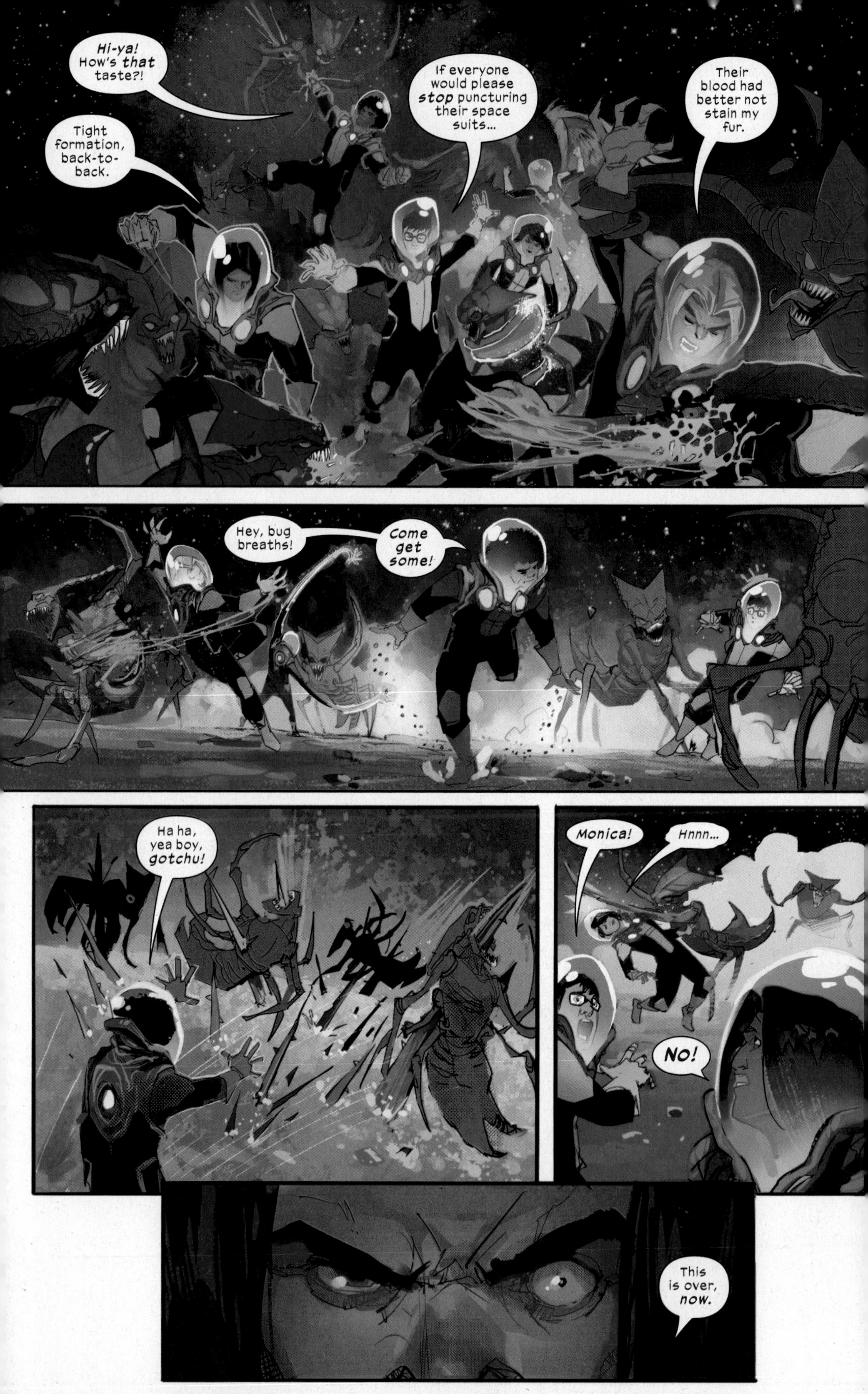

Hi-ya! How's that taste?!
Tight formation, back-to-back.
If everyone would please stop puncturing their space suits...
Their blood had better not stain my fur.
Hey, bug breaths!
Come get some!
Ha ha, yea boy, gotchu!
Monica!
Hnnn...
NO!
This is over, now.

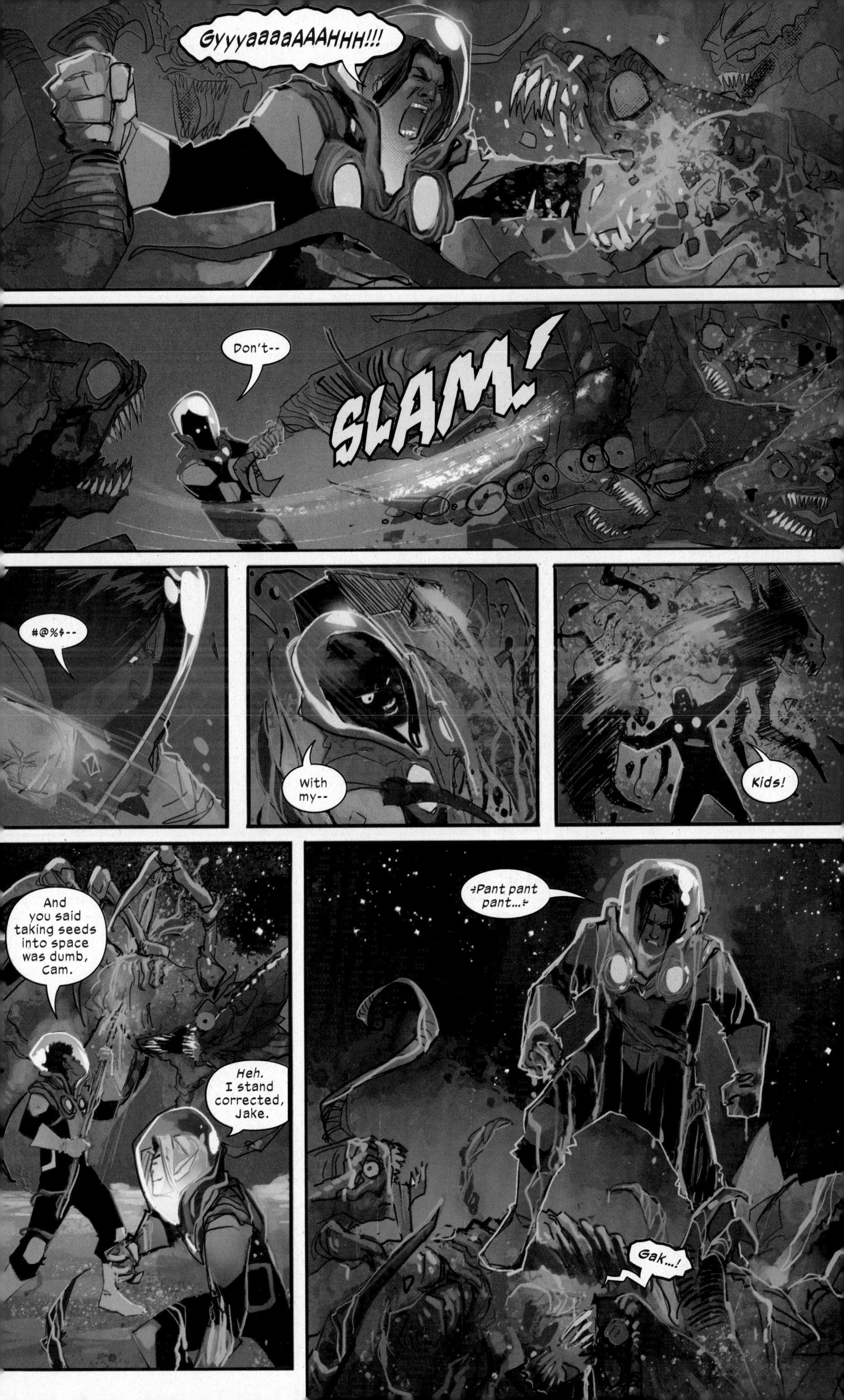

GyyyaaaaAAAHHH!!!
Don't--
SLAM!
#@%$--
With my--
Kids!
And you said taking seeds into space was dumb, Cam.
Heh. I stand corrected, Jake.
Pant pant pant...
Gak...!

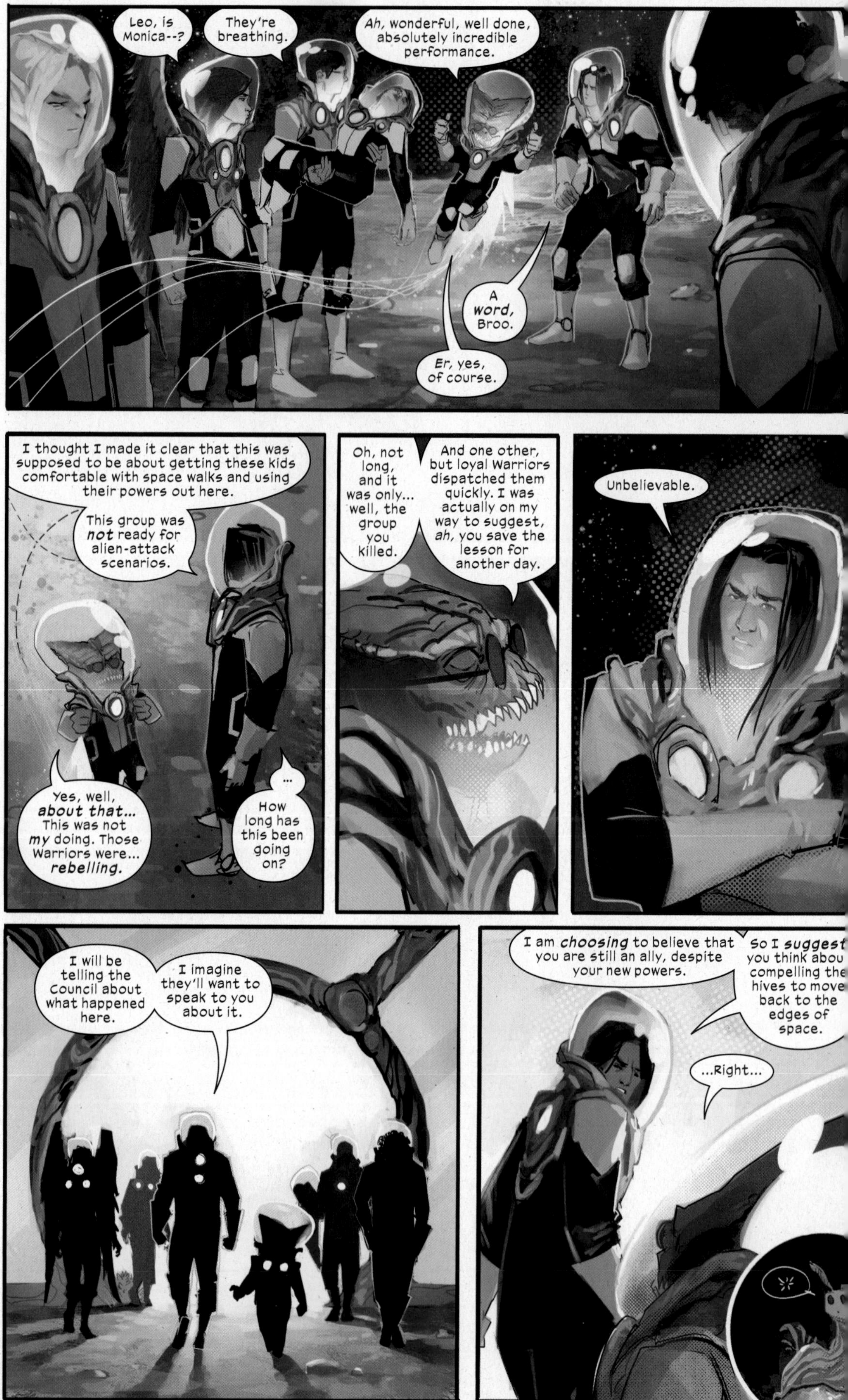

Leo, is Monica--?
They're breathing.
Ah, wonderful, well done, absolutely incredible performance.
A word, Broo.
Er, yes, of course.
I thought I made it clear that this was supposed to be about getting these kids comfortable with space walks and using their powers out here.
This group was not ready for alien-attack scenarios.
Yes, well, about that... This was not my doing. Those Warriors were... rebelling.
...
How long has this been going on?
Oh, not long, and it was only... well, the group you killed.
And one other, but loyal Warriors dispatched them quickly. I was actually on my way to suggest, ah, you save the lesson for another day.
Unbelievable.
I will be telling the Council about what happened here.
I imagine they'll want to speak to you about it.
I am choosing to believe that you are still an ally, despite your new powers.
So I suggest you think abou compelling the hives to move back to the edges of space.
...Right...

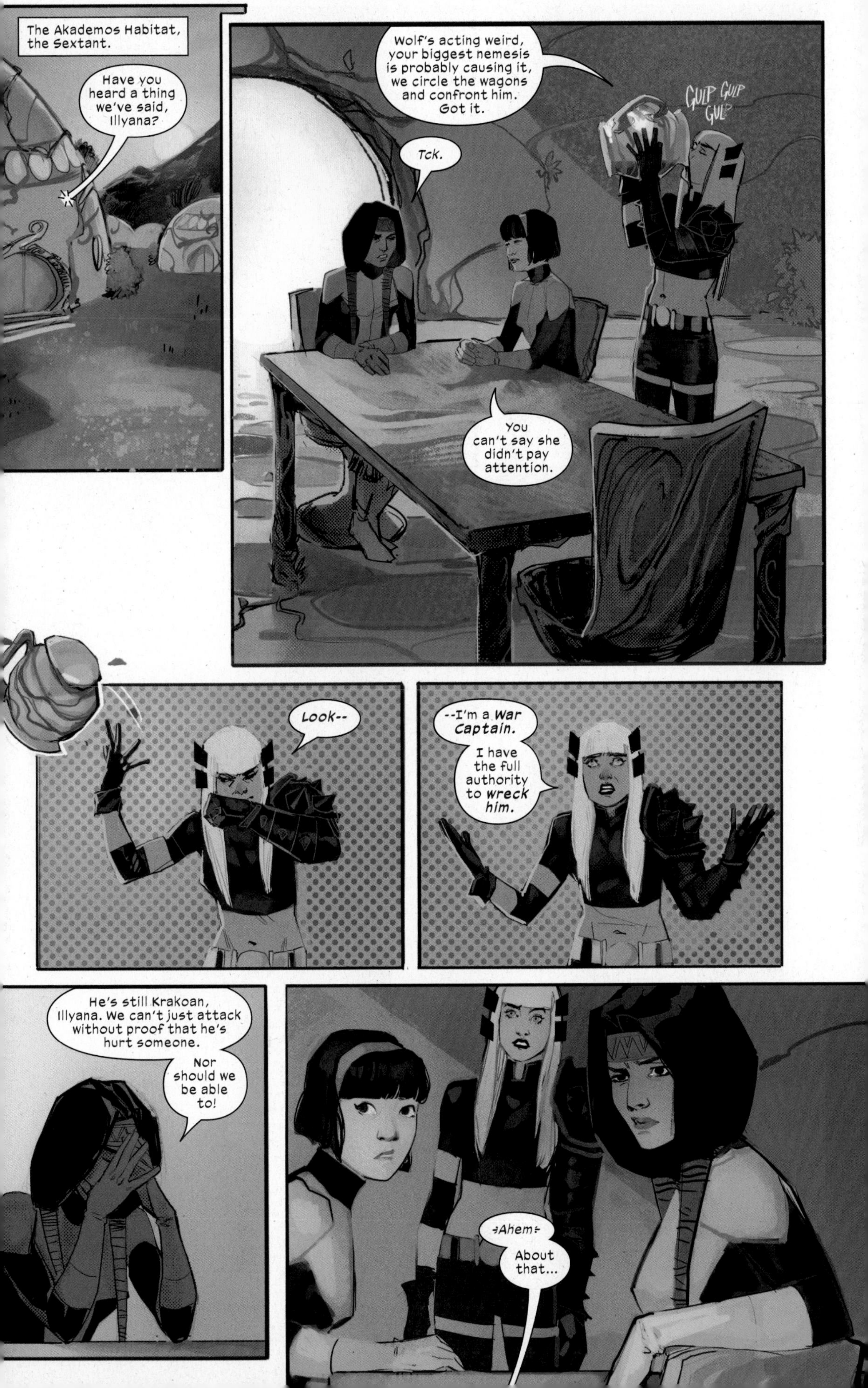
The Akademos Habitat, the Sextant.
Have you heard a thing we've said, Illyana?
Wolf's acting weird, your biggest nemesis is probably causing it, we circle the wagons and confront him. Got it.
GULP GULP GULP
Tck.
You can't say she didn't pay attention.
Look--
--I'm a War Captain.
I have the full authority to wreck him.
He's still Krakoan, Illyana. We can't just attack without proof that he's hurt someone.
Nor should we be able to!
=Ahem=
About that...

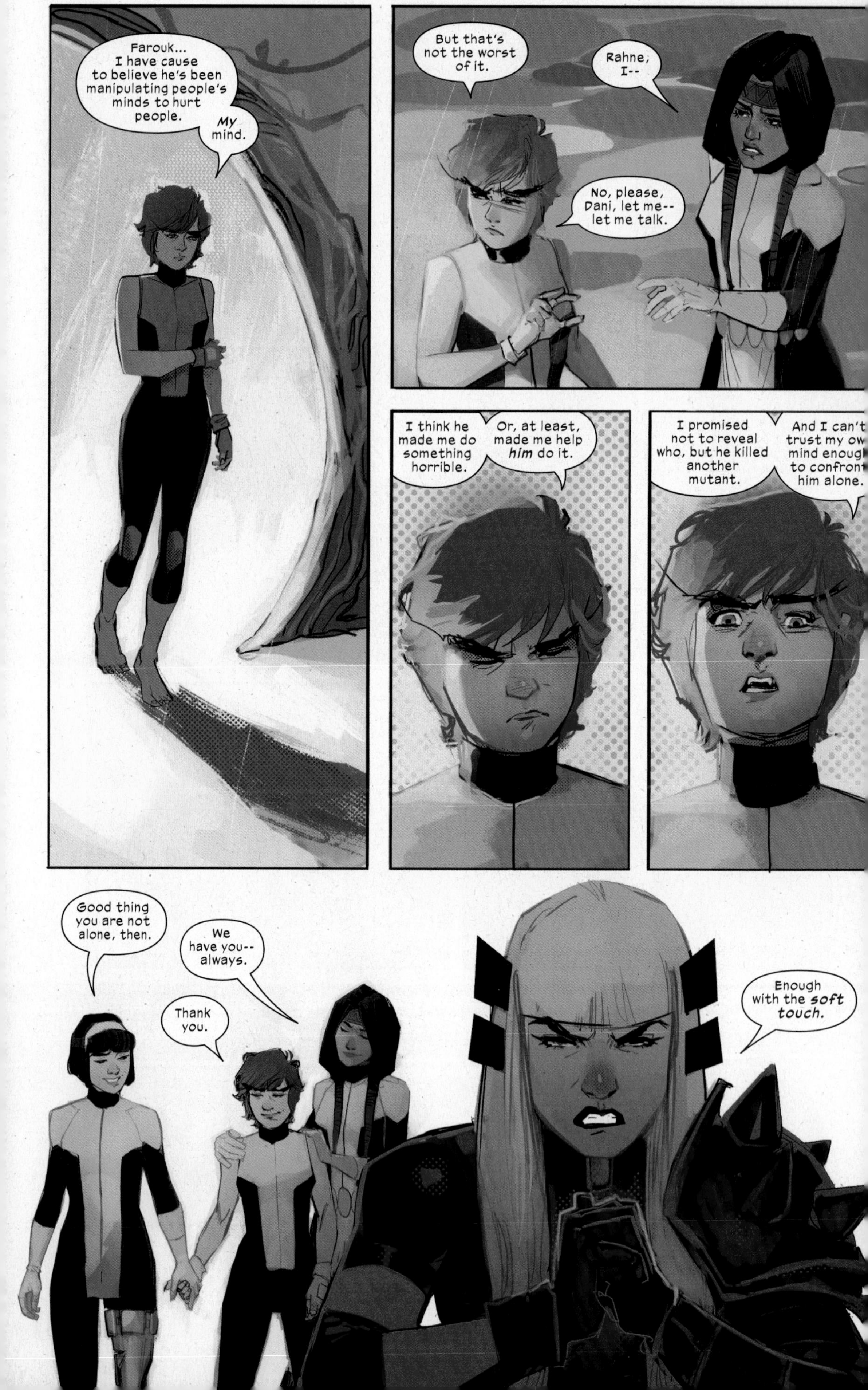
Farouk... I have cause to believe he's been manipulating people's minds to hurt people.
My mind.
But that's not the worst of it.
Rahne, I--
No, please, Dani, let me-- let me talk.
I think he made me do something horrible.
Or, at least, made me help *him* do it.
I promised not to reveal who, but he killed another mutant.
And I can't trust my own mind enough to confront him alone.
Good thing you are not alone, then.
We have you-- always.
Thank you.
Enough with the *soft touch.*

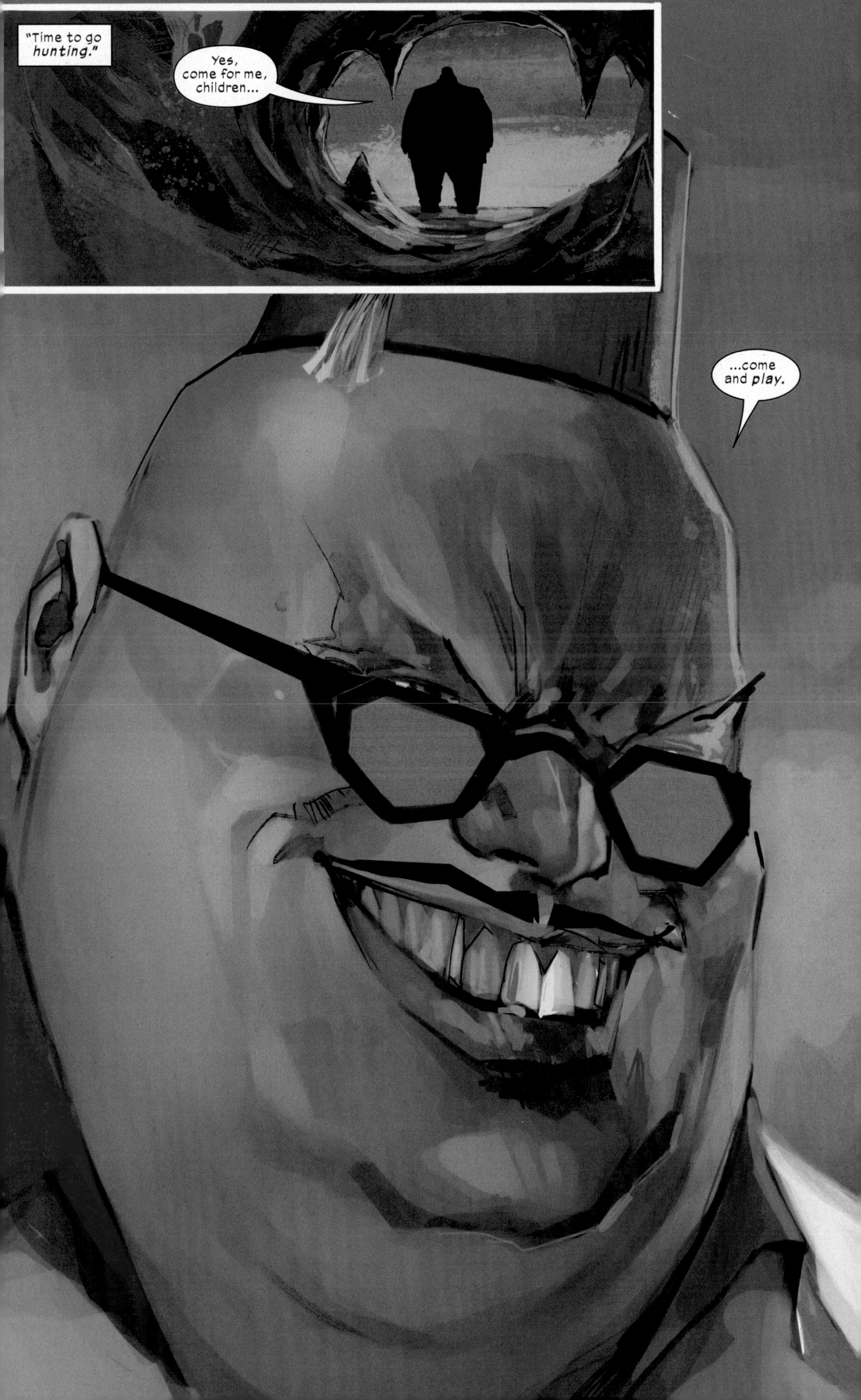
"Time to go *hunting.*"
Yes, come for me, children...
...come and *play.*

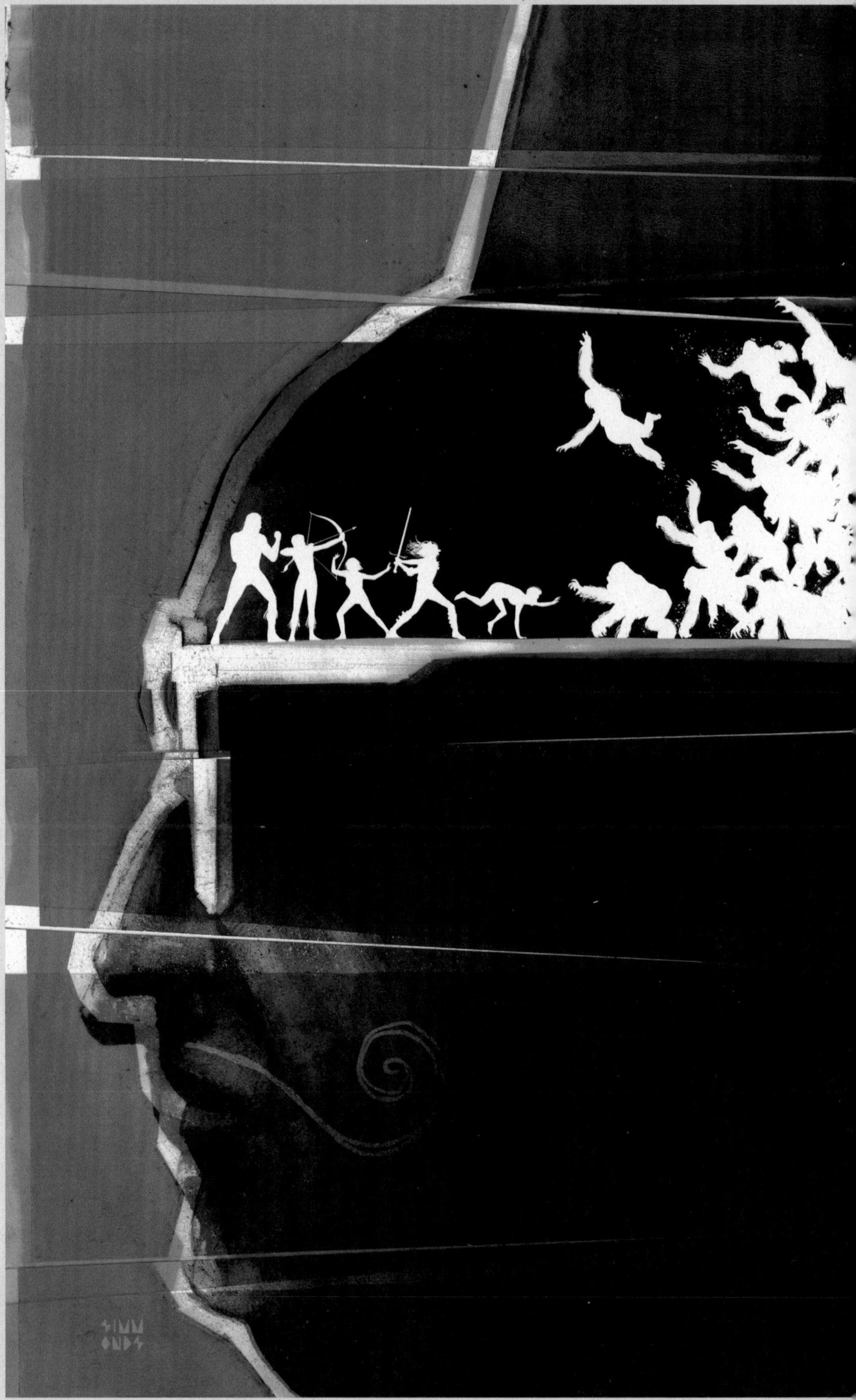
SIMMONDS

Shadows and Mirrors

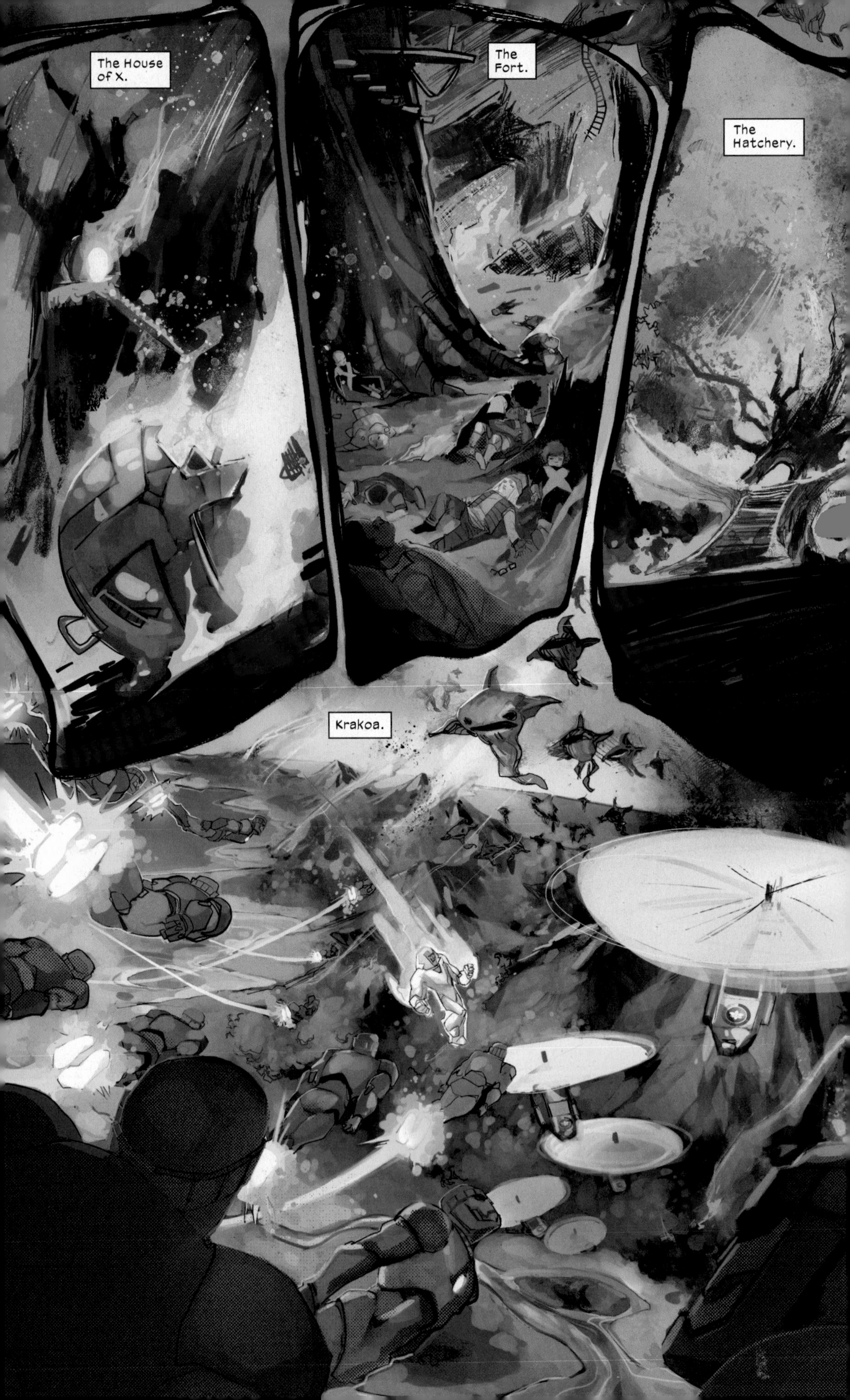

The House of X.
The Fort.
The Hatchery.
Krakoa.

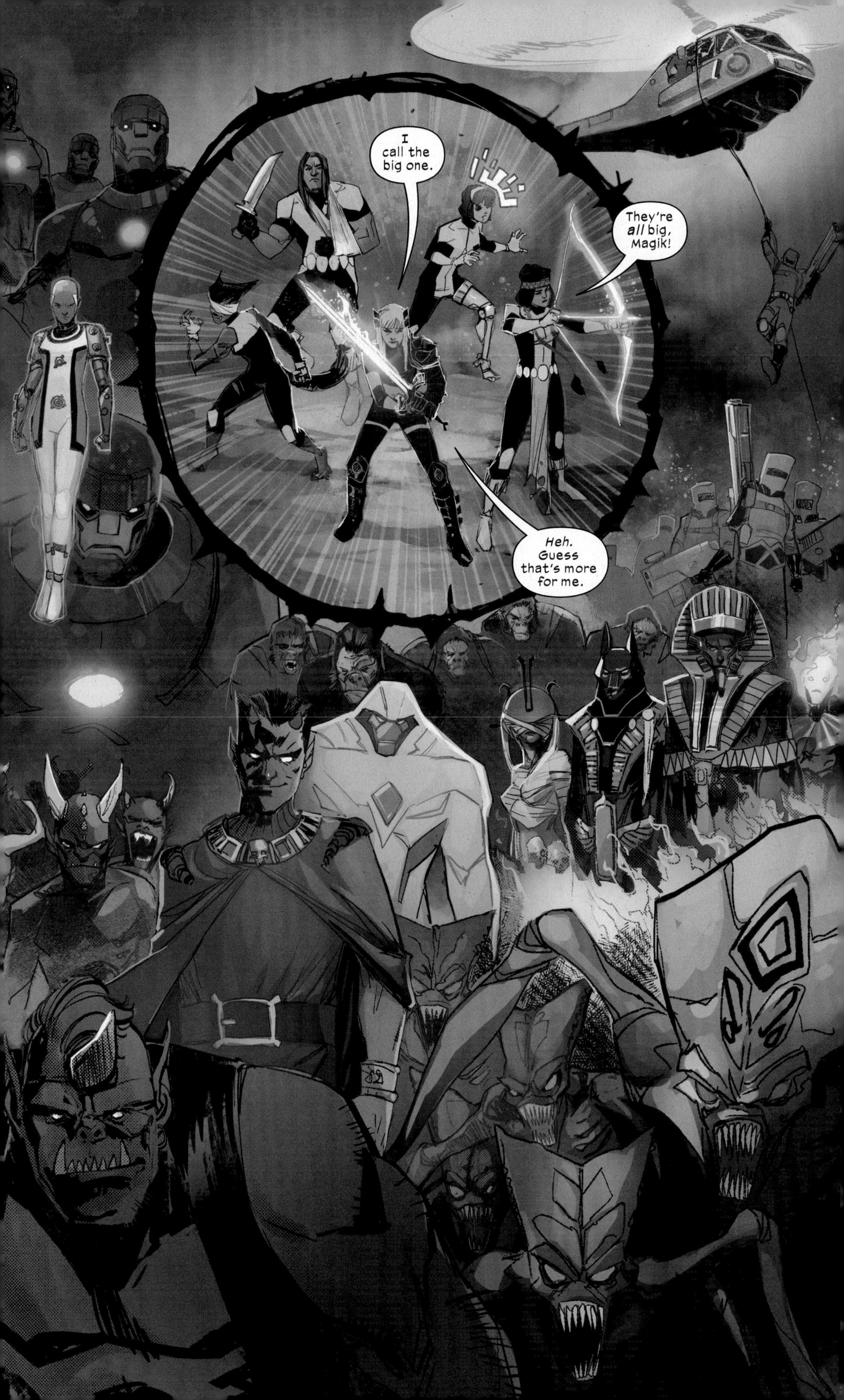
I call the big one.
They're *all* big, Magik!
Heh. Guess that's more for me.

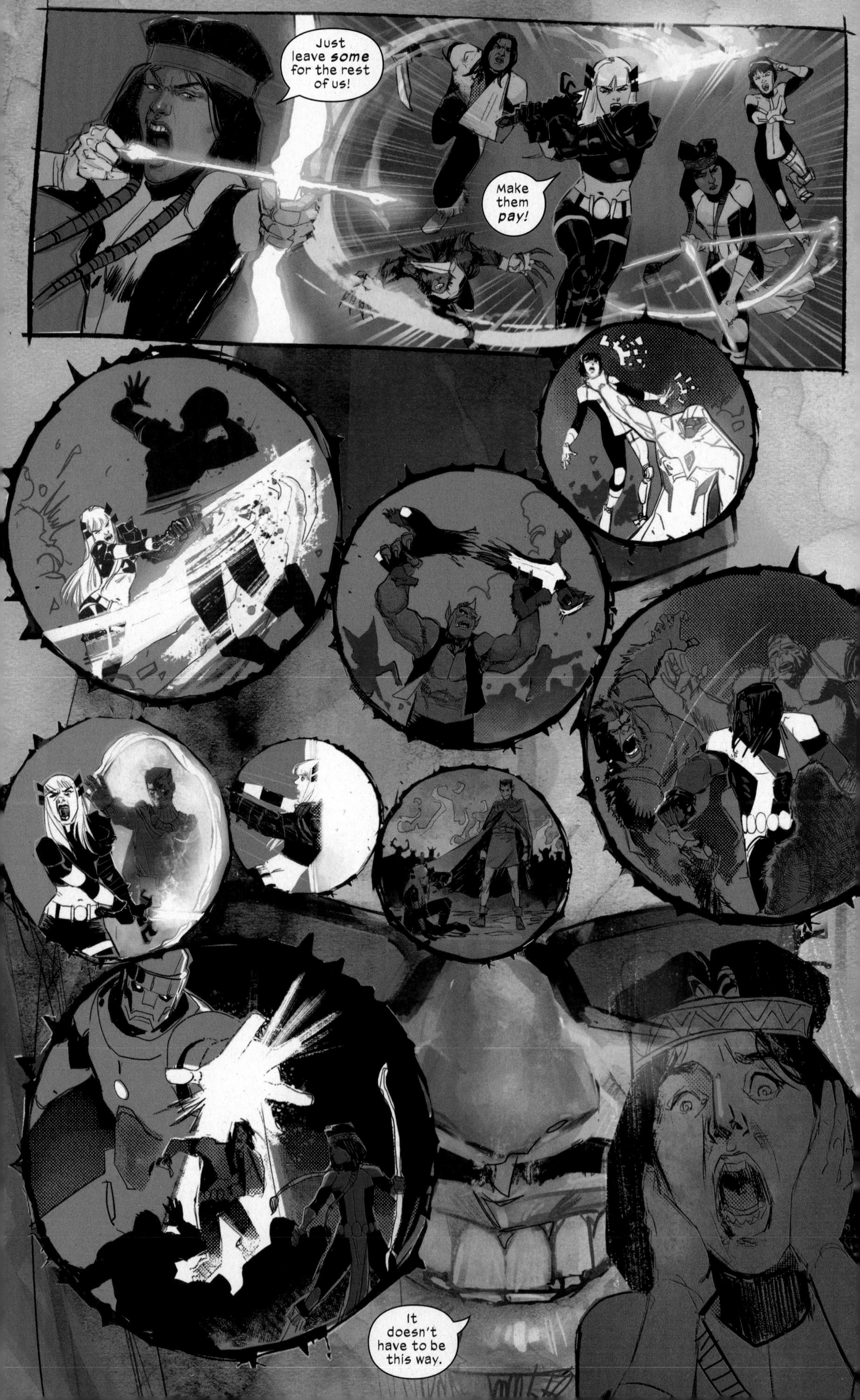
Just leave *some* for the rest of us!
Make them *pay!*
It doesn't have to be this way.

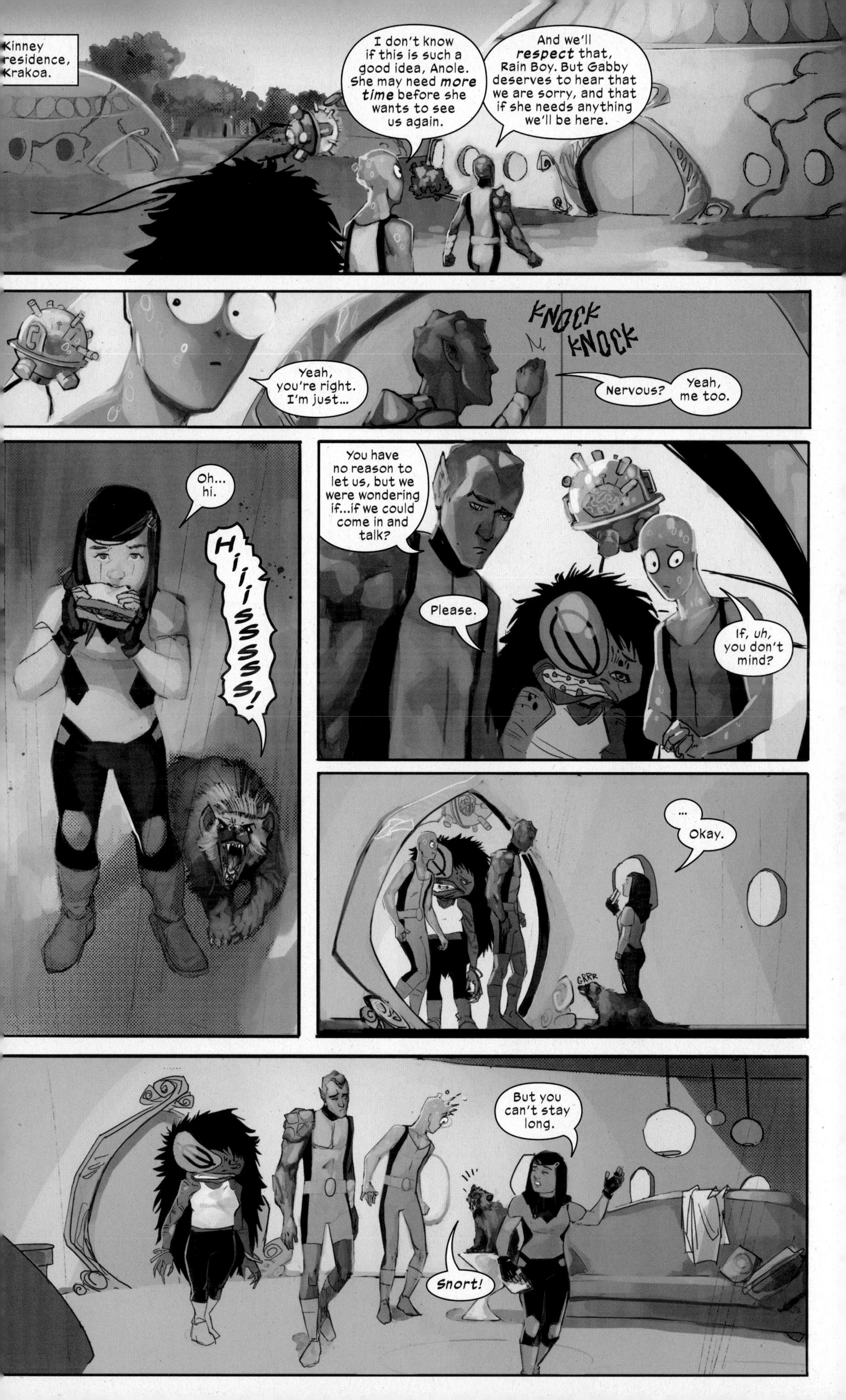
Kinney residence, Krakoa.
I don't know if this is such a good idea, Anole. She may need *more time* before she wants to see us again.
And we'll *respect* that, Rain Boy. But Gabby deserves to hear that we are sorry, and that if she needs anything we'll be here.
Yeah, you're right. I'm just...
KNOCK KNOCK
Nervous? Yeah, me too.
Oh... hi.
Hiiissssss!
You have no reason to let us, but we were wondering if...if we could come in and talk?
Please.
If, uh, you don't mind?
... Okay.
GRRR
But you can't stay long.
Snort!

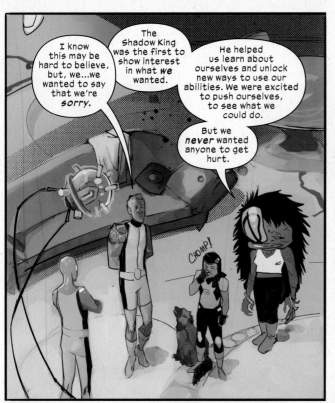

I know this may be hard to believe, but, we...we wanted to say that we're *sorry*.

The Shadow King was the first to show interest in what *we* wanted.

He helped us learn about ourselves and unlock new ways to use our abilities. We were excited to push ourselves, to see what we could do.

But we *never* wanted anyone to get hurt.

CHOMP!

We understand that our part in things may be unforgivable, but you *deserved* to hear that we would do things differently if we could.

You are our friend, and your life is important-- *you* are important. We are truly sorry.

You were trying to tell us something and we didn't listen. You deserved better.

But we hear you *now*.

So... thanks.

I do... ...forgive you, I mean. I do.

Really?

?

You *do?*

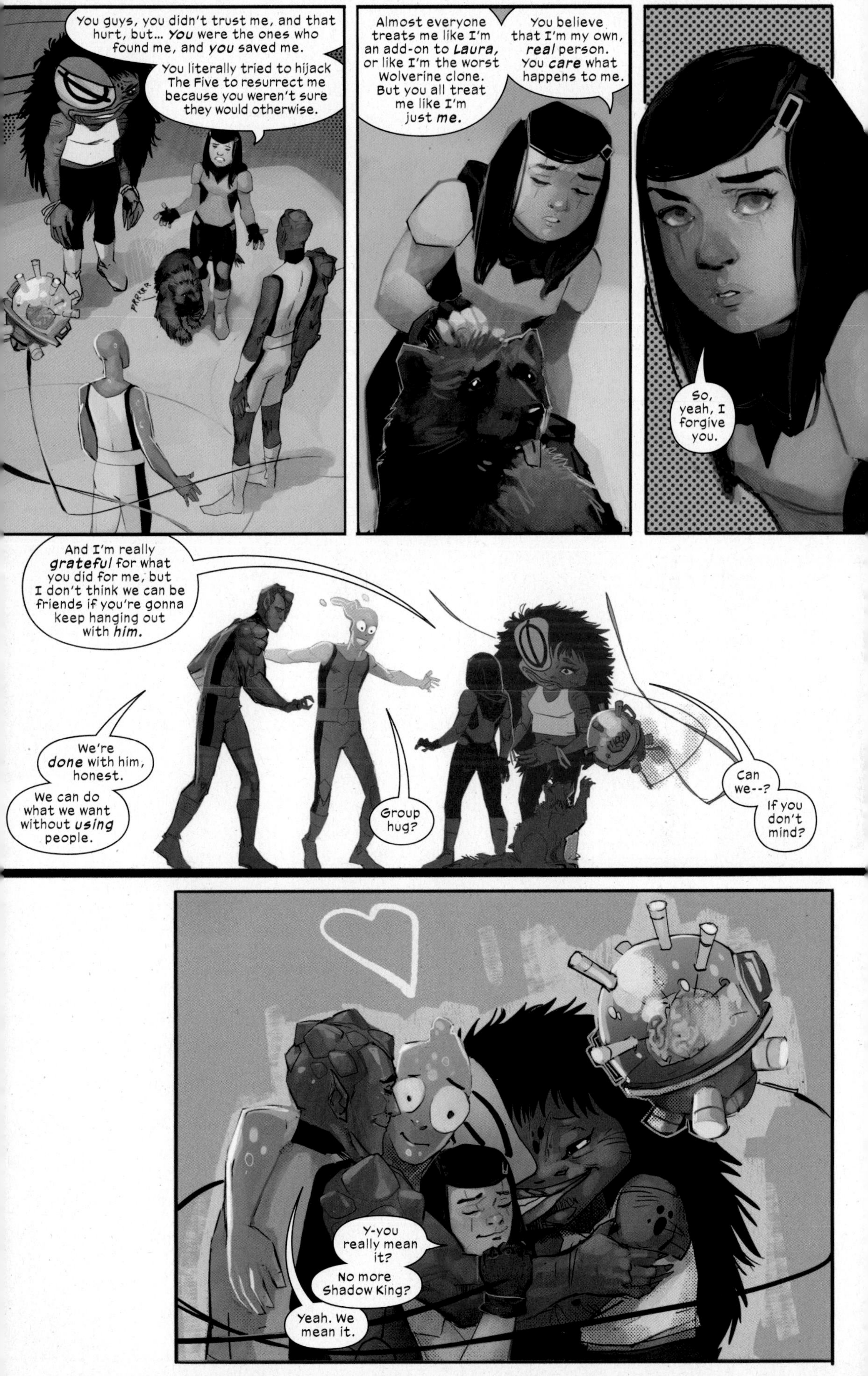

You guys, you didn't trust me, and that hurt, but... *you* were the ones who found me, and *you* saved me.
You literally tried to hijack The Five to resurrect me because you weren't sure they would otherwise.
PRRRR
Almost everyone treats me like I'm an add-on to *Laura,* or like I'm the worst Wolverine clone. But you all treat me like I'm just *me.*
You believe that I'm my own, *real* person. You *care* what happens to me.
So, yeah, I forgive you.
And I'm really *grateful* for what you did for me, but I don't think we can be friends if you're gonna keep hanging out with *him.*
We're *done* with him, honest.
We can do what we want without *using* people.
Group hug?
Can we--?
If you don't mind?
Y-you really mean it?
No more Shadow King?
Yeah. We mean it.

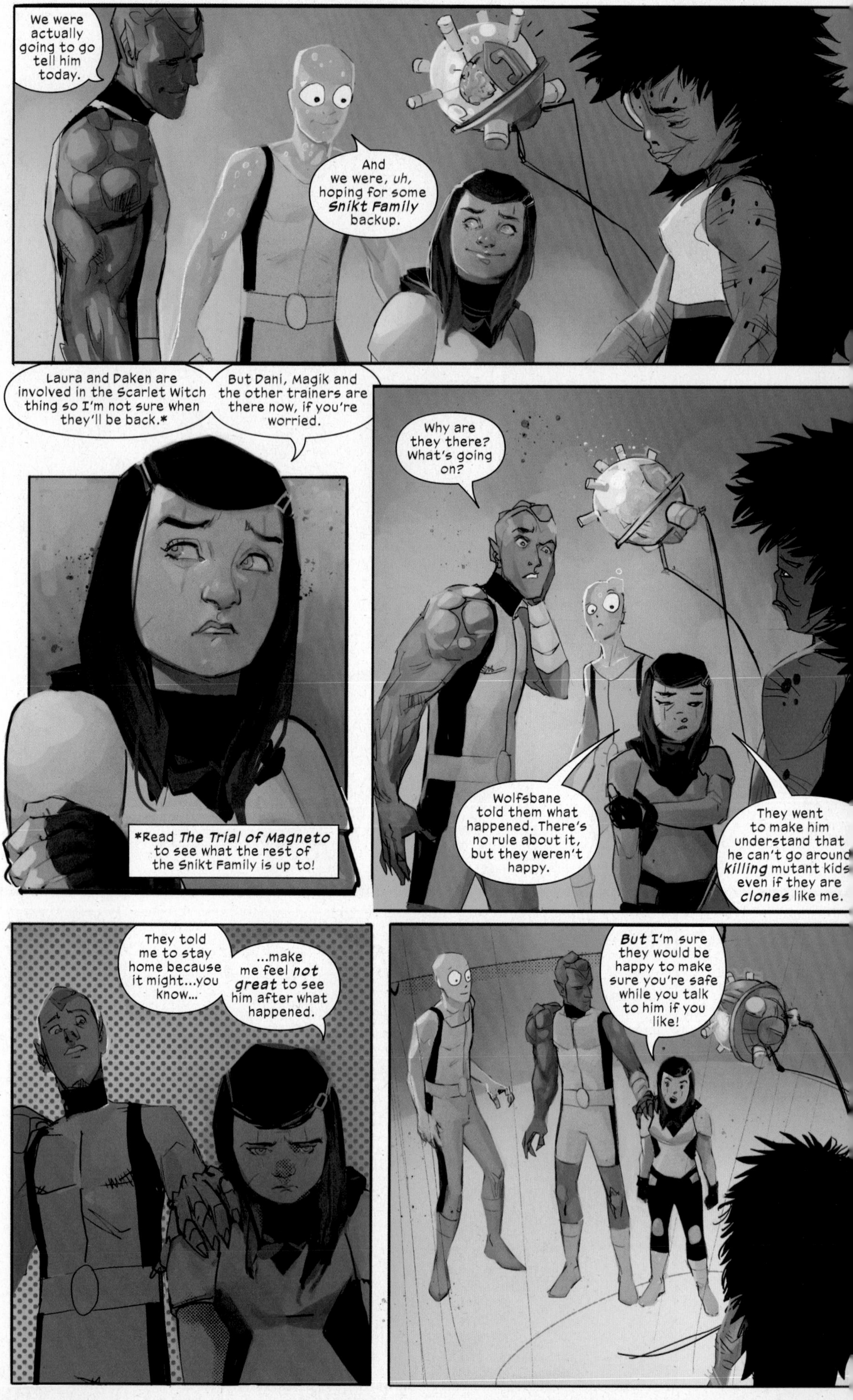
We were actually going to go tell him today.
And we were, *uh*, hoping for some ***Snikt Family*** backup.
Laura and Daken are involved in the Scarlet Witch thing so I'm not sure when they'll be back.*
But Dani, Magik and the other trainers are there now, if you're worried.
*Read *The Trial of Magneto* to see what the rest of the Snikt Family is up to!
Why are they there? What's going on?
Wolfsbane told them what happened. There's no rule about it, but they weren't happy.
They went to make him understand that he can't go around ***killing*** mutant kids even if they are ***clones*** like me.
They told me to stay home because it might...you know...
...make me feel ***not great*** to see him after what happened.
But I'm sure they would be happy to make sure you're safe while you talk to him if you like!

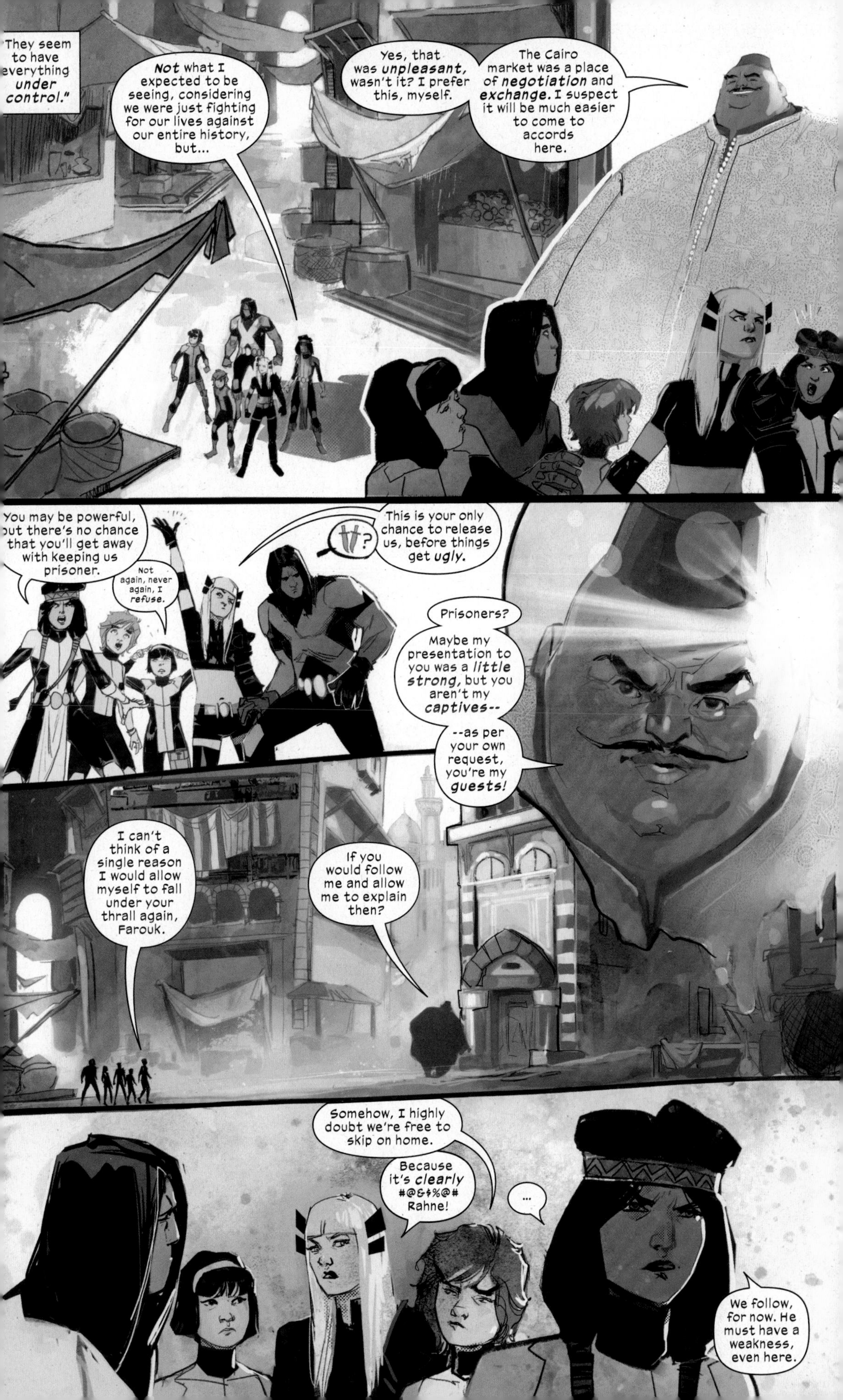
They seem to have everything under control."
Not what I expected to be seeing, considering we were just fighting for our lives against our entire history, but...
Yes, that was unpleasant, wasn't it? I prefer this, myself.
The Cairo market was a place of negotiation and exchange. I suspect it will be much easier to come to accords here.
You may be powerful, but there's no chance that you'll get away with keeping us prisoner.
Not again, never again, I refuse.
This is your only chance to release us, before things get ugly.
?
Prisoners?
Maybe my presentation to you was a little strong, but you aren't my captives--
--as per your own request, you're my guests!
I can't think of a single reason I would allow myself to fall under your thrall again, Farouk.
If you would follow me and allow me to explain then?
Somehow, I highly doubt we're free to skip on home.
Because it's clearly #@&$%@# Rahne!
...
We follow, for now. He must have a weakness, even here.

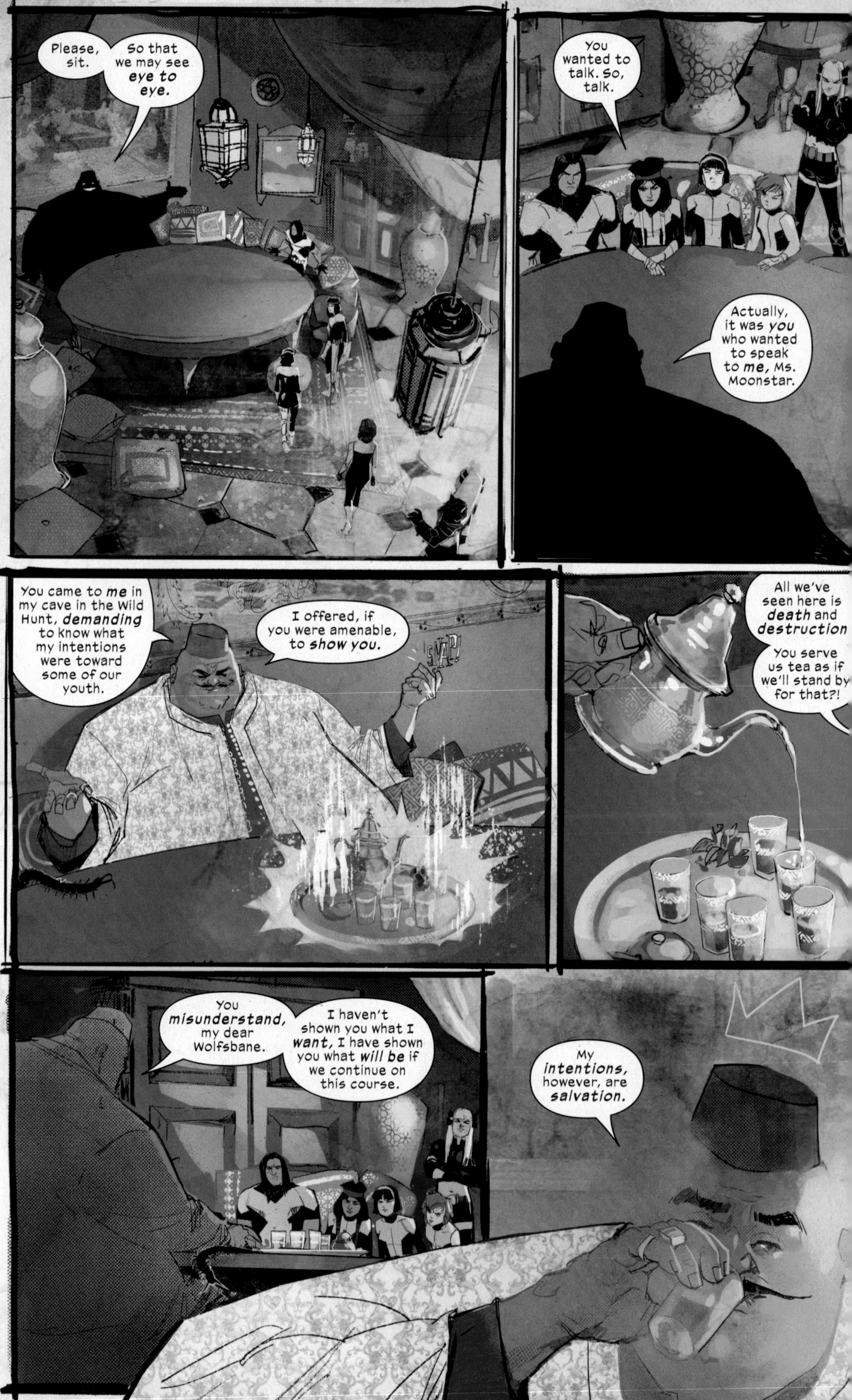

Please, sit.
So that we may see *eye to eye.*
You wanted to talk. So, talk.
Actually, it was *you* who wanted to speak to *me,* Ms. Moonstar.
You came to *me* in my cave in the Wild Hunt, *demanding* to know what my intentions were toward some of our youth.
I offered, if you were amenable, to *show you.*
SNAP!
All we've seen here is *death* and *destruction*
You serve us tea as if we'll stand by for that?!
You *misunderstand,* my dear Wolfsbane.
I haven't shown you what I *want,* I have shown you what *will be* if we continue on this course.
My *intentions,* however, are *salvation.*

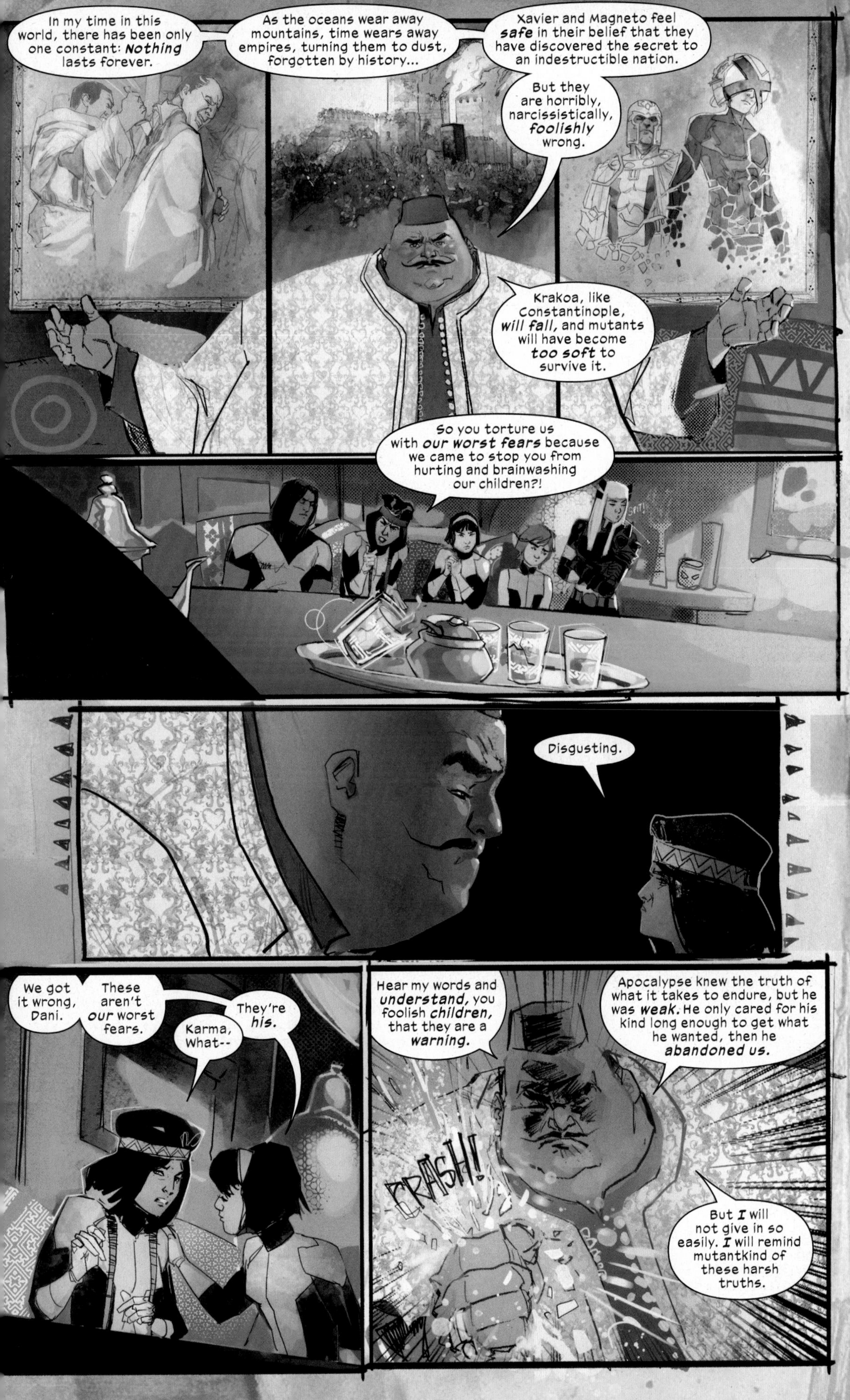
In my time in this world, there has been only one constant: Nothing lasts forever.
As the oceans wear away mountains, time wears away empires, turning them to dust, forgotten by history...
Xavier and Magneto feel safe in their belief that they have discovered the secret to an indestructible nation.
But they are horribly, narcissistically, foolishly wrong.
Krakoa, like Constantinople, will fall, and mutants will have become too soft to survive it.
So you torture us with our worst fears because we came to stop you from hurting and brainwashing our children?!
Disgusting.
We got it wrong, Dani.
These aren't our worst fears.
They're his.
Karma, What--
Hear my words and understand, you foolish children, that they are a warning.
Apocalypse knew the truth of what it takes to endure, but he was weak. He only cared for his kind long enough to get what he wanted, then he abandoned us.
CRASH!
But I will not give in so easily. I will remind mutantkind of these harsh truths.

REBELLION OF THE HOST

The boy slumbers, his dreams sweet and gentle to keep him docile -- dormant. But sometimes, sometimes he stirs...

-

There is a child, a creature like the boy but different. Stronger? Desire for their power rises like a tide in the Shadow, but...something rises in them, like a wave of white noise.

When it clears, the child is gone.

-

The boy's dreams have turned turbulent, but still he slumbers. Sometimes, he thinks he is awake, but the horror of what he has become is so deep that he is sure he must be dreaming.

-

The girl picks the right pocket. Another one like them -- a mutant, as they call themselves now. The Shadow is pleased, reels the man into his web like a greedy spider.

The man is powerful, but nothing compared to the combined might of the boy and the Shadow.

But, as they battle, once again, the Shadow is set upon by a muzzy wave of nothingness. The Shadow fights it, retains most of his control, but the man manages to use the distraction to claim victory. For now...

-

There is a girl nearby now, and she is frightened and desperately sad. The boy comforts her as well as he can, but her presence is muddled, as if they are on opposite sides of thick glass.

When the girl's friends come for her, the boy thinks she would be happier if they took her away.

The boy strains to wave long enough to --

-- the Shadow sees it coming this time and snatches the boy up, dragging him to the center of things.

The market is in ruins, and the sky closes in on the boy, raining down terror.

-

The boy does not sleep now, but neither is he free.

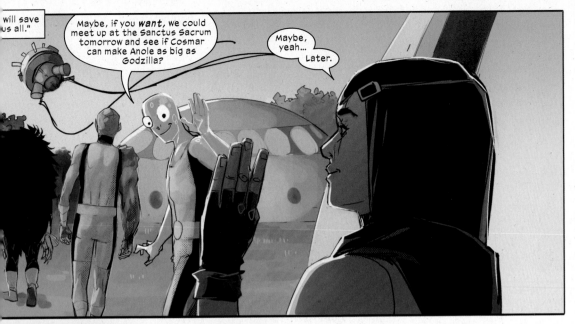

"...will save us all."

Maybe, if you *want*, we could meet up at the Sanctus Sacrum tomorrow and see if Cosmar can make Anole as big as Godzilla?

Maybe... Later.

I should stay home, like Wolfsbane said, right?

They'll be okay? Right?

Huff...

I would feel really guilty and confused and *weird* if I were in their place.

They should have listened to me in the first place, but they're willing to not talk to him anymore because he hurt me. That *does* count for a lot.

I should go *with them!*

I should be allowed to tell the Shadow King to *get bent,* for me from me!

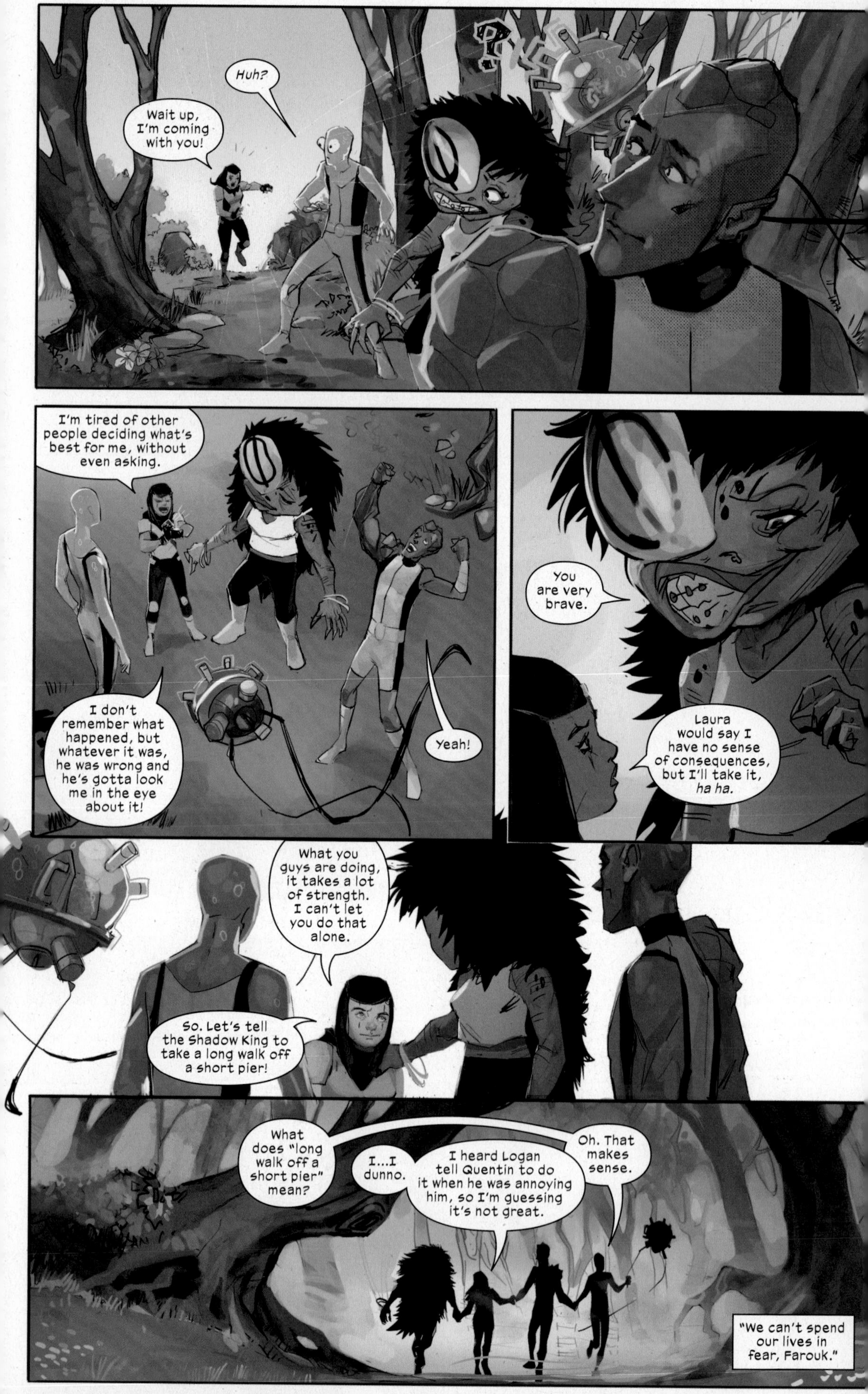

Wait up, I'm coming with you!
Huh?
I'm tired of other people deciding what's best for me, without even asking.
I don't remember what happened, but whatever it was, he was wrong and he's gotta look me in the eye about it!
Yeah!
You are very brave.
Laura would say I have no sense of consequences, but I'll take it, *ha ha.*
What you guys are doing, it takes a lot of strength. I can't let you do that alone.
So. Let's tell the Shadow King to take a long walk off a short pier!
What does "long walk off a short pier" mean?
I...I dunno.
I heard Logan tell Quentin to do it when he was annoying him, so I'm guessing it's not great.
Oh. That makes sense.
"We can't spend our lives in fear, Farouk."

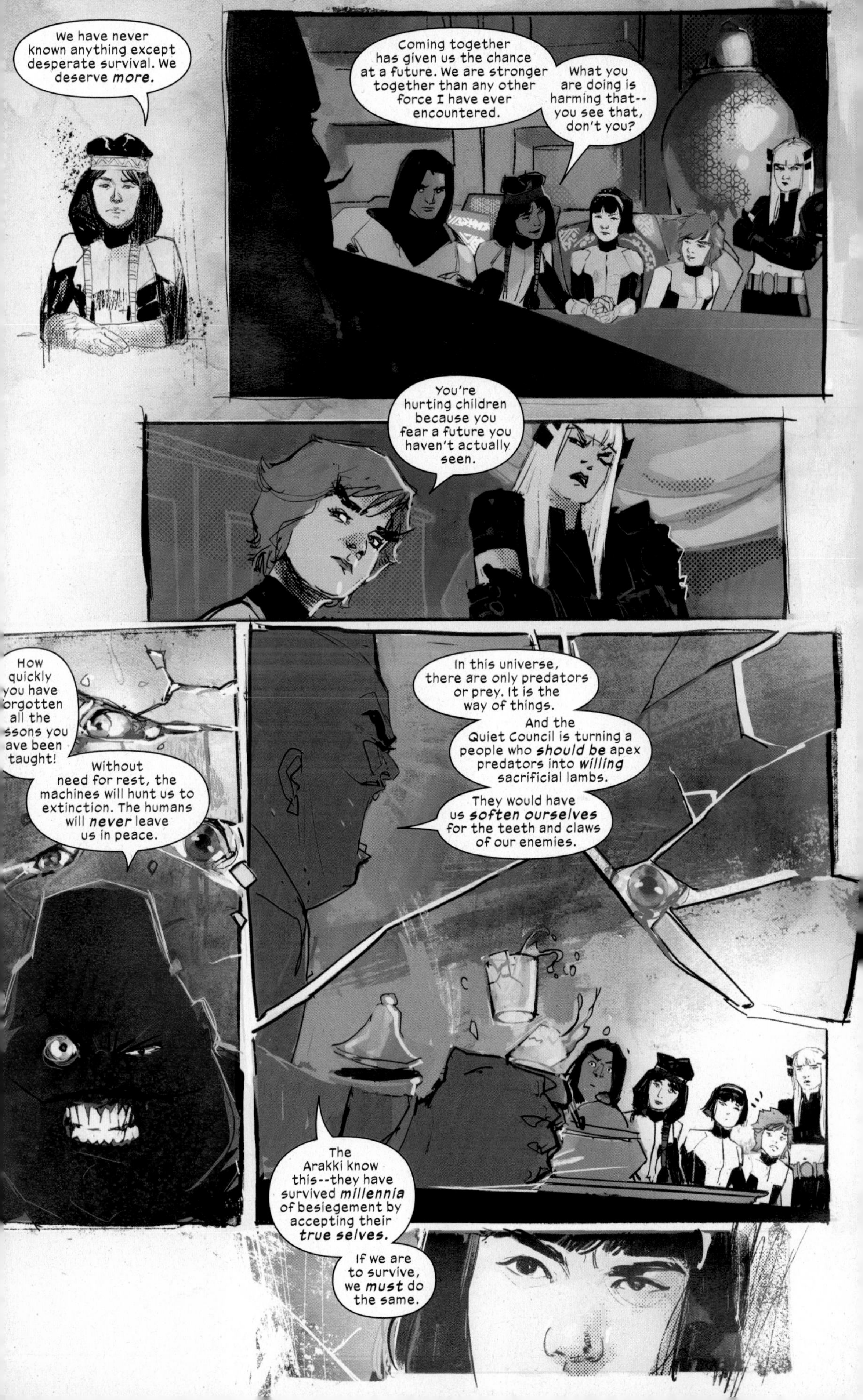
We have never known anything except desperate survival. We deserve *more.*
Coming together has given us the chance at a future. We are stronger together than any other force I have ever encountered.
What you are doing is harming that--you see that, don't you?
You're hurting children because you fear a future you haven't actually seen.
How quickly you have orgotten all the ssons you ave been taught!
Without need for rest, the machines will hunt us to extinction. The humans will *never* leave us in peace.
In this universe, there are only predators or prey. It is the way of things.
And the Quiet Council is turning a people who *should be* apex predators into *willing* sacrificial lambs.
They would have us *soften ourselves* for the teeth and claws of our enemies.
The Arakki know this--they have survived *millennia* of besiegement by accepting their *true selves.*
If we are to survive, we *must* do the same.

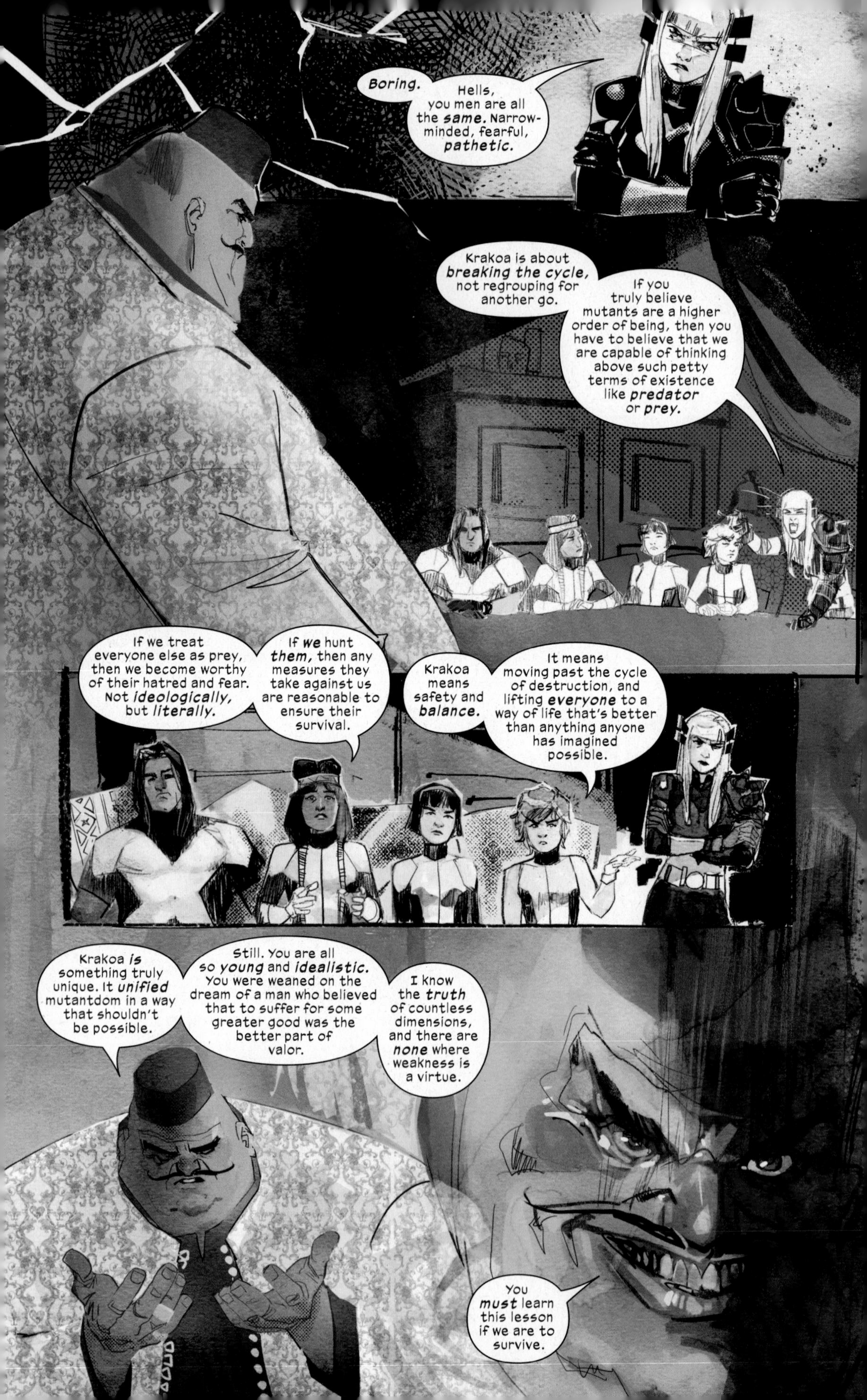
Boring.
Hells, you men are all the same. Narrow-minded, fearful, pathetic.
Krakoa is about breaking the cycle, not regrouping for another go.
If you truly believe mutants are a higher order of being, then you have to believe that we are capable of thinking above such petty terms of existence like predator or prey.
If we treat everyone else as prey, then we become worthy of their hatred and fear. Not ideologically, but literally.
If we hunt them, then any measures they take against us are reasonable to ensure their survival.
Krakoa means safety and balance.
It means moving past the cycle of destruction, and lifting everyone to a way of life that's better than anything anyone has imagined possible.
Krakoa is something truly unique. It unified mutantdom in a way that shouldn't be possible.
Still. You are all so young and idealistic. You were weaned on the dream of a man who believed that to suffer for some greater good was the better part of valor.
I know the truth of countless dimensions, and there are none where weakness is a virtue.
You must learn this lesson if we are to survive.

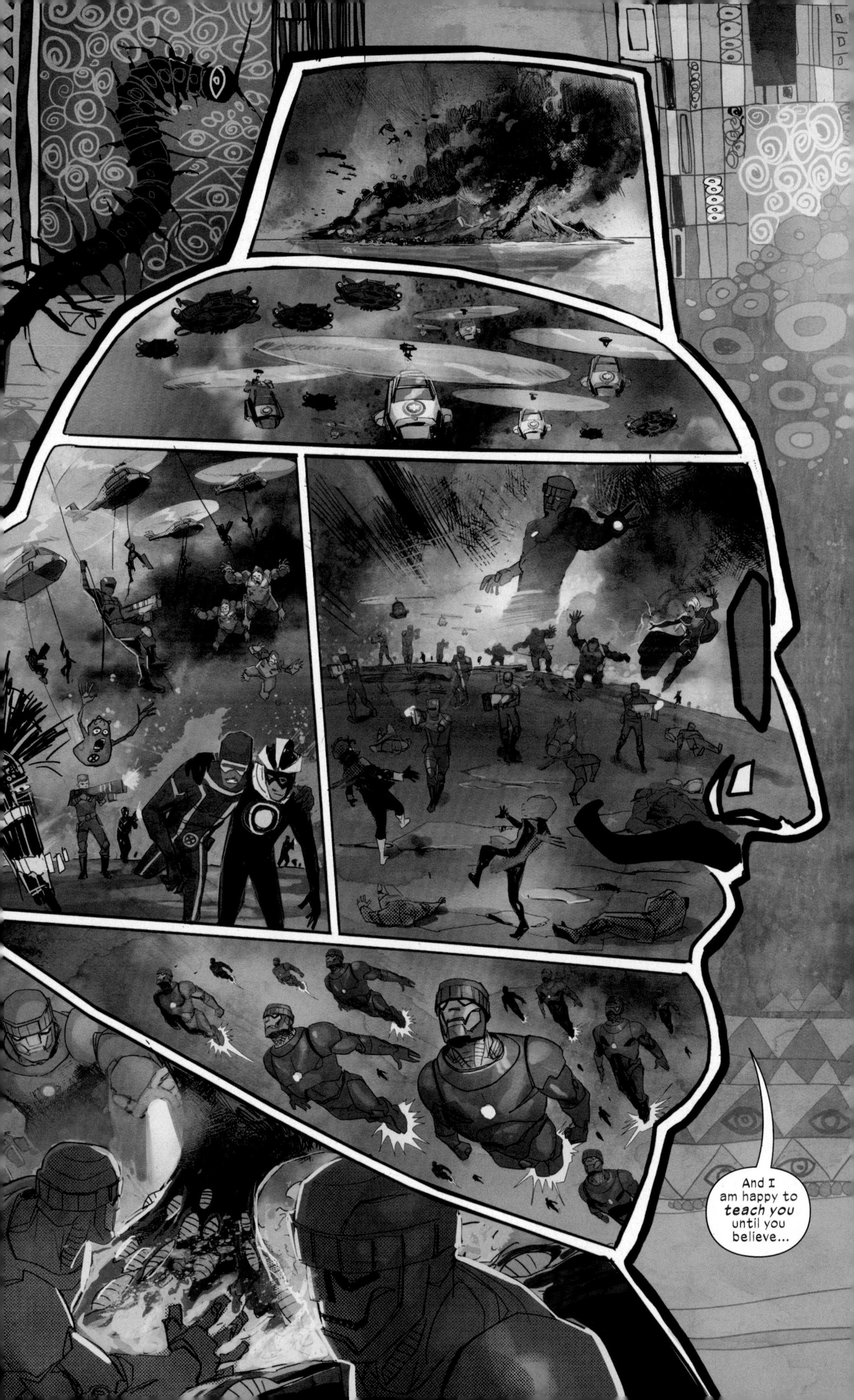
And I am happy to *teach you* until you believe...

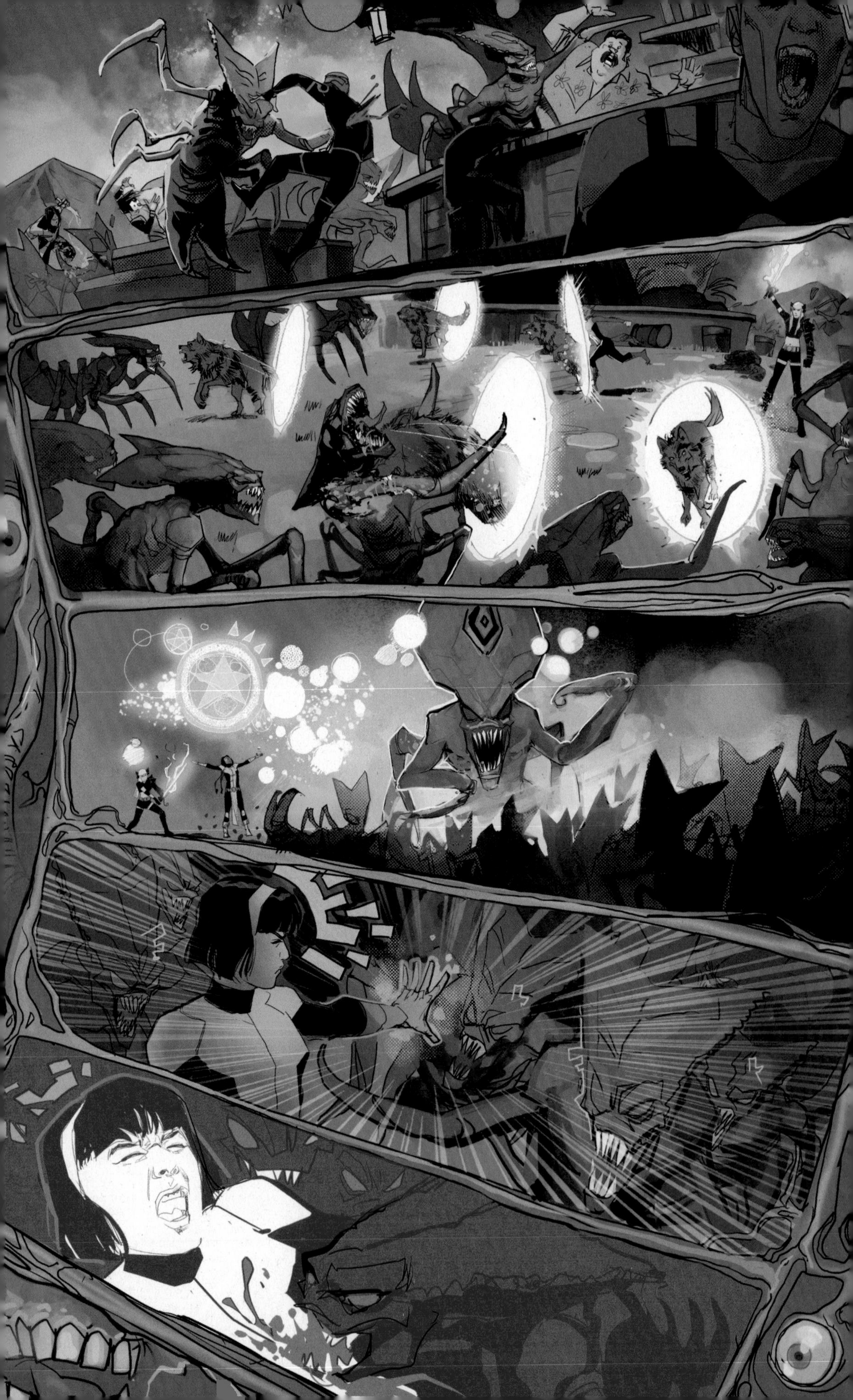

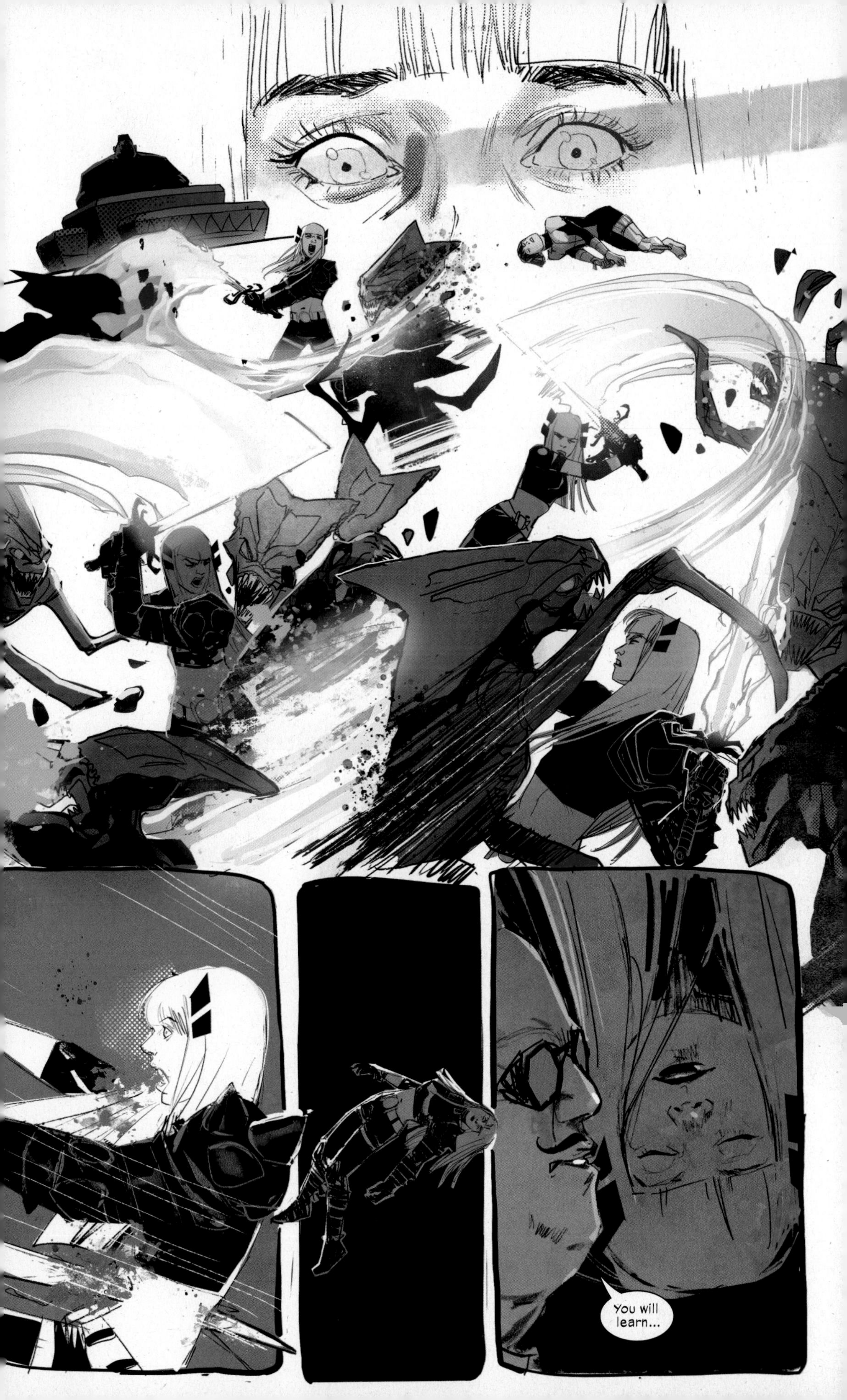
You will learn...

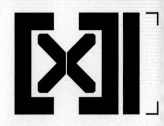

STRATEGIES & TACTICS

DEMONSTRATION 002: 45 MINUTES

Synergies: Mirage/Magik - "solidification" and destruction of constructs.

Last mutants standing: Mirage.

Next demonstration: Start all separately, at random locations.

DEMONSTRATION 14: 32 MINUTES

Synergies: Mirage/Karma – mental manipulation of constructs (semi-successful).

Last mutants standing: Mirage and Karma.

Next demonstration: Start Warpath and Magik in the Arbor Magna, Karma and Wolfsbane in the Wild hunt, and Mirage in House of M.

DEMONSTRATION 015: 4 HOURS 38 MINUTES

Synergies: No synergies attempted.

Last mutants standing: Most of the team died early. Magik and Warpath managed to make a temporary stronghold of the Council Chambers. They proceeded to hack away at all presented threats for hours, until Magik broke the line to pursue her brother.

Next demonstration: Start Magik and Warpath in separate areas. Warpath in The Fort (loses focus in the presence of dead children), Magik in "the Hole."

DEMONSTRATION 023: 5 MINUTES 36 SECONDS

Synergies: Unclear.

Last mutants standing: All. Mirage and Karma in close proximity when an anomaly appeared. (Were they attempting a new synergy?) Another presence (multiple?) detected. Brief nothingness.

Next demonstration: The New Mutants are unaccounted for.

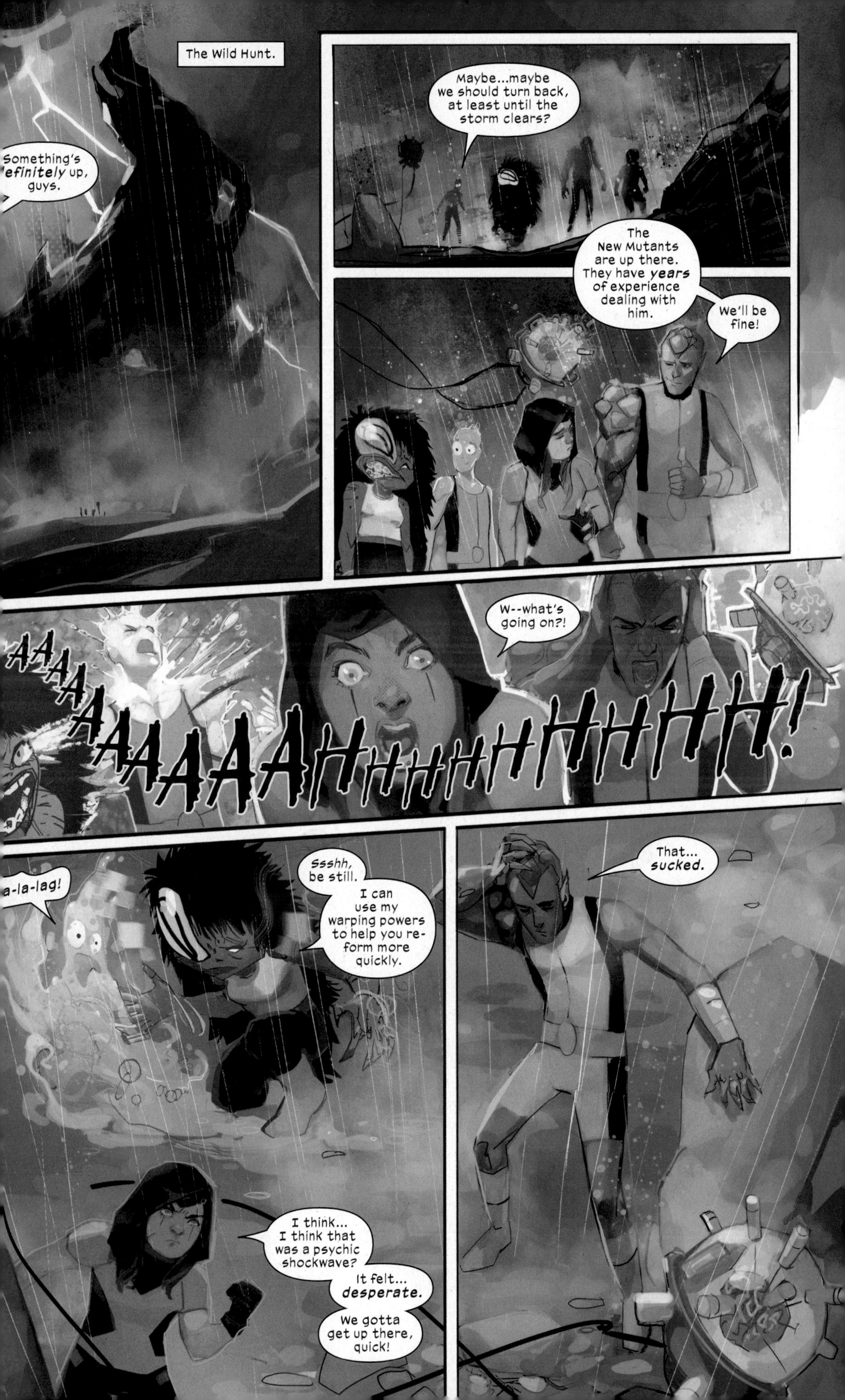

The Wild Hunt.
Something's *definitely* up, guys.
Maybe...maybe we should turn back, at least until the storm clears?
The New Mutants are up there. They have *years* of experience dealing with him.
We'll be fine!
W--what's going on?!
AAAAAAAAAAAAHHHHHHHHHHHH!
a-la-lag!
Ssshh, be still.
I can use my warping powers to help you re-form more quickly.
That... *sucked.*
I think... I think that was a psychic shockwave?
It felt... *desperate.*
We gotta get up there, quick!

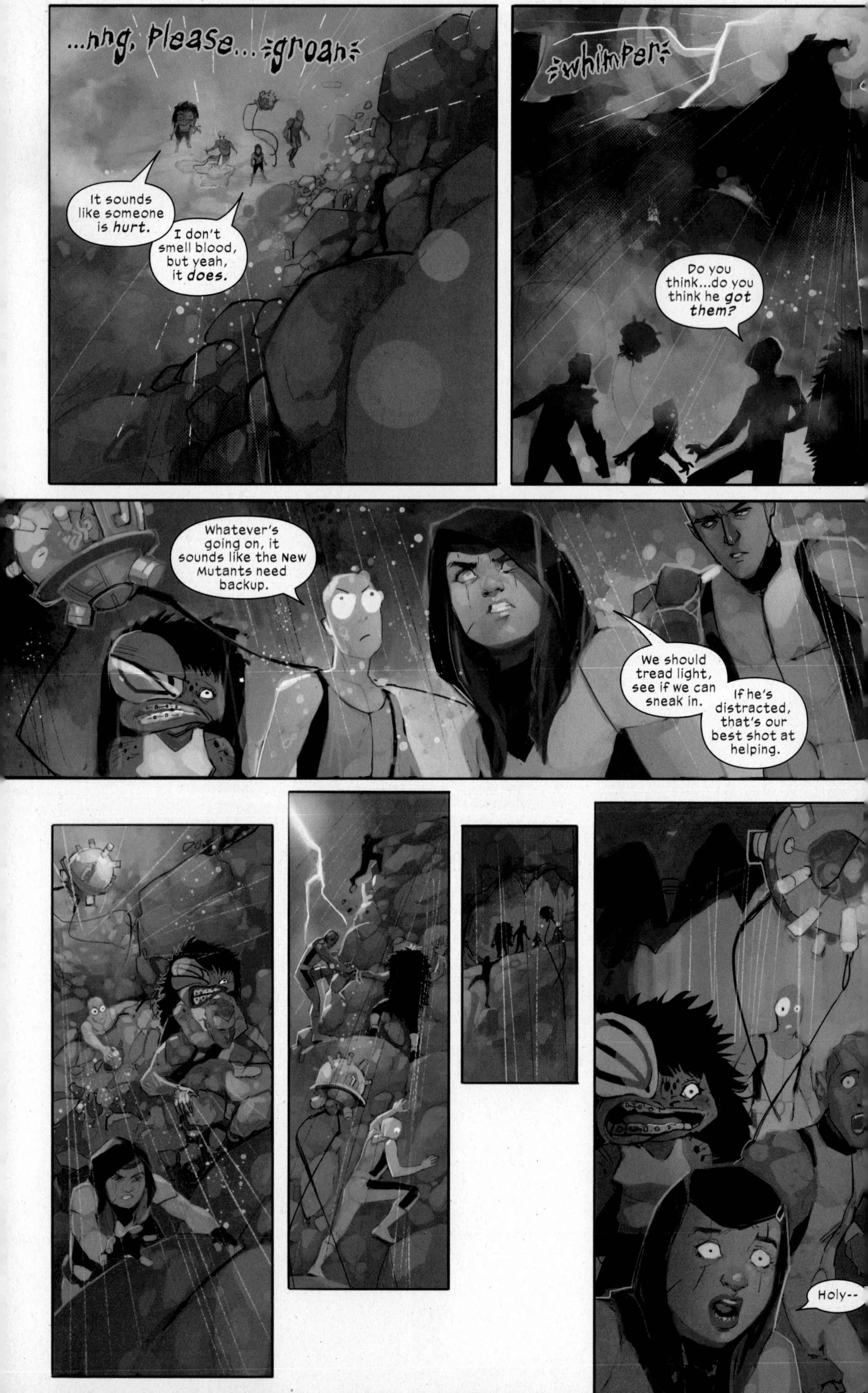
...hng, please... groan
It sounds like someone is hurt.
I don't smell blood, but yeah, it does.
whimper
Do you think...do you think he got them?
Whatever's going on, it sounds like the New Mutants need backup.
We should tread light, see if we can sneak in.
If he's distracted, that's our best shot at helping.
Holy--

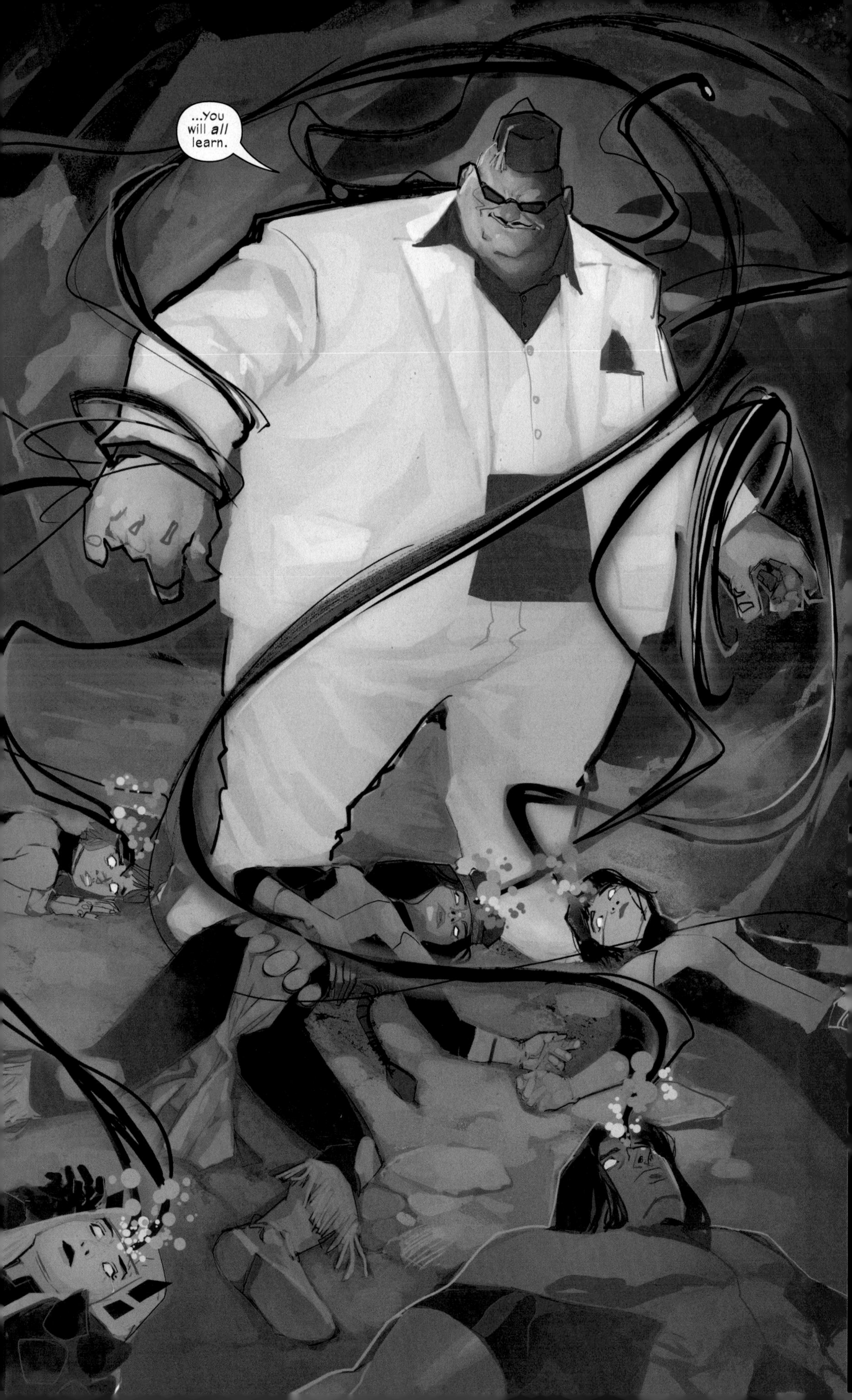
...You will *all* learn.

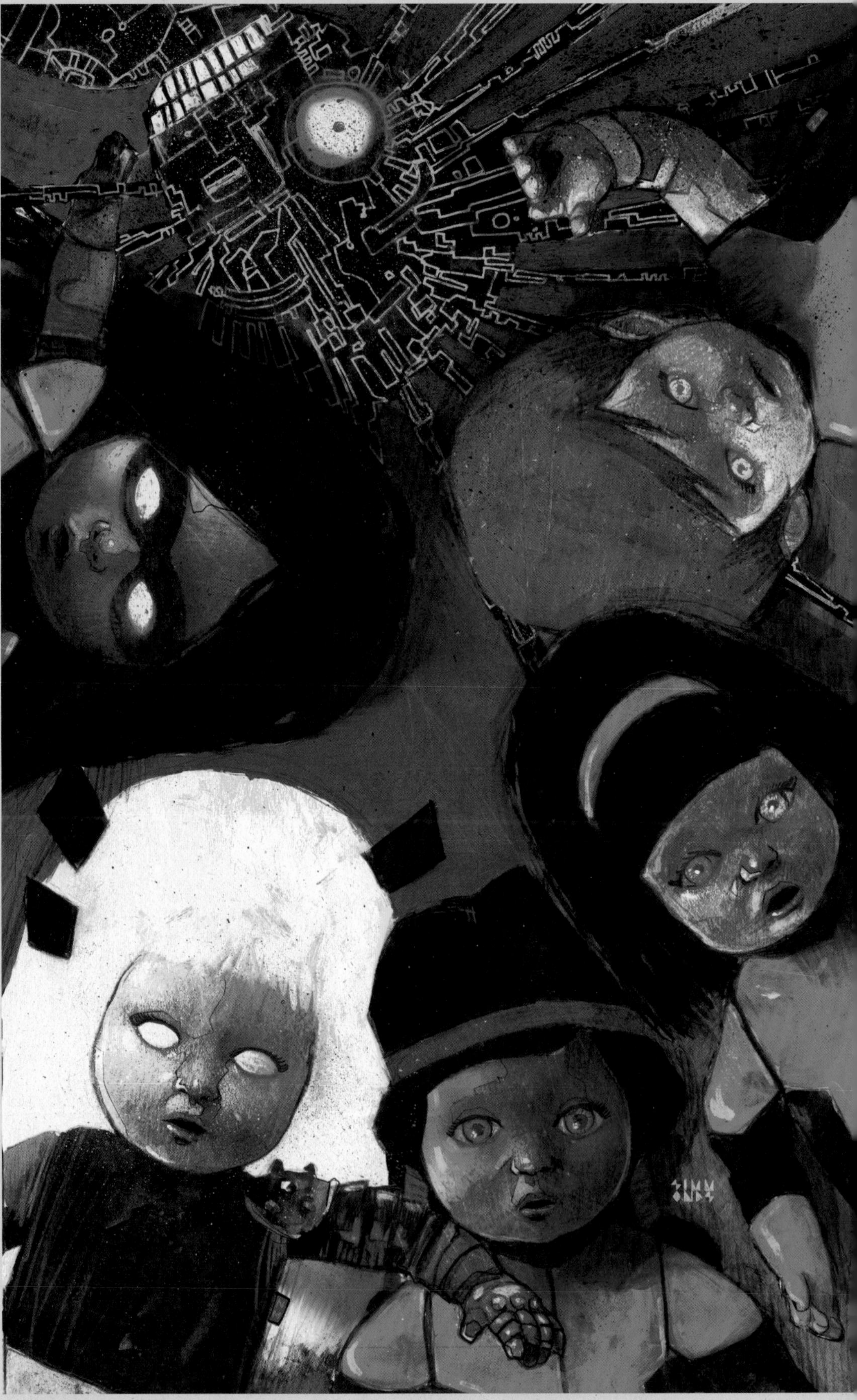

The Truth Shall Set Them Free...

[reign_of_x]

[kra_]
[koa_]

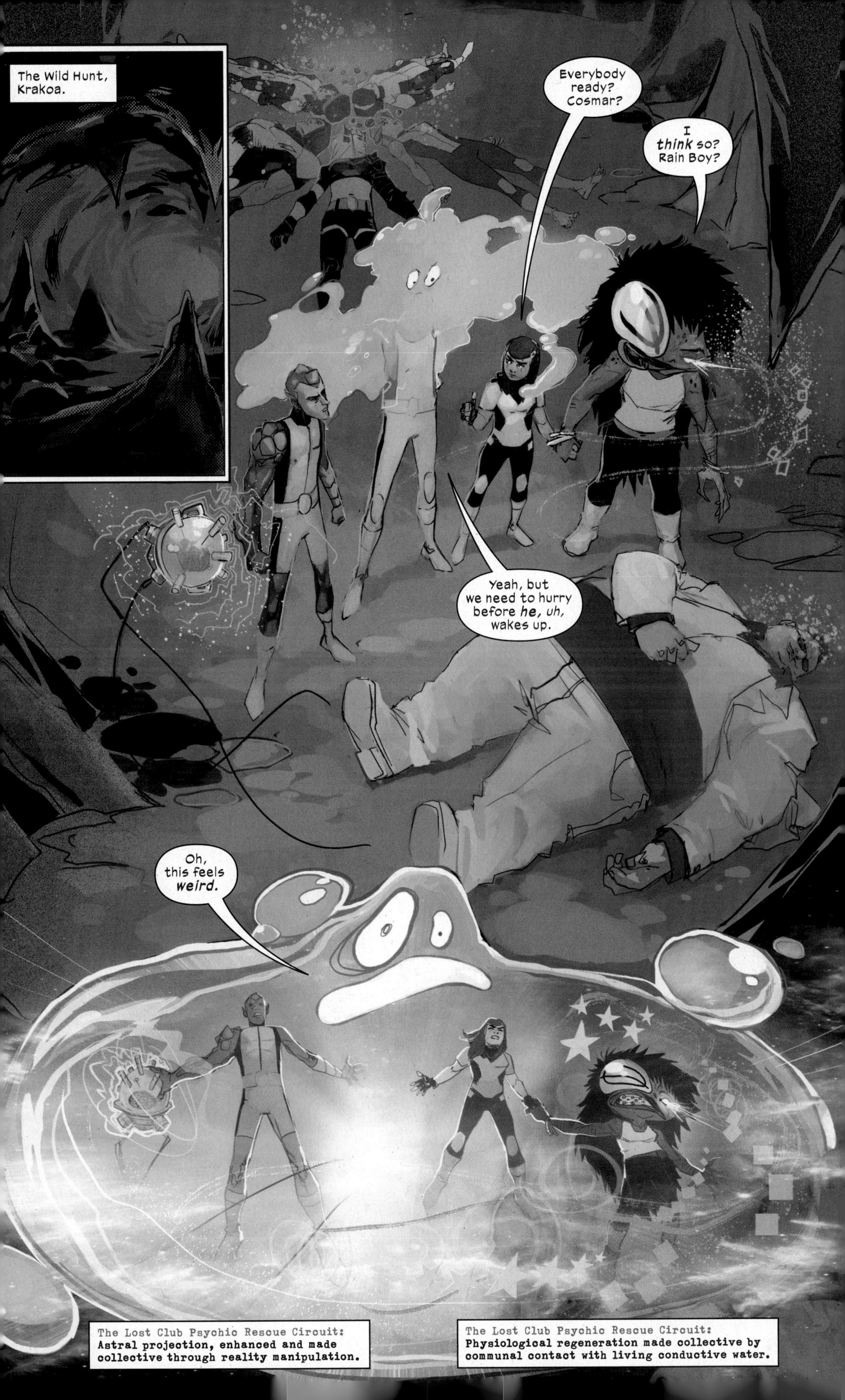

The Wild Hunt, Krakoa.
Everybody ready? Cosmar?
I *think* so? Rain Boy?
Yeah, but we need to hurry before *he*, *uh*, wakes up.
Oh, this feels *weird.*
The Lost Club Psychic Rescue Circuit: Astral projection, enhanced and made collective through reality manipulation.
The Lost Club Psychic Rescue Circuit: Physiological regeneration made collective by communal contact with living conductive water.

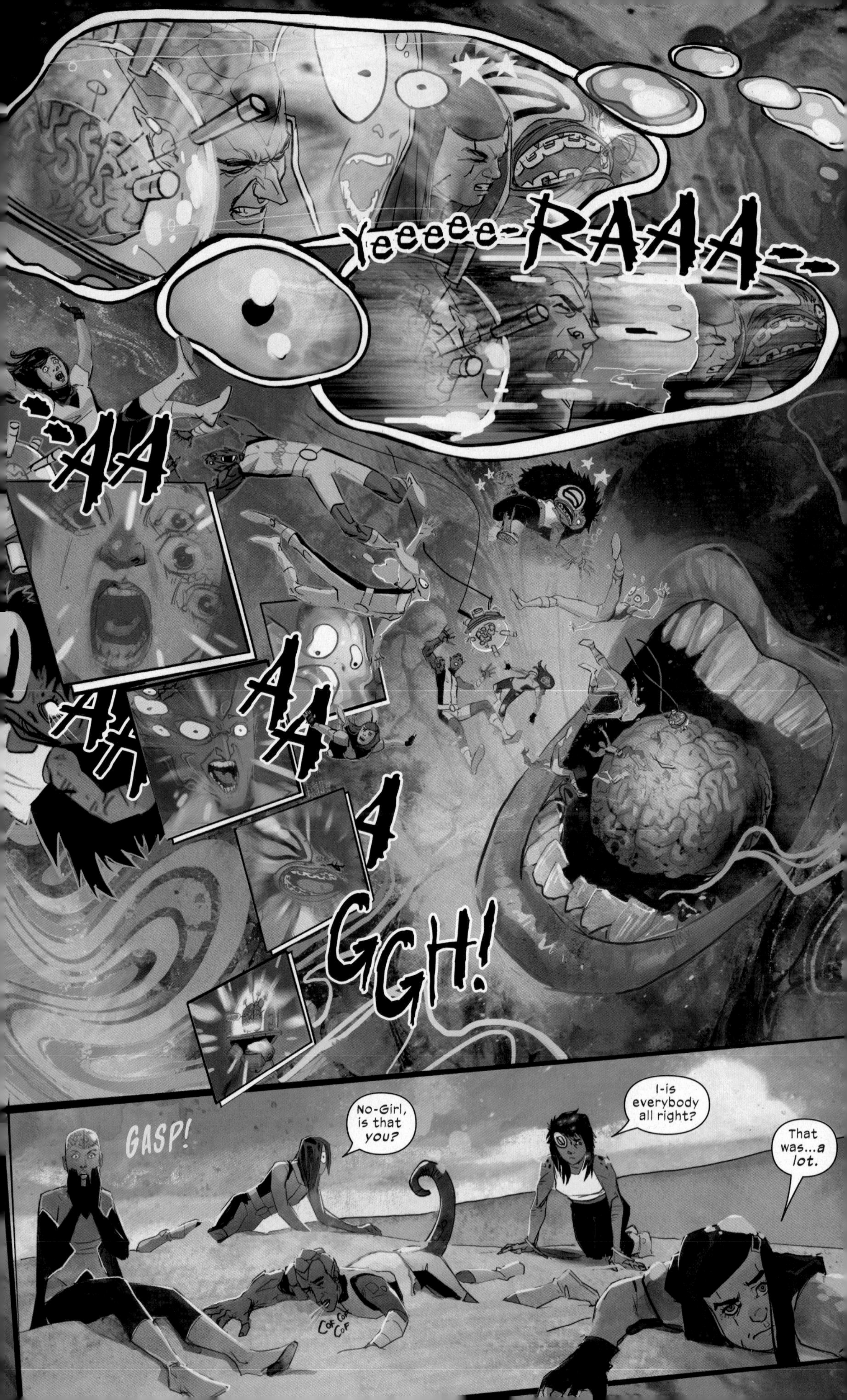
Yeeeee-RAAA--
AA
AA
AA
A
GGH!
GASP!
No-Girl, is that *you?*
I-is everybody all right?
That was...a *lot.*
COF COF COF

THE BOY & THE BEAST -- ACT 2, SCENE 3452

AMAHL FAROUK, *the boy, waits as* SHADOW KING, *an echo of the beast, materializes.*

Shadow King
You think yourself clever, boy -- obscuring the New Mutants from me.

Amahl Farouk
I didn't do anything. [*pause*] Maybe you aren't as powerful as you believe.

Shadow King
Even in your little cage, I feel the fight in your spirit. It is why I CHOSE YOU, boy. It is why I even got a toehold in this sad little dimension. It is why I will return.

Amahl Farouk
You're nothing but the echo of an evil being. You aren't even real!

Shadow King
And yet, I have you trapped. And yet, I have TAINTED every action AMAHL FAROUK has taken. Why do you think that is?

Amahl Farouk
I...I...

Shadow King
Could it be that the reasonable part of you long ago realized that it was ME who made you able to survive? Could it be, perhaps, that the TRUTH is that you would be NOTHING without the Shadow King?

Amahl Farouk
I HATE YOU. [*pause*] You're right, I AM keeping you from SEEING. And soon, the New Mutants will come; they will wash away the last of you, and it will be as if you NEVER WERE.

Shadow King
Do you truly believe the idea to bring them here was YOURS, boy? Did you think I was not whispering in your ear all along? [*pause*] Did it not occur to you that I have KNOWN these children the way I know YOU? That the Shadow King didn't leave little pieces of himself in them, dormant and waiting for the right moment to bloom? [*Amahl begins to weep, Shadow King laughs*] I am an echo, but one that you keep alive. I am YOU at your best. And I will THRIVE while you wither and DIE.

SHADOW KING *exits,* AMAHL FAROUK *is left weeping bitterly.*

After a moment, Amahl wipes his eyes, a determined look on his face.

The Shadows creep in. Fade to black.

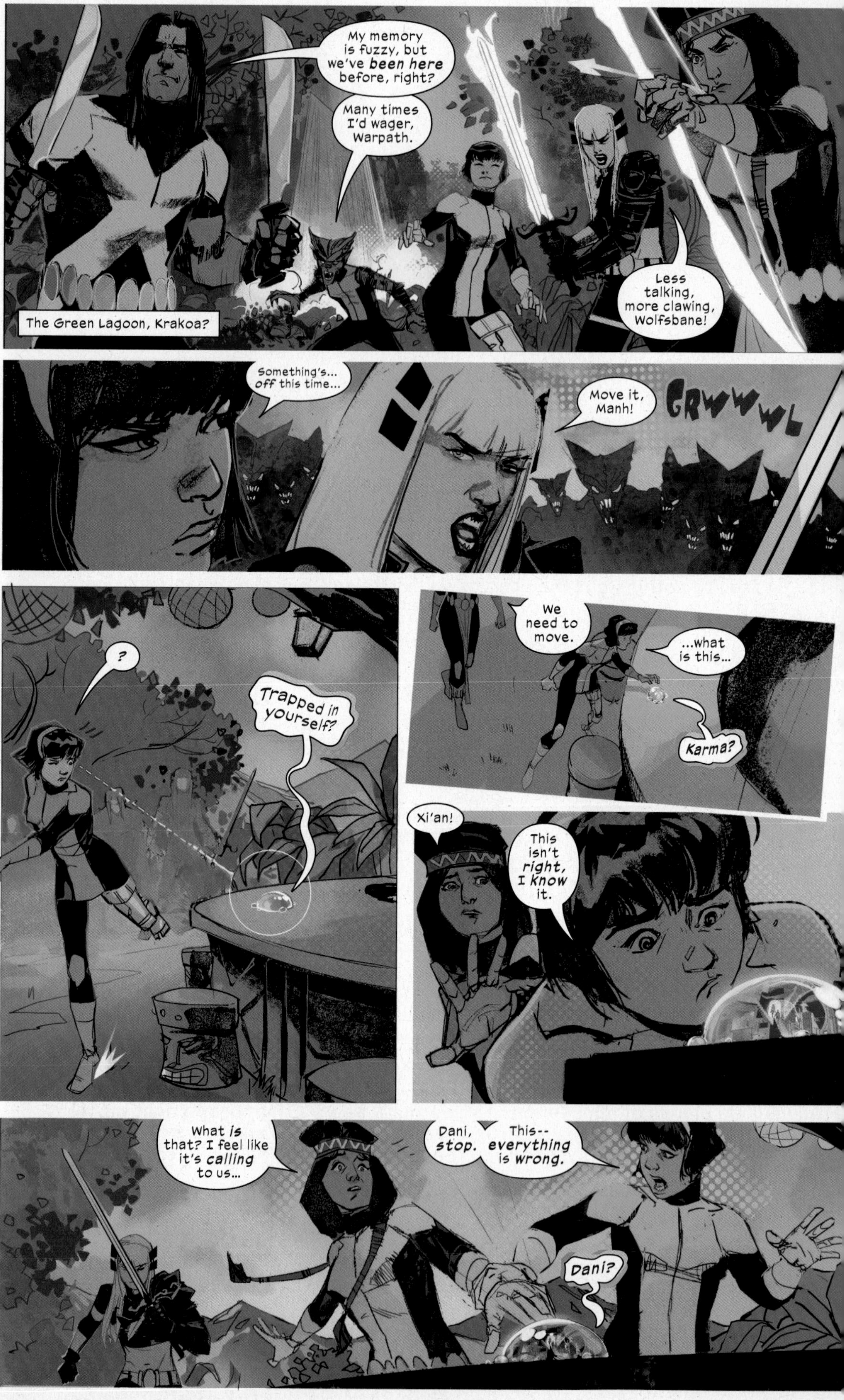
My memory is fuzzy, but we've *been here* before, right?
Many times I'd wager, Warpath.
Less talking, more clawing, Wolfsbane!
The Green Lagoon, Krakoa?
Something's... *off* this time...
Move it, Manh!
GRWWWL
?
Trapped in yourself?
We need to move.
...what is this...
Karma?
Xi'an!
This isn't *right*, I *know* it.
What *is* that? I feel like it's *calling* to us...
Dani, *stop*.
This-- *everything* is *wrong*.
Dani?

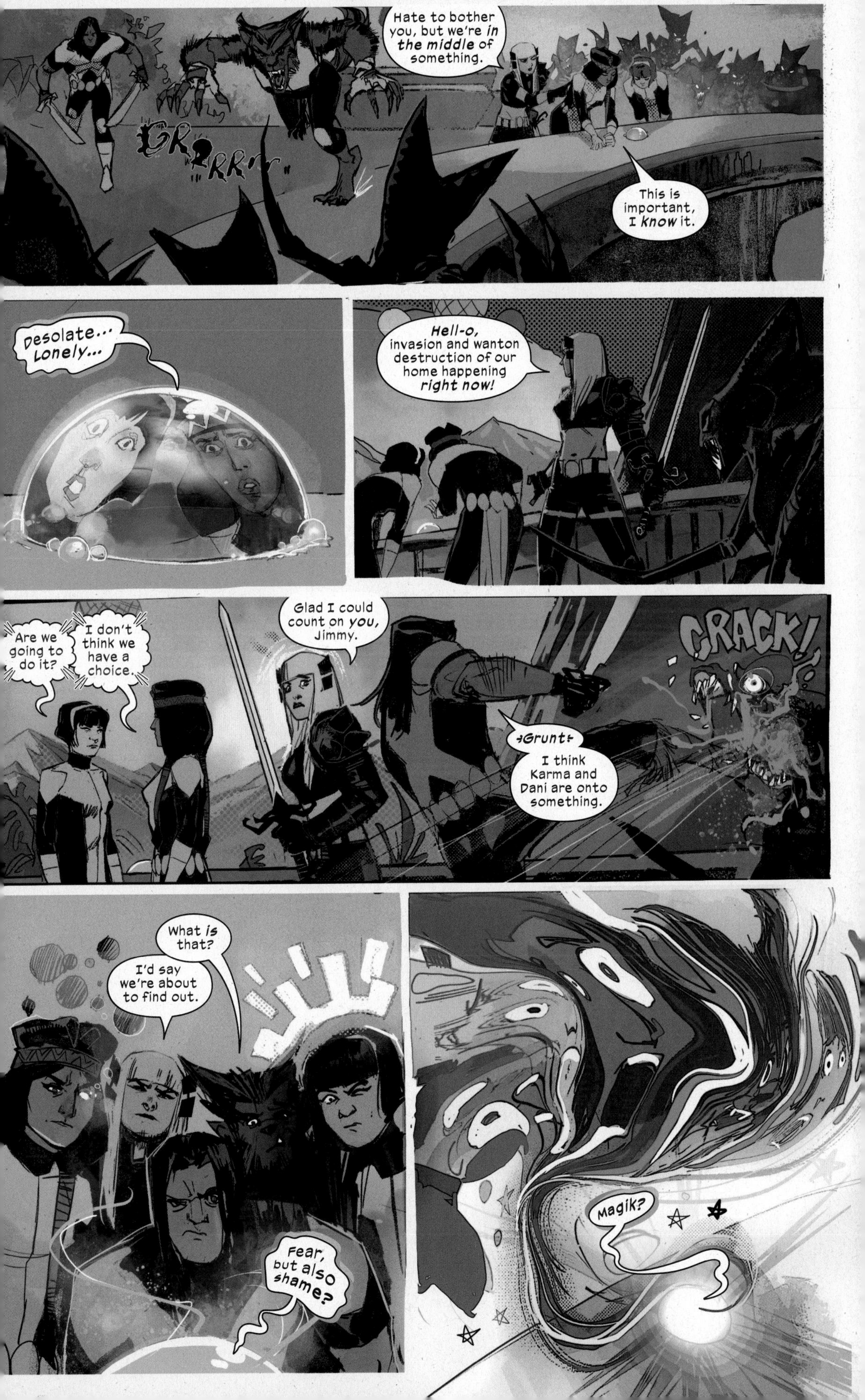
Hate to bother you, but we're *in the middle* of something.
GRRRRR
This is important, *I know* it.
Desolate... Lonely...
Hell-o, invasion and wanton destruction of our home happening *right now!*
Are we going to do it?
I don't think we have a choice.
Glad I could count on *you,* Jimmy.
CRACK!
-Grunt-
I think Karma and Dani are onto something.
What *is* that?
I'd say we're about to find out.
Fear, but also *shame?*
Magik?

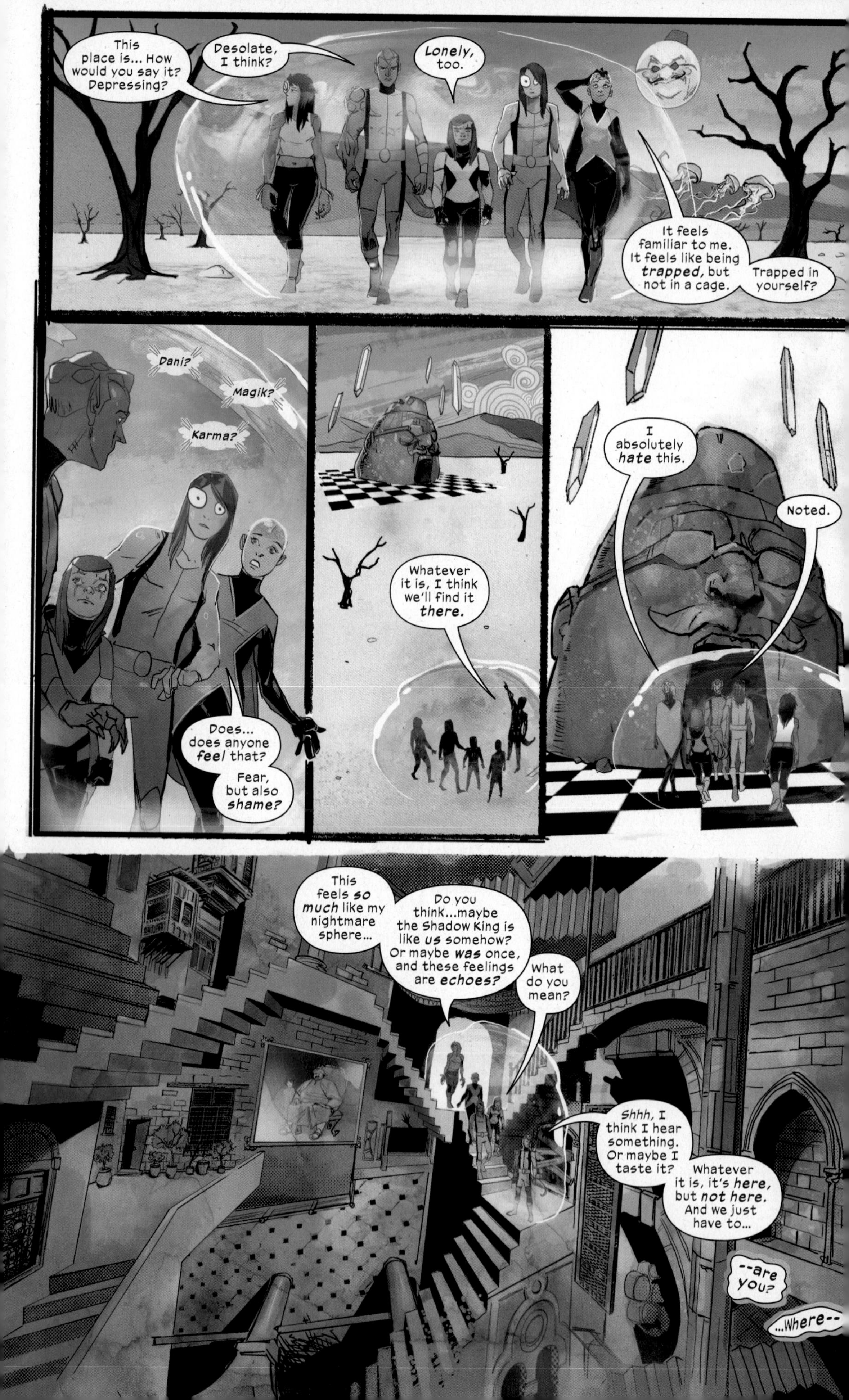
This place is... How would you say it? Depressing?
Desolate, I think?
Lonely, too.
It feels familiar to me. It feels like being trapped, but not in a cage.
Trapped in yourself?
Dani?
Magik?
Karma?
Does... does anyone feel that?
Fear, but also shame?
Whatever it is, I think we'll find it there.
I absolutely hate this.
Noted.
This feels so much like my nightmare sphere...
Do you think...maybe the Shadow King is like us somehow? Or maybe was once, and these feelings are echoes?
What do you mean?
Shhh, I think I hear something. Or maybe I taste it?
Whatever it is, it's here, but not here. And we just have to...
--are you?
...Where--

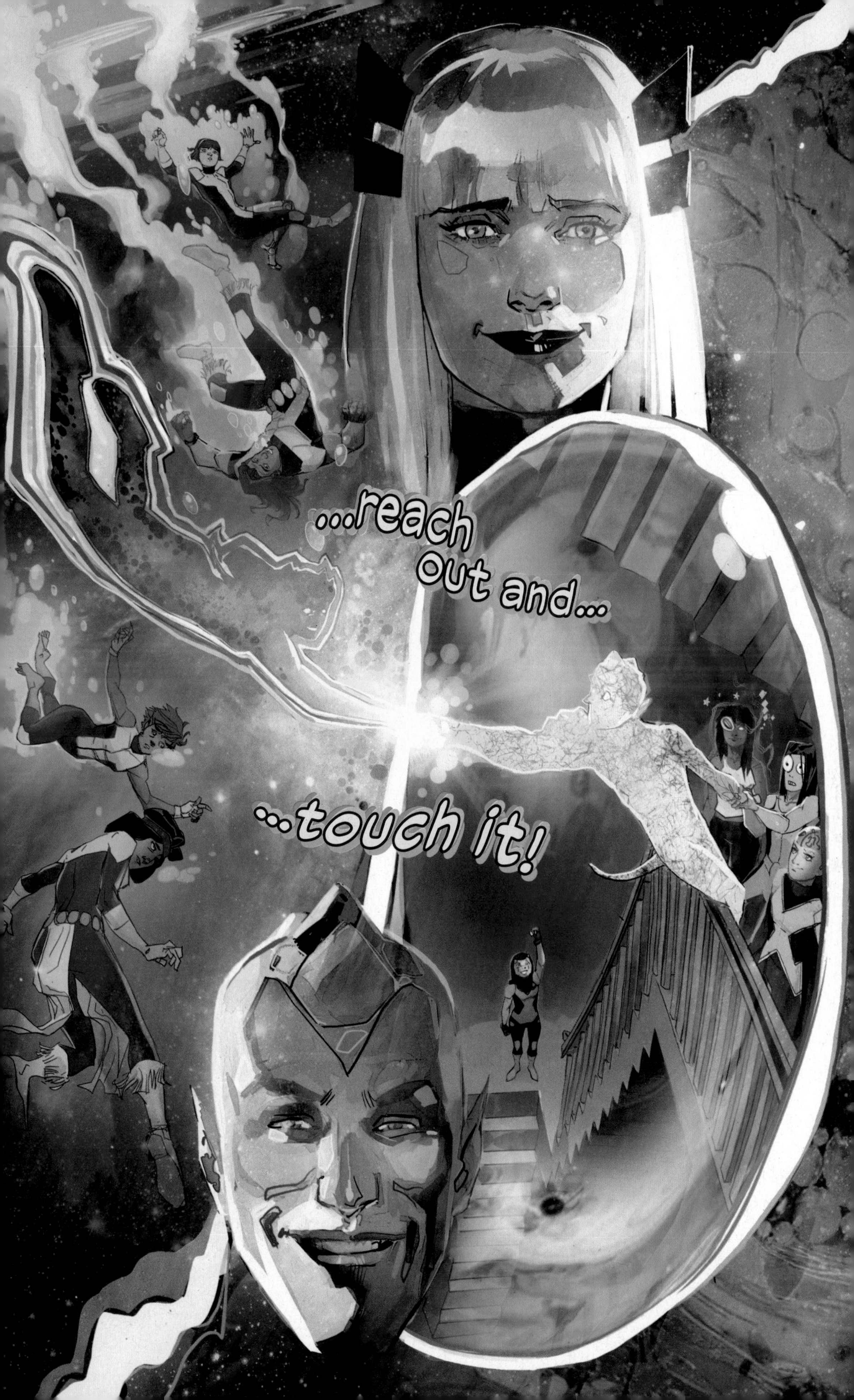
...reach out and...
...touch it!

HEROES & SHADOWS -- ACT 1, SCENE 2

NEW MUTANTS (DANI, KARMA, MAGIK, WARPATH, WOLFSBANE) *arrive into the non-Euclidean space to meet the* LOST CLUB (ANOLE, COSMAR, NO-GIRL, RAIN BOY, SCOUT).

Scout & Anole
That was AWESOME!

> **Warpath**
> What, exactly, WAS that?

No-Girl
If I had to guess, I would say that our [*indicates The Lost Club*] combined need to find you interacted with Cosmar's warping powers to pierce through the reality of Shadow King's astral plane.

> **Cosmar**
> It wasn't just ME. I felt another presence, someone OUTSIDE all of this guiding my powers.

Karma
I have as well. I KNOW this presence, but I hesitate to say it is the Shadow King...It seems to be HELPFUL. I think it may be why we were able to ESCAPE the loop.

> **Magik**
> Why assume we've escaped the loop? Just because this seems different doesn't mean it isn't another of Farouk's manipulations.

Rain Boy
You say that as if there's nothing in him that could be good, but I don't think that's fair? He did bad stuff, but I think he really DID care about us, even if it was in a messed up way.

> **Magik**
> As someone who has A LOT of experience being trapped in a liminal space being tortured and manipulated by its ruler, I think I earned the right to be aggressively suspicious. ESPECIALLY considering what the adults here just went through...I lost count of how many cycles we spent watching everything we care about destroyed.

No-Girl
And as someone who knows what it is like to be TRAPPED in her own mind and MANIPULATED to do horrible things -- while still trying to FIGHT BACK -- I think I have earned the right to say things may not be as black and white as you think they are.

> **Scout** [*coming to stand between the New Mutants and the Lost Club*]
> Look, what the Shadow King did to us -- to Karma, and Rahne, and ME -- was WRONG. That's not the problem. But there seems to be something else happening here too, WE [*gestures to the lost Club*] can sense it. Maybe you can't because you already decided what everything means.

No-Girl
I know what it is to be left behind. All I ask is that you consider that maybe we would be doing the same HERE.

> **Dani**
> No one is denying things are complicated, No-Girl. But that doesn't stop them from being DANGEROUS. And sometimes SAFETY has to be the priority.

Wolfsbane
I think what would be best, perhaps, is to find a way out of here. We can regroup then, all right?

> **Magik**
> We need to find a way OUT of this maze then. Anyone have any ideas?

Anole
Maybe...but if we don't figure out what is actually happening here, we may not be able to.

> **Warpath**
> If your powers combined were able to connect US like this, ALL of our powers combined may be able to break us free.

Wolfsbane
I think I can find a staging area, a weak point to attempt a break. [*pause*] This way!

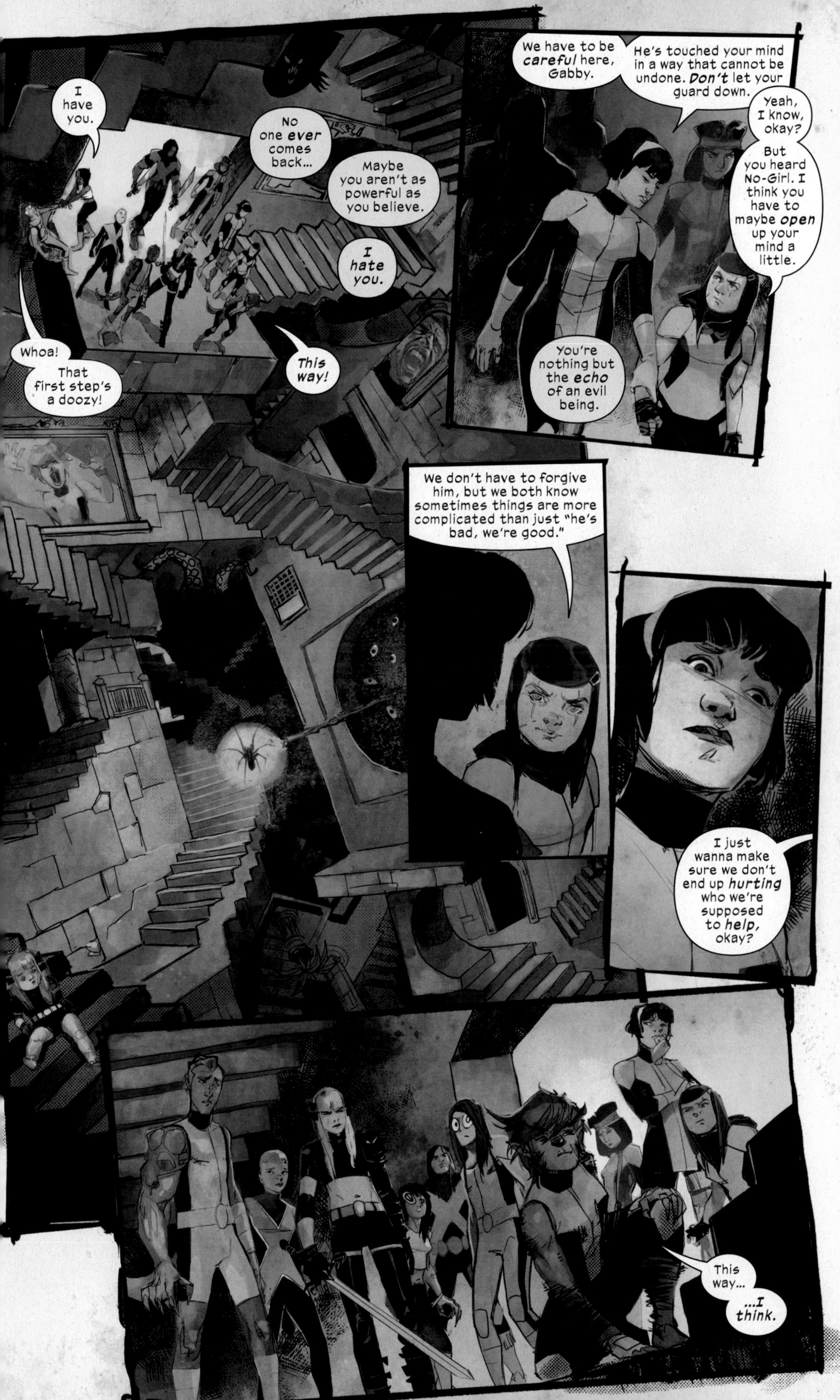
I have you.
No one ever comes back...
Maybe you aren't as powerful as you believe.
I hate you.
Whoa! That first step's a doozy!
This way!
We have to be careful here, Gabby.
He's touched your mind in a way that cannot be undone. Don't let your guard down.
Yeah, I know, okay?
But you heard No-Girl. I think you have to maybe open up your mind a little.
You're nothing but the echo of an evil being.
We don't have to forgive him, but we both know sometimes things are more complicated than just "he's bad, we're good."
I just wanna make sure we don't end up hurting who we're supposed to help, okay?
This way...
...I think.

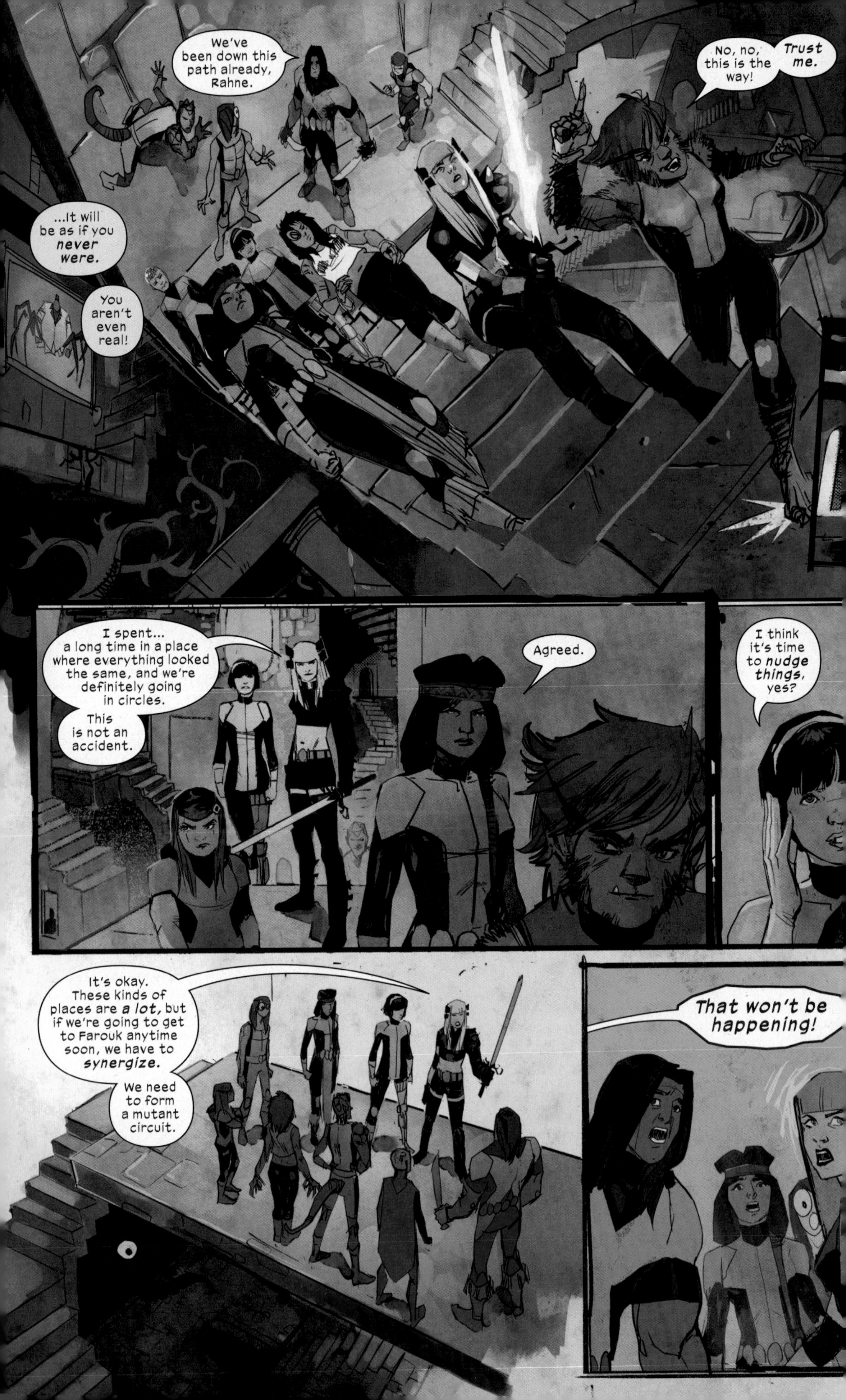
We've been down this path already, Rahne.
No, no, this is the way!
Trust me.
...It will be as if you never were.
You aren't even real!
I spent... a long time in a place where everything looked the same, and we're definitely going in circles.
This is not an accident.
Agreed.
I think it's time to nudge things, yes?
It's okay. These kinds of places are a lot, but if we're going to get to Farouk anytime soon, we have to synergize.
We need to form a mutant circuit.
That won't be happening!

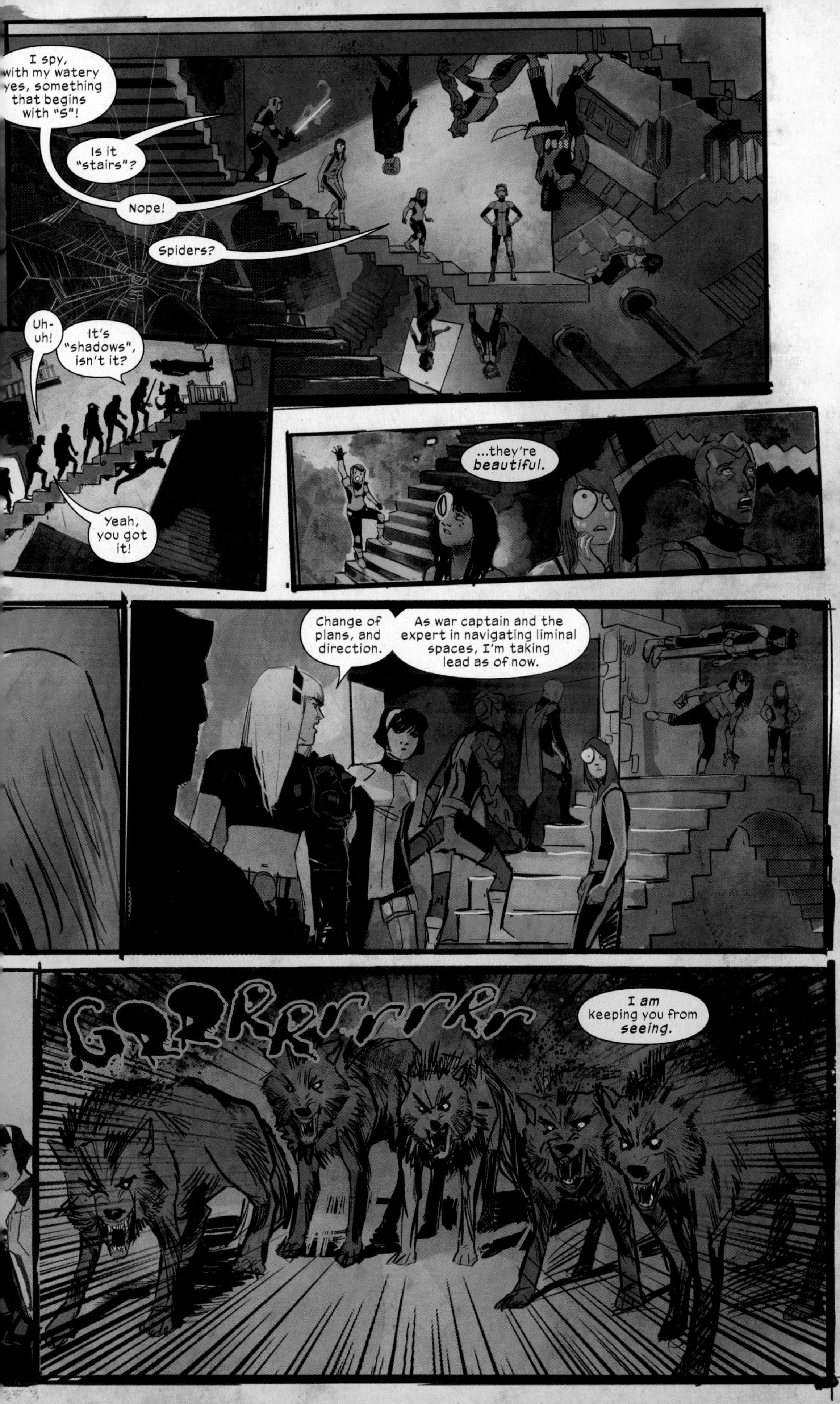
I spy, with my watery yes, something that begins with "S"!
Is it "stairs"?
Nope!
Spiders?
Uh-uh!
It's "shadows", isn't it?
Yeah, you got it!
...they're *beautiful*.
Change of plans, and direction.
As war captain and the expert in navigating liminal spaces, I'm taking lead as of now.
GRRRrrrrRr
I am keeping you from *seeing*.

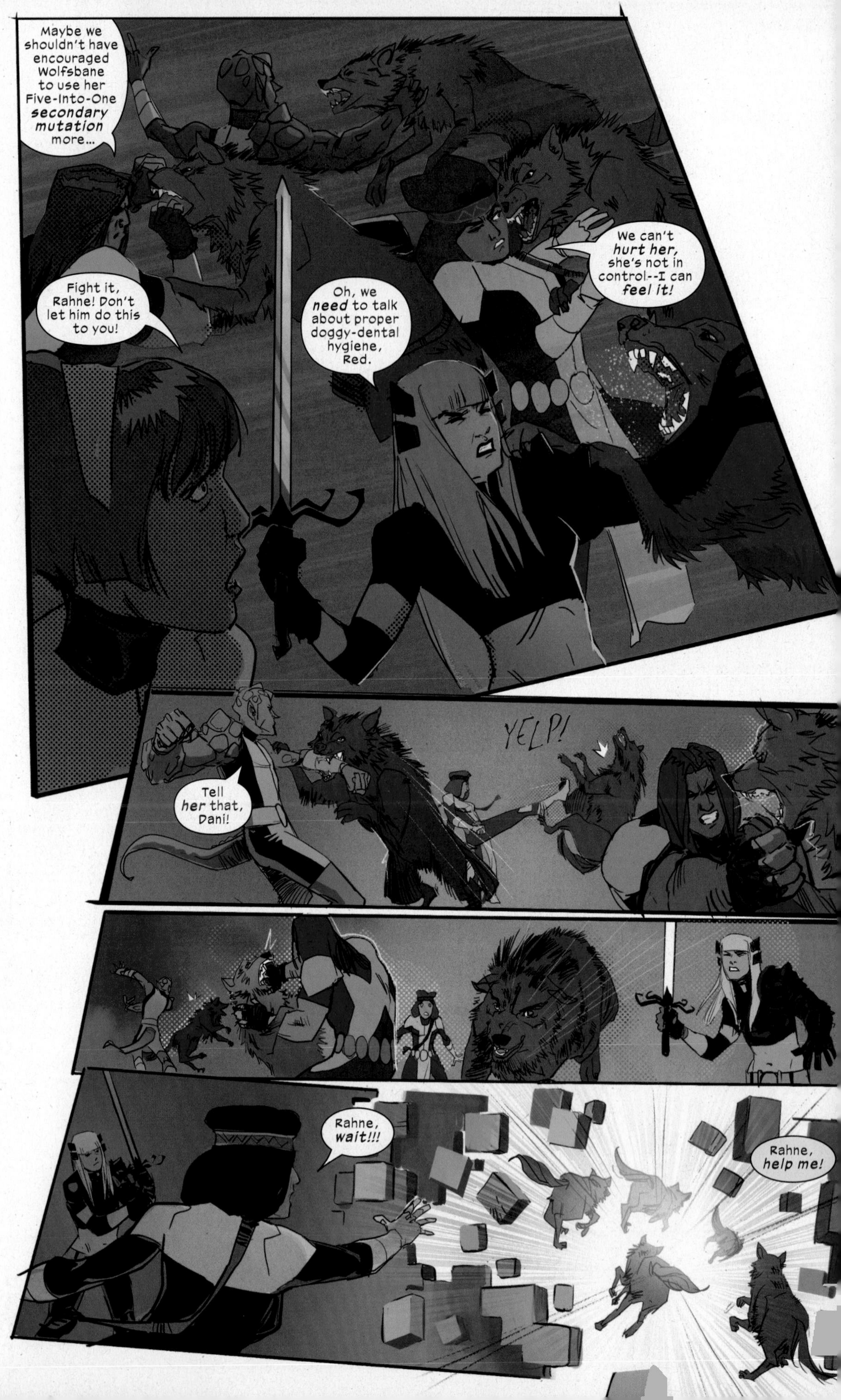

Maybe we shouldn't have encouraged Wolfsbane to use her Five-Into-One *secondary mutation* more...
We can't *hurt her,* she's not in control--I can *feel it!*
Fight it, Rahne! Don't let him do this to you!
Oh, we *need* to talk about proper doggy-dental hygiene, Red.
Tell *her* that, Dani!
YELP!
Rahne, *wait!!!*
Rahne, *help me!*

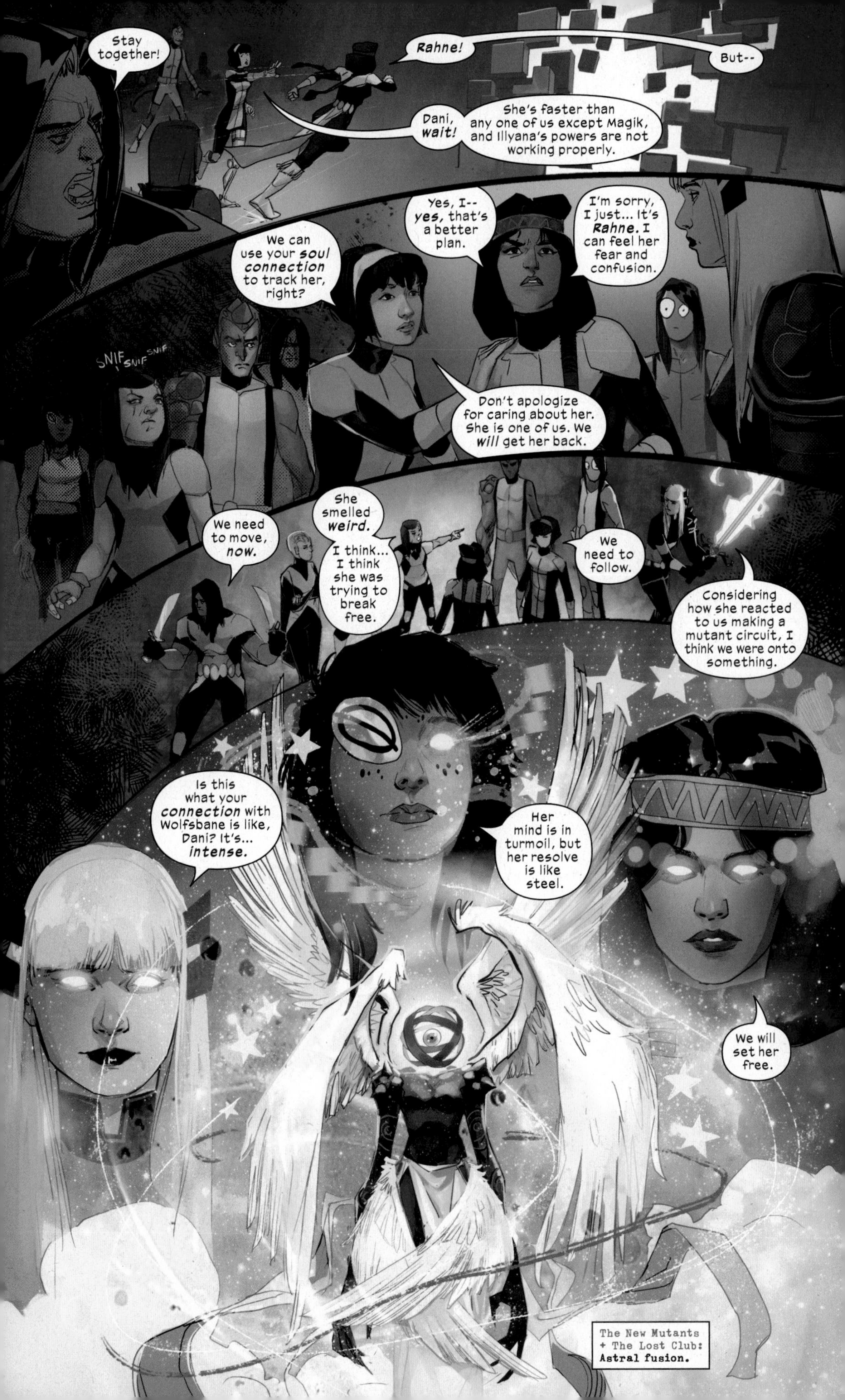
Stay together!
Rahne!
But--
Dani, wait!
She's faster than any one of us except Magik, and Illyana's powers are not working properly.
We can use your soul connection to track her, right?
Yes, I-- yes, that's a better plan.
I'm sorry, I just... It's Rahne. I can feel her fear and confusion.
SNIF SNIF SNIF
Don't apologize for caring about her. She is one of us. We will get her back.
We need to move, now.
She smelled weird.
I think... I think she was trying to break free.
We need to follow.
Considering how she reacted to us making a mutant circuit, I think we were onto something.
Is this what your connection with Wolfsbane is like, Dani? It's... intense.
Her mind is in turmoil, but her resolve is like steel.
We will set her free.
The New Mutants + The Lost Club: Astral fusion.

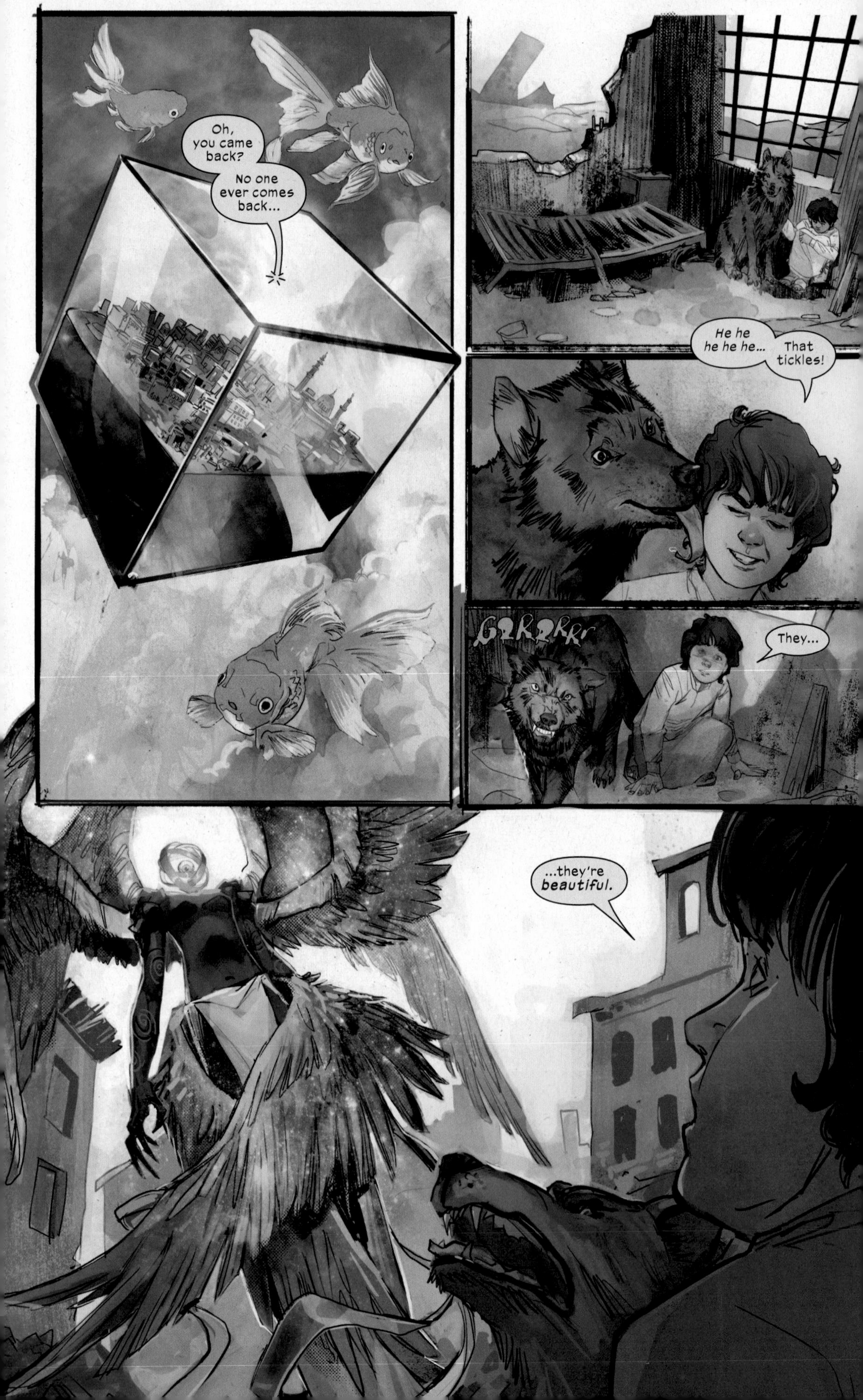
Oh, you came back?
No one ever comes back...
He he he he he...
That tickles!
GRRRRR
They...
...they're *beautiful*.

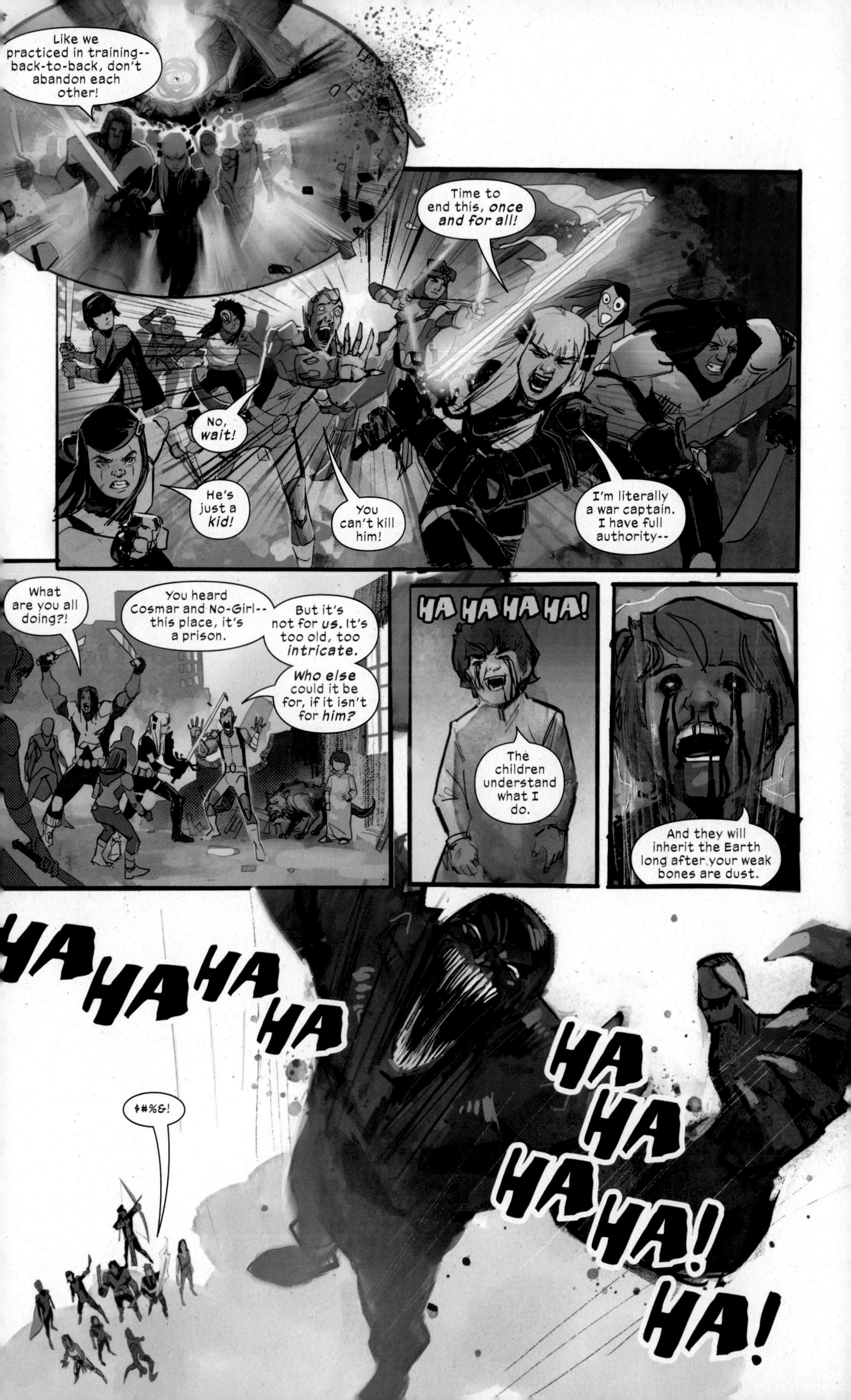
Like we practiced in training-- back-to-back, don't abandon each other!
Time to end this, once and for all!
No, wait!
He's just a kid!
You can't kill him!
I'm literally a war captain. I have full authority--
What are you all doing?!
You heard Cosmar and No-Girl-- this place, it's a prison.
But it's not for us. It's too old, too intricate.
Who else could it be for, if it isn't for him?
HA HA HA HA!
The children understand what I do.
And they will inherit the Earth long after your weak bones are dust.
HA HA HA HA HA
HA HA HA HA! HA!
$#%&!

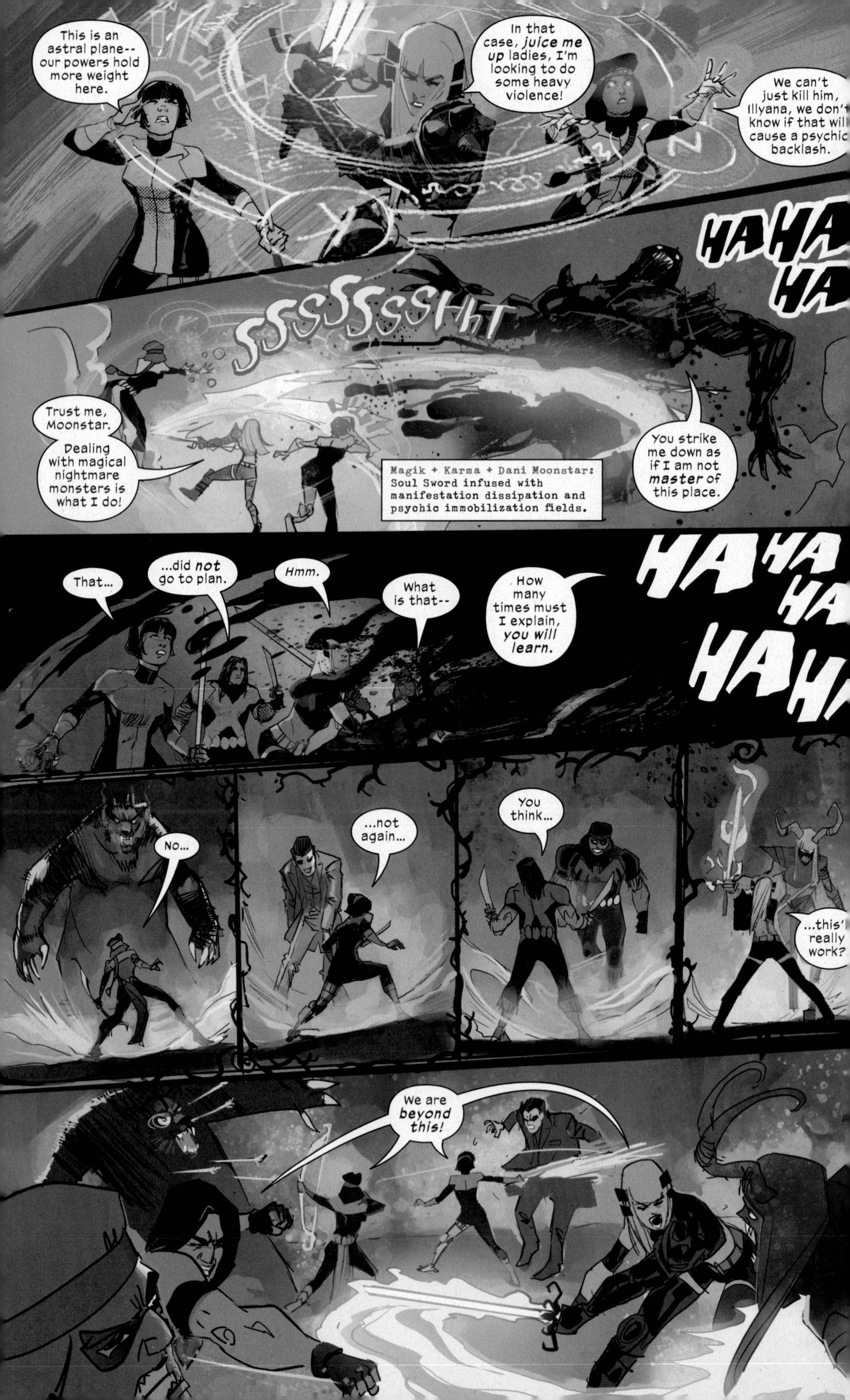
This is an astral plane--our powers hold more weight here.
In that case, *juice me up* ladies, I'm looking to do some heavy violence!
We can't just kill him, Illyana, we don't know if that will cause a psychic backlash.
HAHA HA
SSSSSSSHHT
Trust me, Moonstar.
Dealing with magical nightmare monsters is what I do!
Magik + Karma + Dani Moonstar: Soul Sword infused with manifestation dissipation and psychic immobilization fields.
You strike me down as if I am not *master* of this place.
HAHA HA HAHA
That...
...did *not* go to plan.
Hmm.
What is that--
How many times must I explain, *you will learn.*
No...
...not again...
You think...
...this really work?
We are *beyond this!*

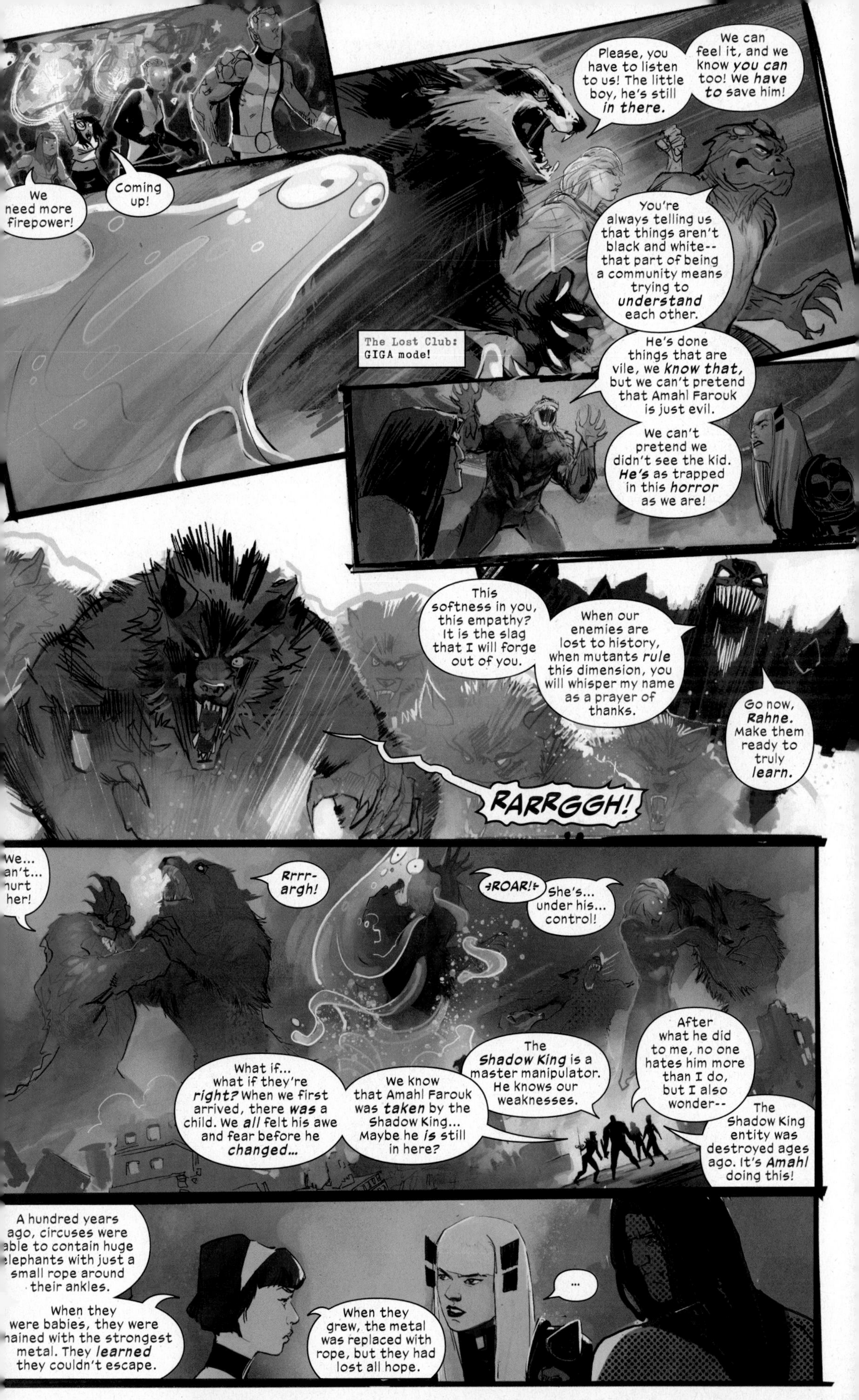
Please, you have to listen to us! The little boy, he's still in there.
We can feel it, and we know you can too! We have to save him!
We need more firepower!
Coming up!
You're always telling us that things aren't black and white-- that part of being a community means trying to understand each other.
The Lost Club: GIGA mode!
He's done things that are vile, we know that, but we can't pretend that Amahl Farouk is just evil.
We can't pretend we didn't see the kid. He's as trapped in this horror as we are!
This softness in you, this empathy? It is the slag that I will forge out of you.
When our enemies are lost to history, when mutants rule this dimension, you will whisper my name as a prayer of thanks.
Go now, Rahne. Make them ready to truly learn.
RARRGGH!
We... an't... hurt her!
Rrrr-argh!
ROAR!
She's... under his... control!
What if... what if they're right? When we first arrived, there was a child. We all felt his awe and fear before he changed...
We know that Amahl Farouk was taken by the Shadow King... Maybe he is still in here?
The Shadow King is a master manipulator. He knows our weaknesses.
After what he did to me, no one hates him more than I do, but I also wonder--
The Shadow King entity was destroyed ages ago. It's Amahl doing this!
A hundred years ago, circuses were able to contain huge elephants with just a small rope around their ankles.
When they were babies, they were hained with the strongest metal. They learned they couldn't escape.
When they grew, the metal was replaced with rope, but they had lost all hope.
...

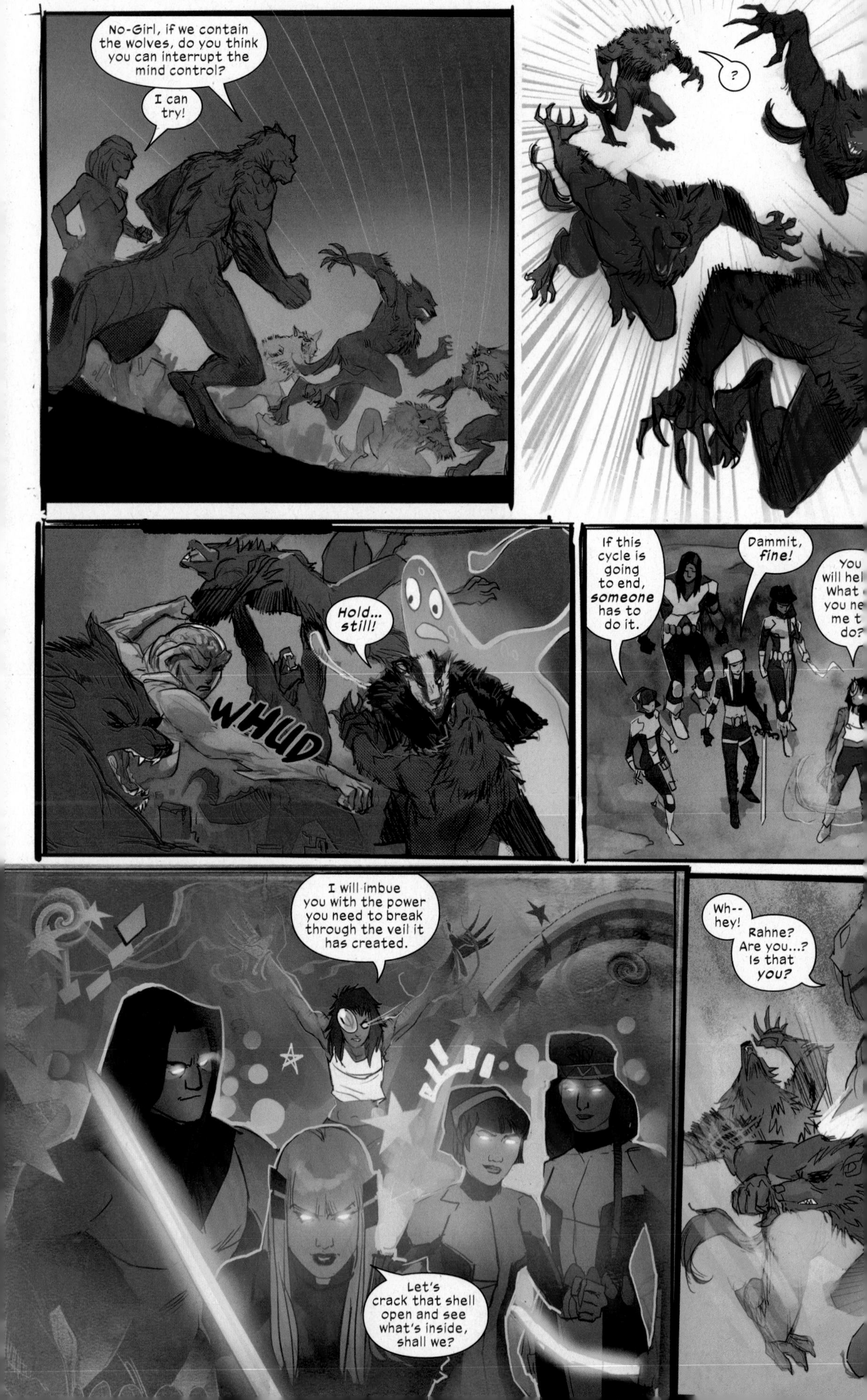

No-Girl, if we contain the wolves, do you think you can interrupt the mind control?
I can try!
?
Hold... still!
WHUD
If this cycle is going to end, *someone* has to do it.
Dammit, *fine!*
You will hel What you ne me t do?
I will imbue you with the power you need to break through the veil it has created.
Let's crack that shell open and see what's inside, shall we?
Wh-- hey!
Rahne? Are you...? Is that *you?*

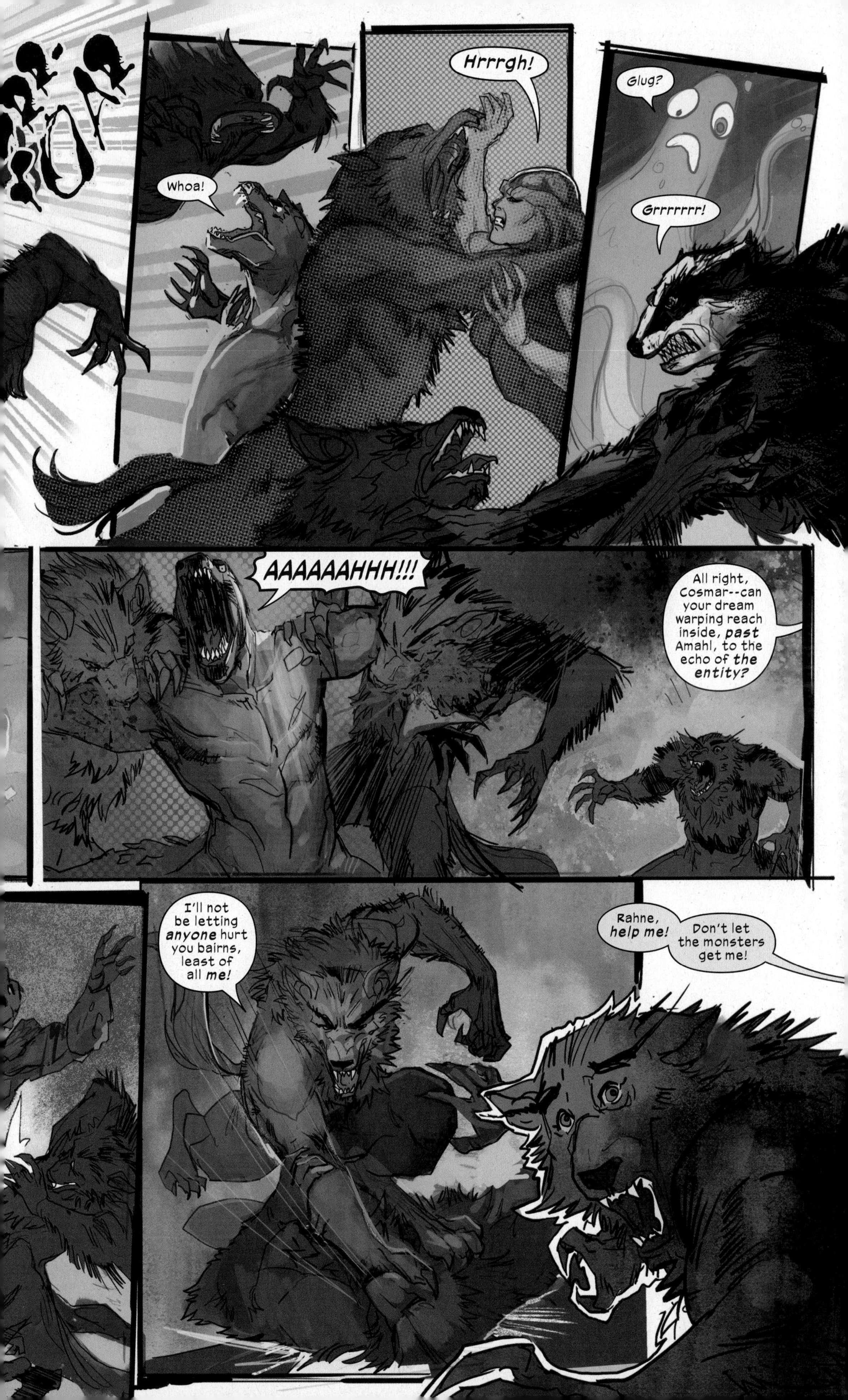
RRROAR
Whoa!
Hrrrgh!
Glug?
Grrrrrrr!
AAAAAAHHH!!!
All right, Cosmar--can your dream warping reach inside, past Amahl, to the echo of the entity?
I'll not be letting anyone hurt you bairns, least of all me!
Rahne, help me!
Don't let the monsters get me!

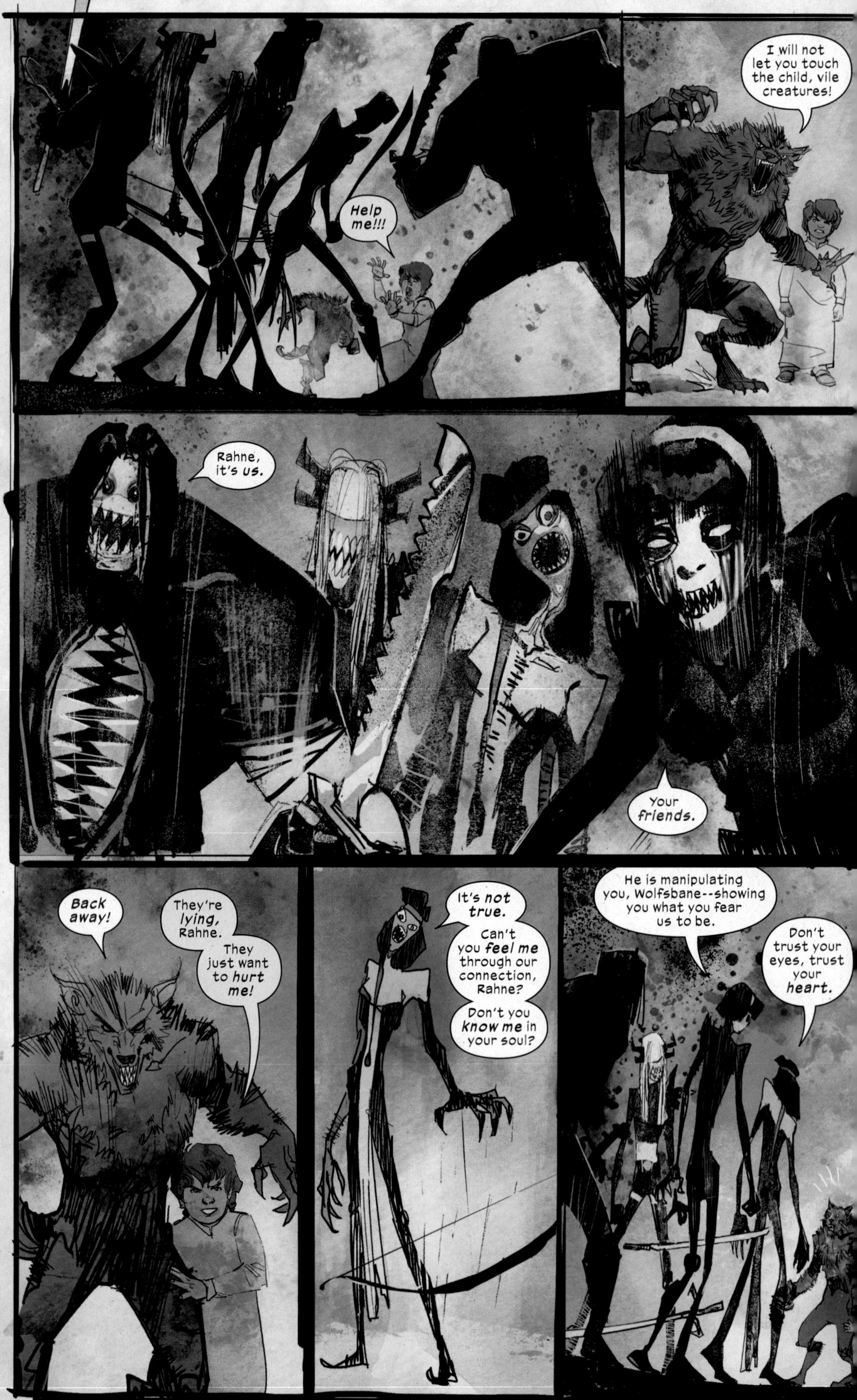
Help me!!!
I will not let you touch the child, vile creatures!
Rahne, it's us.
Your friends.
Back away!
They're lying, Rahne.
They just want to hurt me!
It's not true.
Can't you feel me through our connection, Rahne?
Don't you know me in your soul?
He is manipulating you, Wolfsbane--showing you what you fear us to be.
Don't trust your eyes, trust your heart.

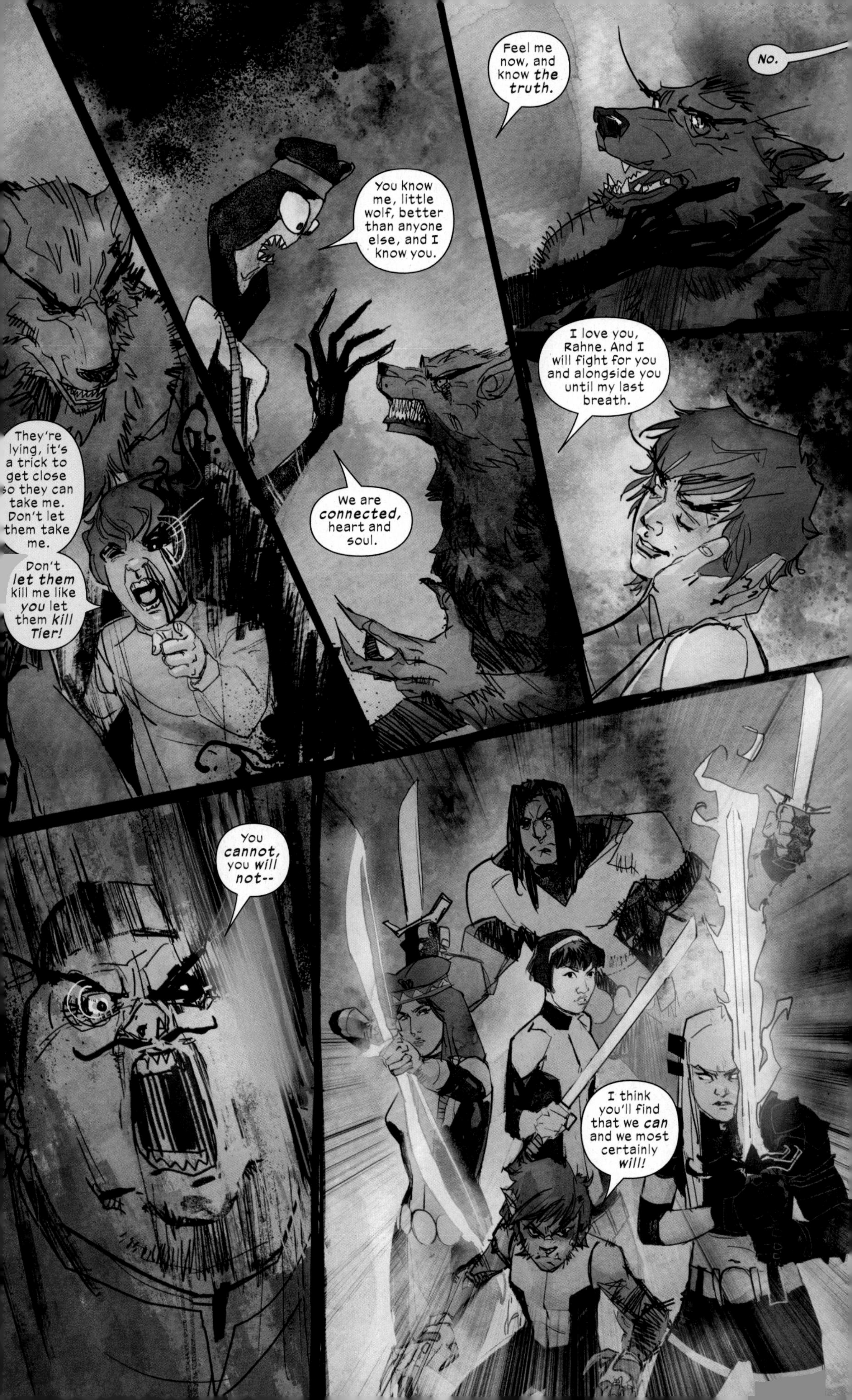

You know me, little wolf, better than anyone else, and I know you.
Feel me now, and know the truth.
No.
They're lying, it's a trick to get close so they can take me. Don't let them take me.
Don't let them kill me like you let them kill Tier!
We are connected, heart and soul.
I love you, Rahne. And I will fight for you and alongside you until my last breath.
You cannot, you will not--
I think you'll find that we can and we most certainly will!

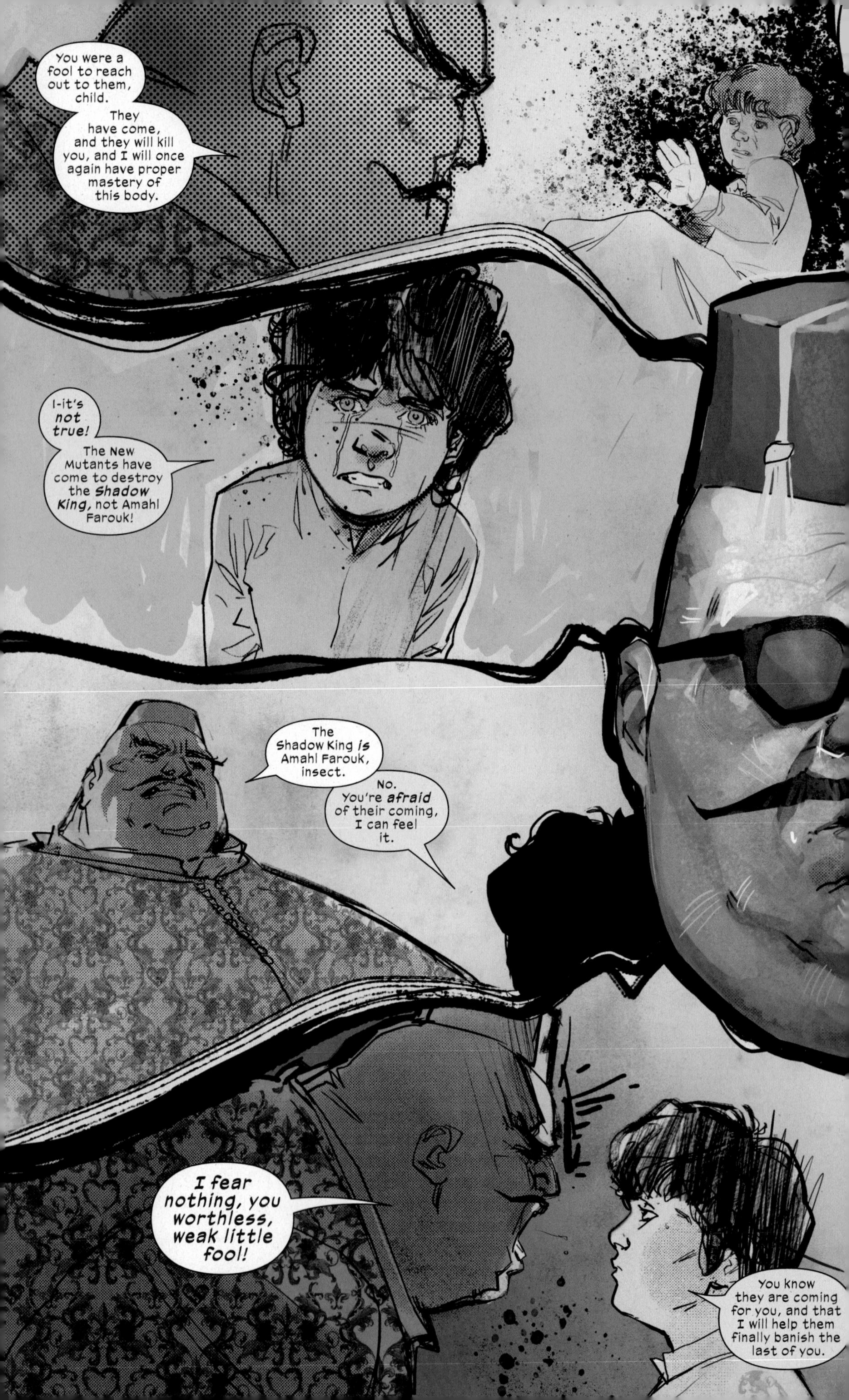

You were a fool to reach out to them, child.
They have come, and they will kill you, and I will once again have proper mastery of this body.
I-it's *not true!*
The New Mutants have come to destroy the *Shadow King,* not Amahl Farouk!
The Shadow King *is* Amahl Farouk, insect.
No. You're *afraid* of their coming, I can feel it.
I fear nothing, you worthless, weak little fool!
You know they are coming for you, and that I will help them finally banish the last of you.

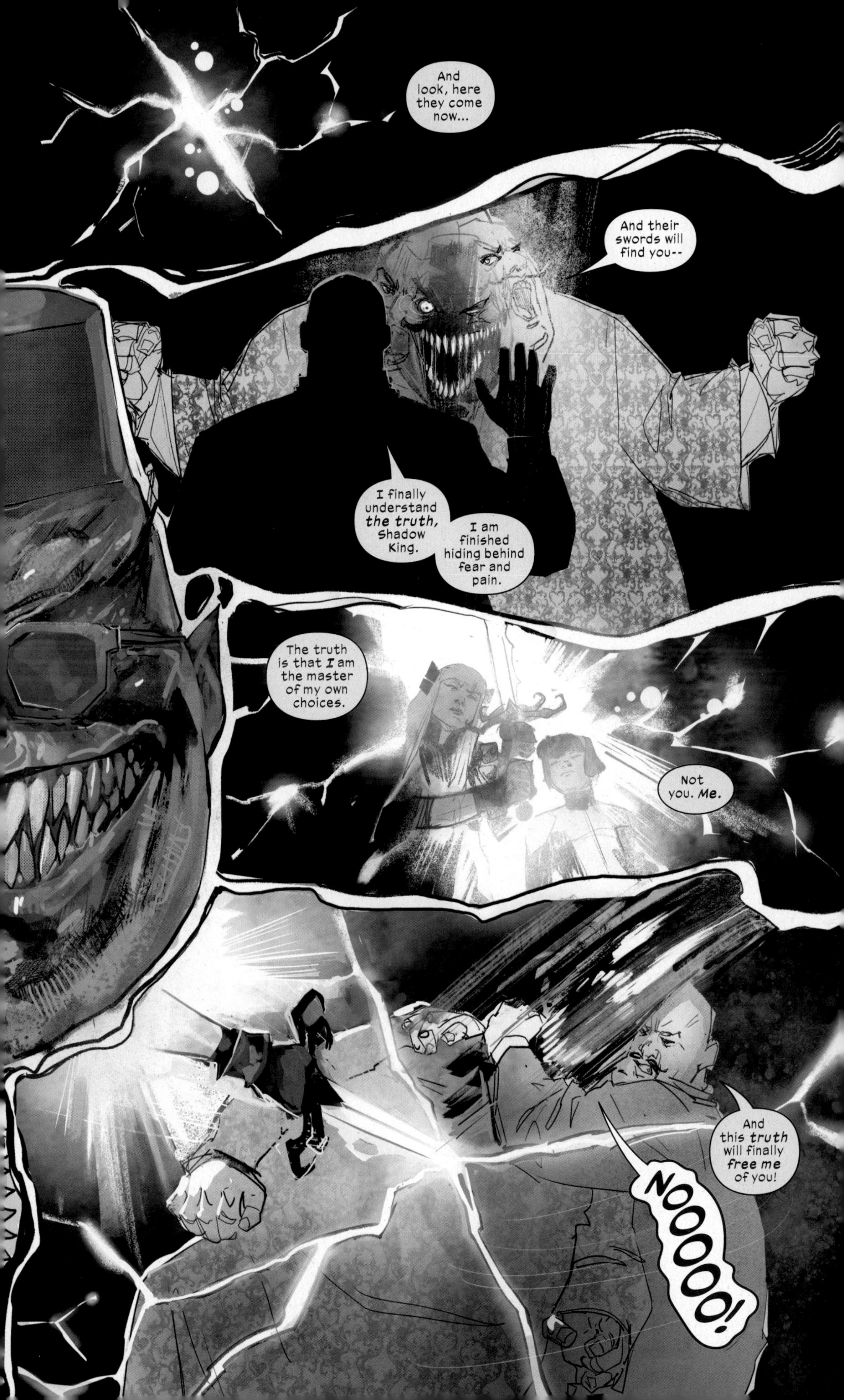
And look, here they come now...
And their swords will find you--
I finally understand *the truth,* Shadow King.
I am finished hiding behind fear and pain.
The truth is that *I* am the master of my own choices.
Not you. *Me.*
And this *truth* will finally *free me* of you!
NOOOOO!

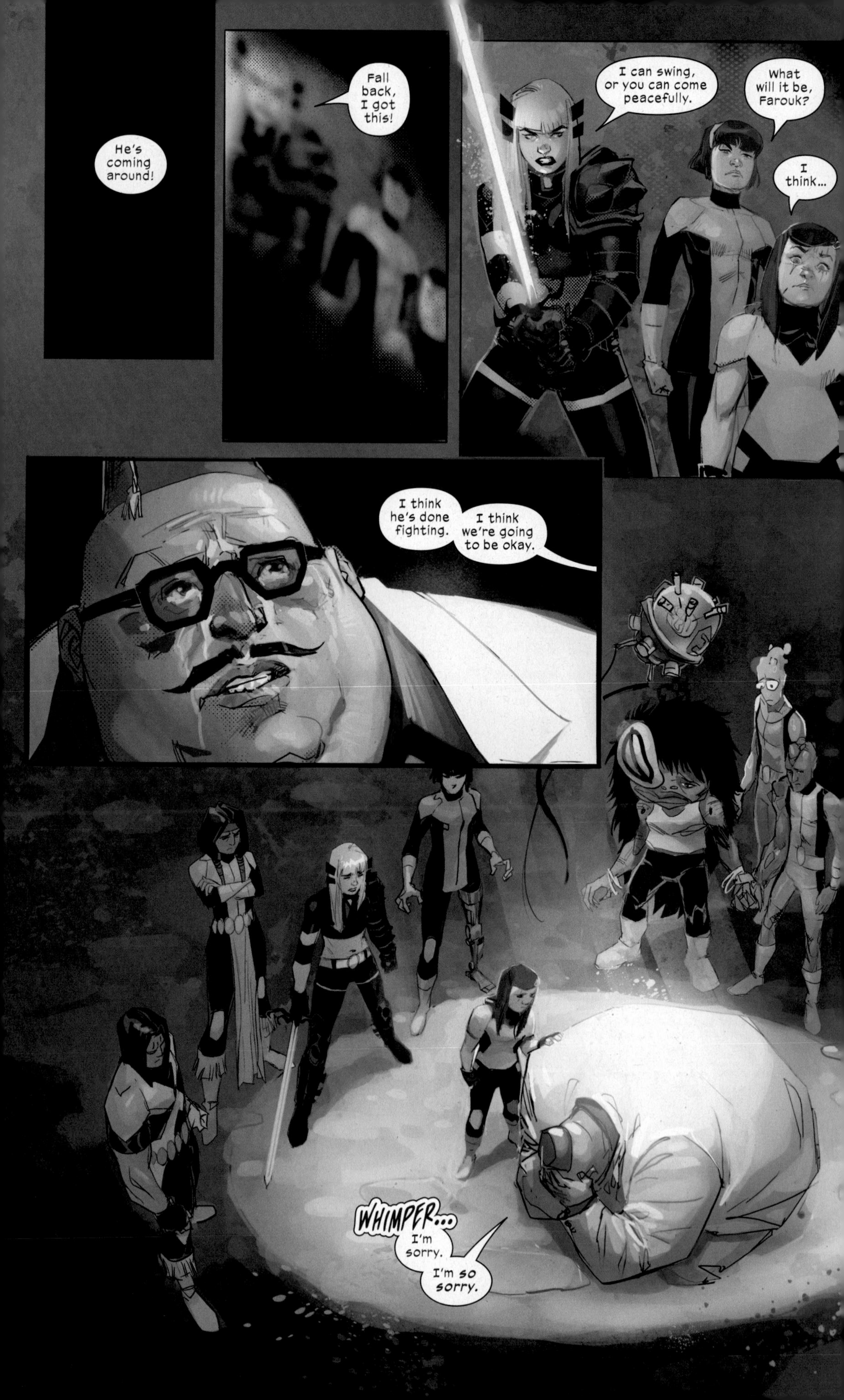
He's coming around!
Fall back, I got this!
I can swing, or you can come peacefully.
What will it be, Farouk?
I think...
I think he's done fighting.
I think we're going to be okay.
WHIMPER...
I'm sorry.
I'm so sorry.

[reign_of_x]

[kra_]
[koa_]

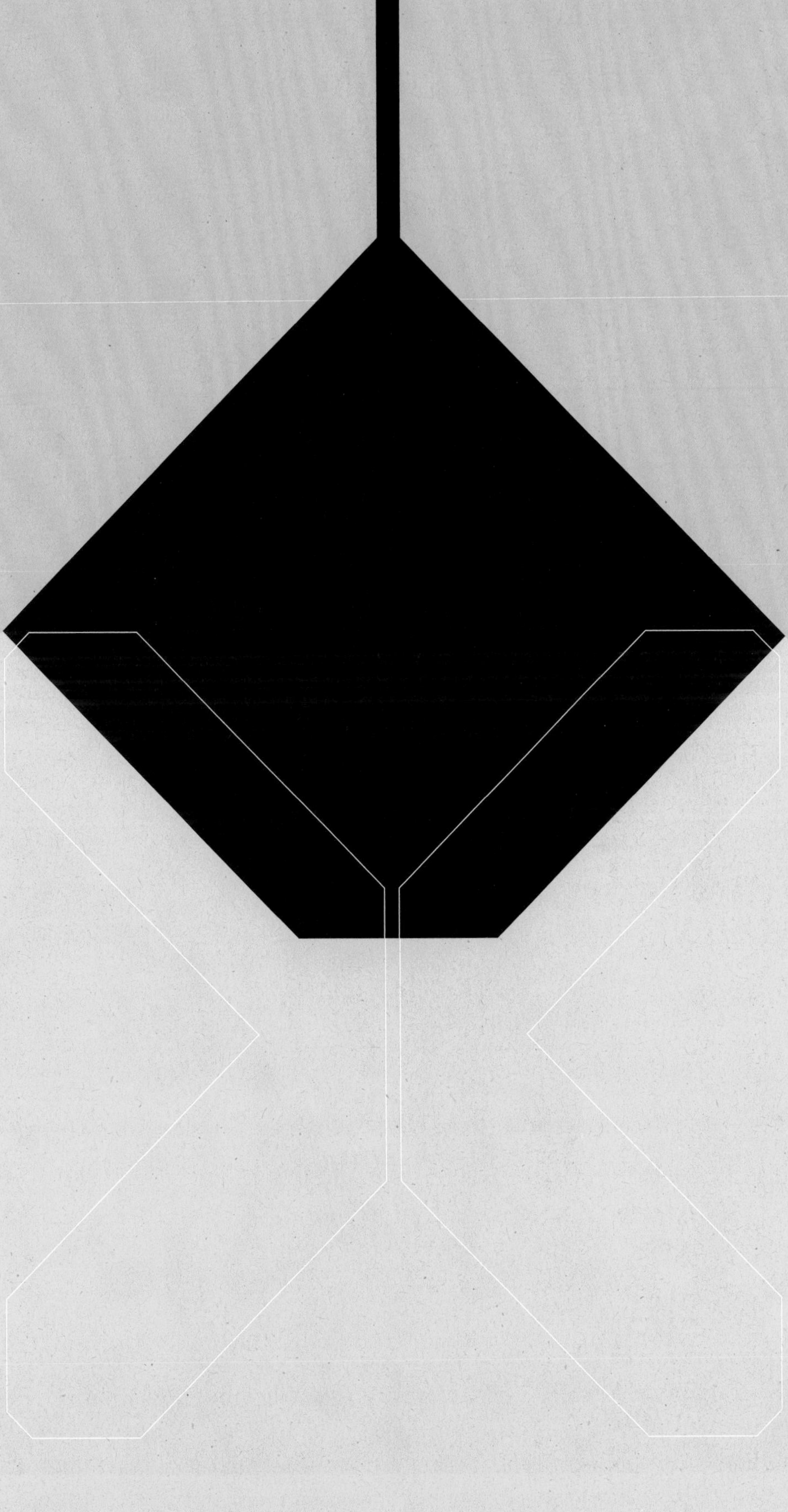

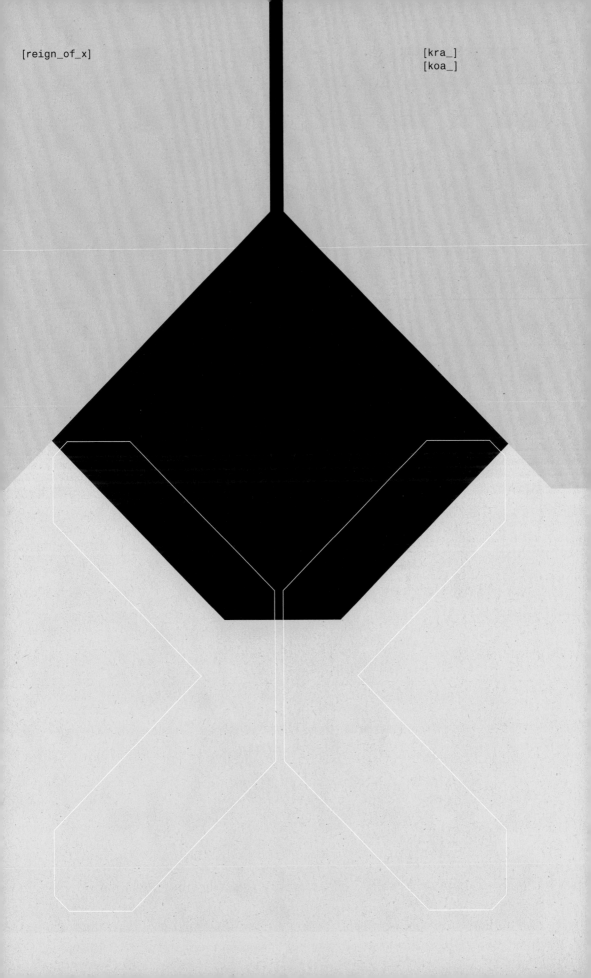

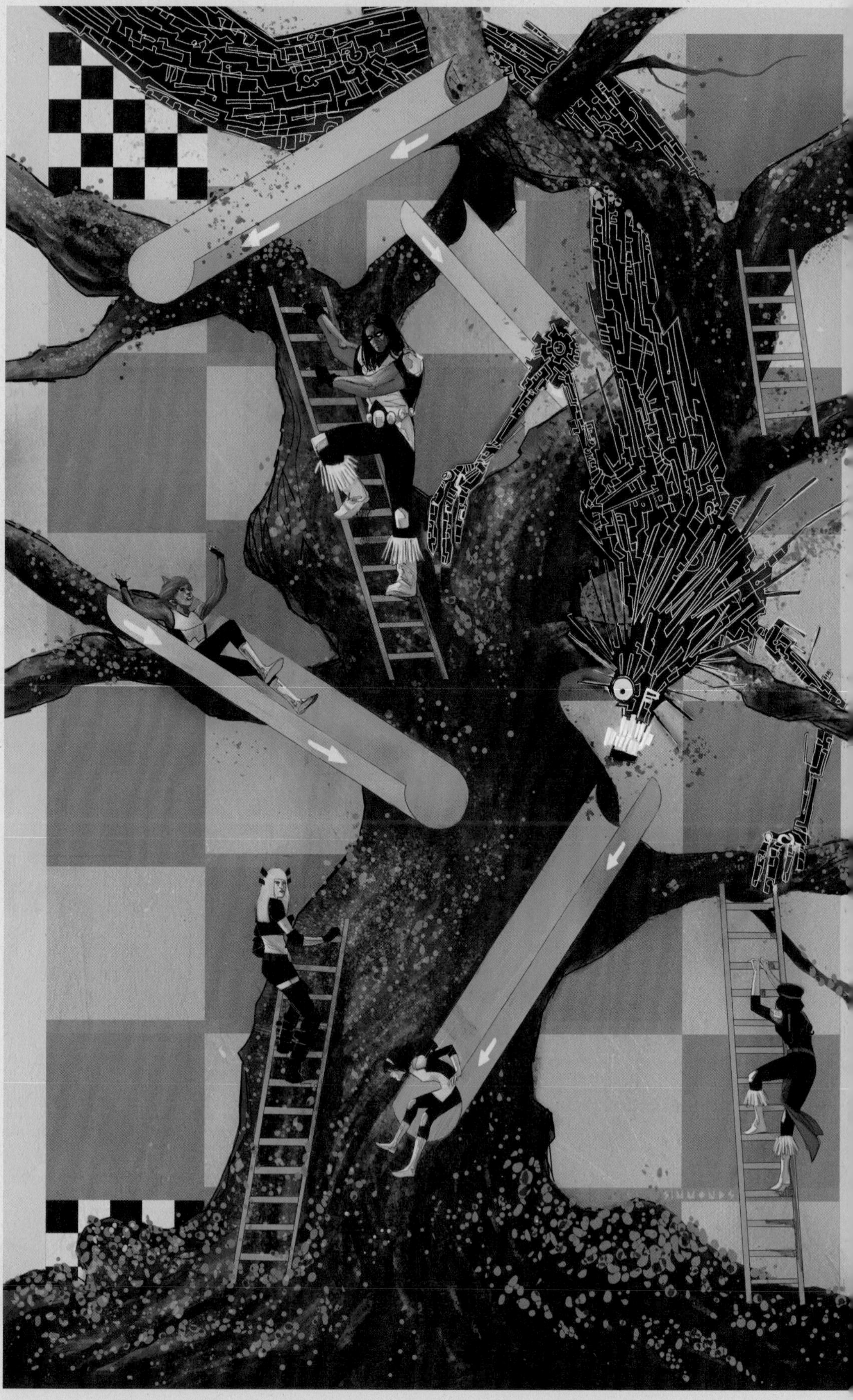
SIMMONDS

What is Deserved

[reign_of_x]

[kra_]
[koa_]

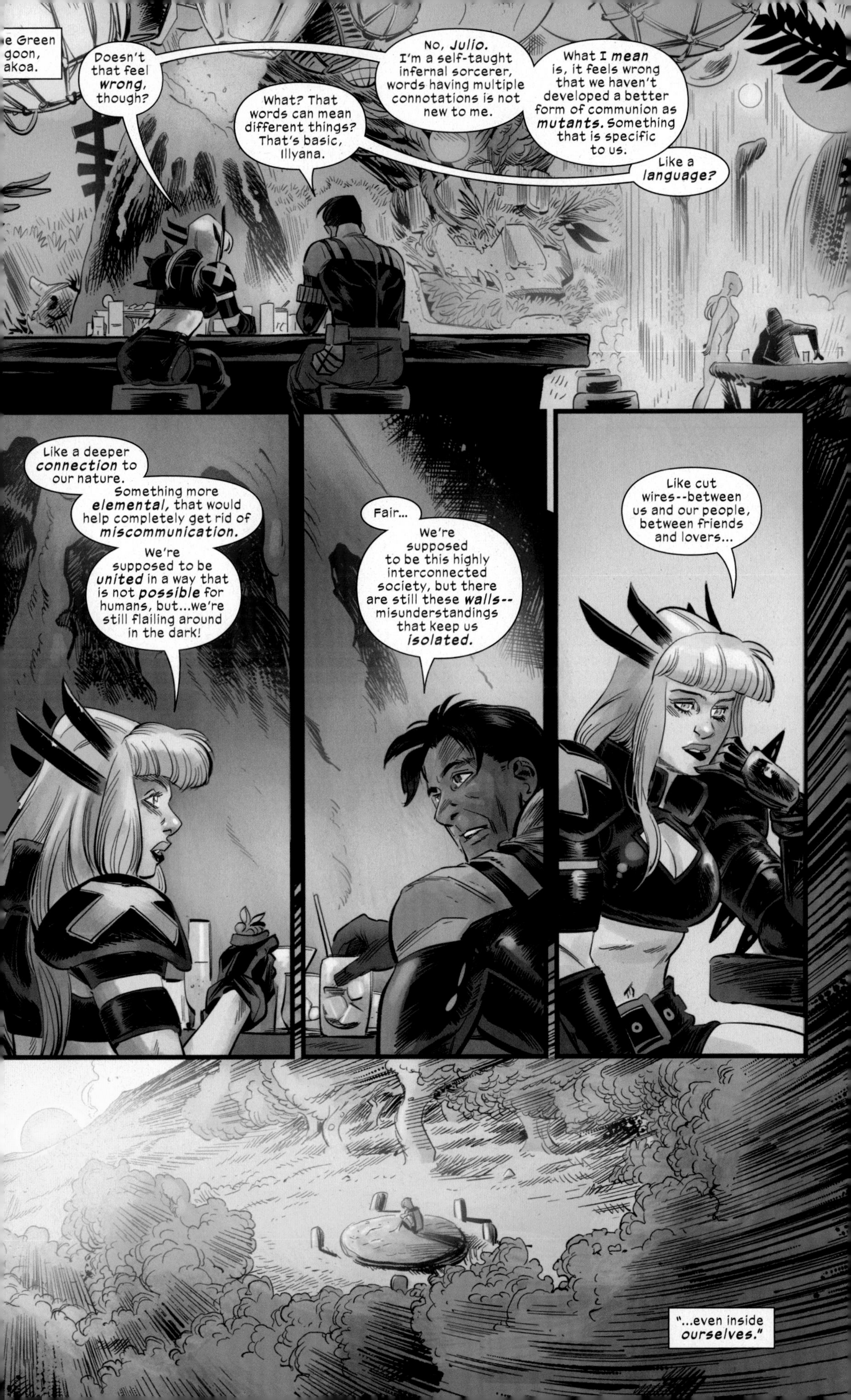
e Green goon, akoa.
Doesn't that feel wrong, though?
What? That words can mean different things? That's basic, Illyana.
No, Julio. I'm a self-taught infernal sorcerer, words having multiple connotations is not new to me.
What I mean is, it feels wrong that we haven't developed a better form of communion as mutants. Something that is specific to us.
Like a language?
Like a deeper connection to our nature.
Something more elemental, that would help completely get rid of miscommunication.
We're supposed to be united in a way that is not possible for humans, but...we're still flailing around in the dark!
Fair...
We're supposed to be this highly interconnected society, but there are still these walls--misunderstandings that keep us isolated.
Like cut wires--between us and our people, between friends and lovers...
"...even inside ourselves."

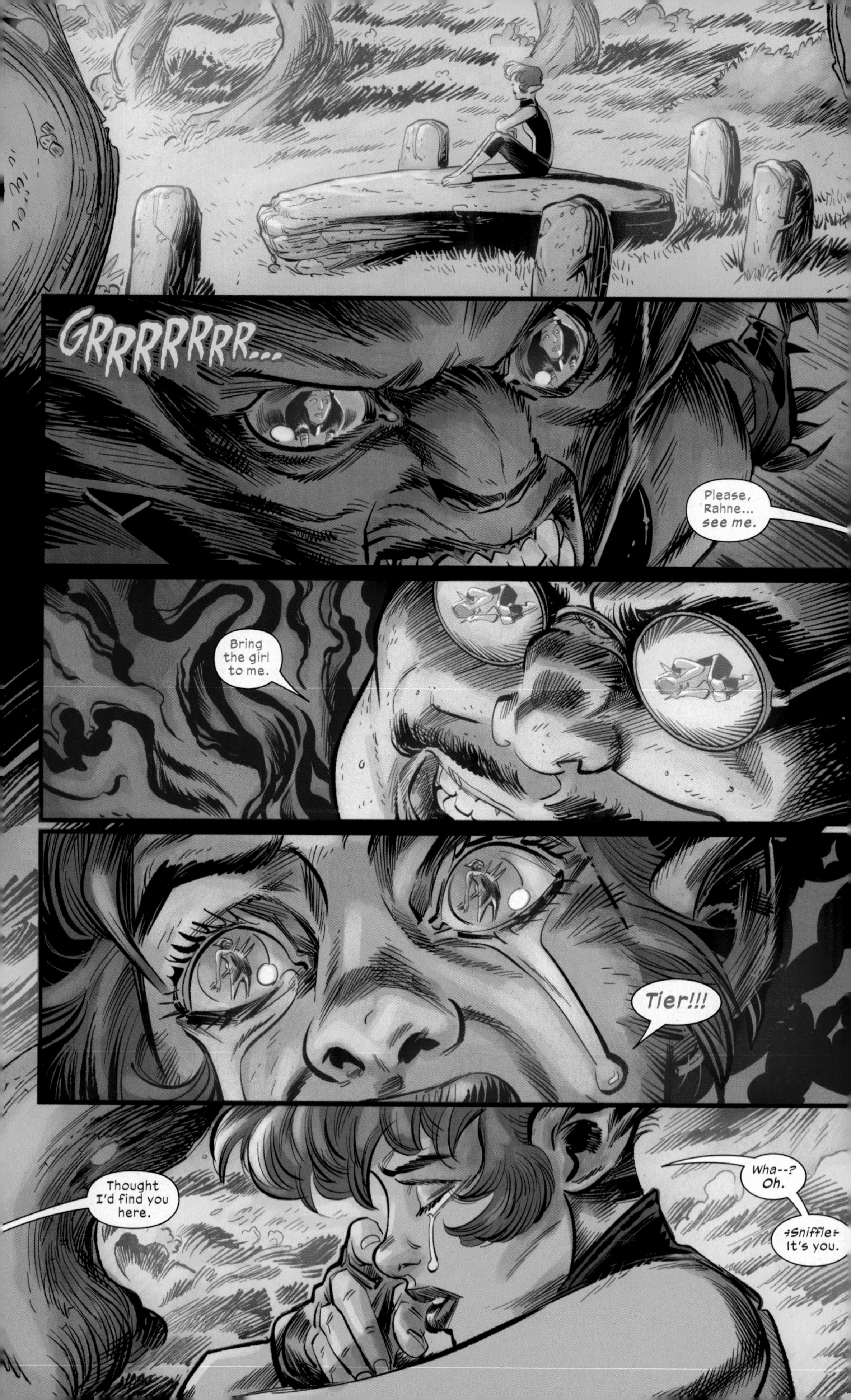
GRRRRRRR...
Please, Rahne... see me.
Bring the girl to me.
Tier!!!
Thought I'd find you here.
Wha--? Oh.
⸗Sniffle⸗ It's you.

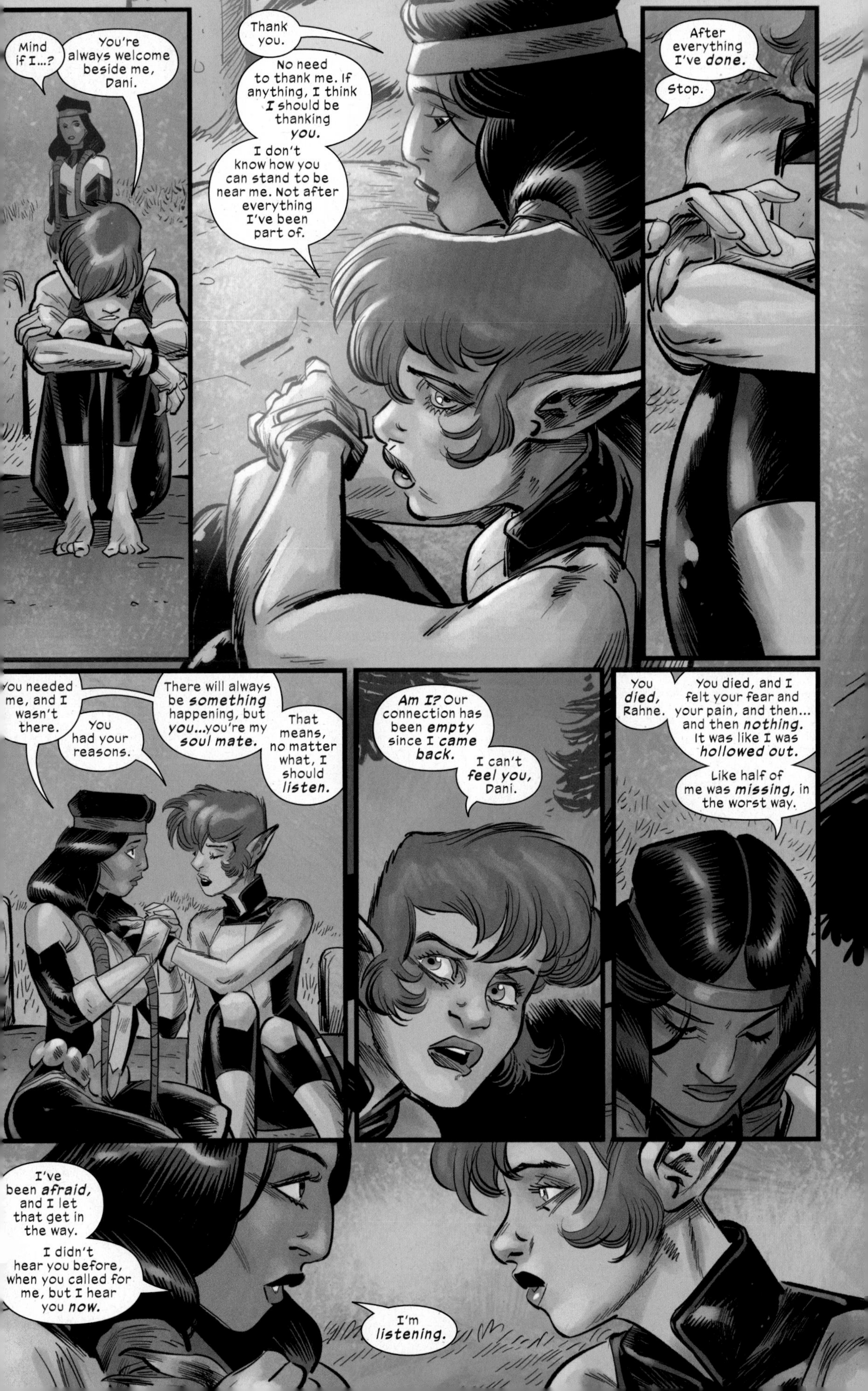
Mind if I...?
You're always welcome beside me, Dani.
Thank you.
No need to thank me. If anything, I think I should be thanking you.
I don't know how you can stand to be near me. Not after everything I've been part of.
After everything I've done.
Stop.
You needed me, and I wasn't there.
You had your reasons.
There will always be something happening, but you...you're my soul mate.
That means, no matter what, I should listen.
Am I? Our connection has been empty since I came back.
I can't feel you, Dani.
You died, Rahne.
You died, and I felt your fear and your pain, and then... and then nothing. It was like I was hollowed out.
Like half of me was missing, in the worst way.
I've been afraid, and I let that get in the way.
I didn't hear you before, when you called for me, but I hear you now.
I'm listening.

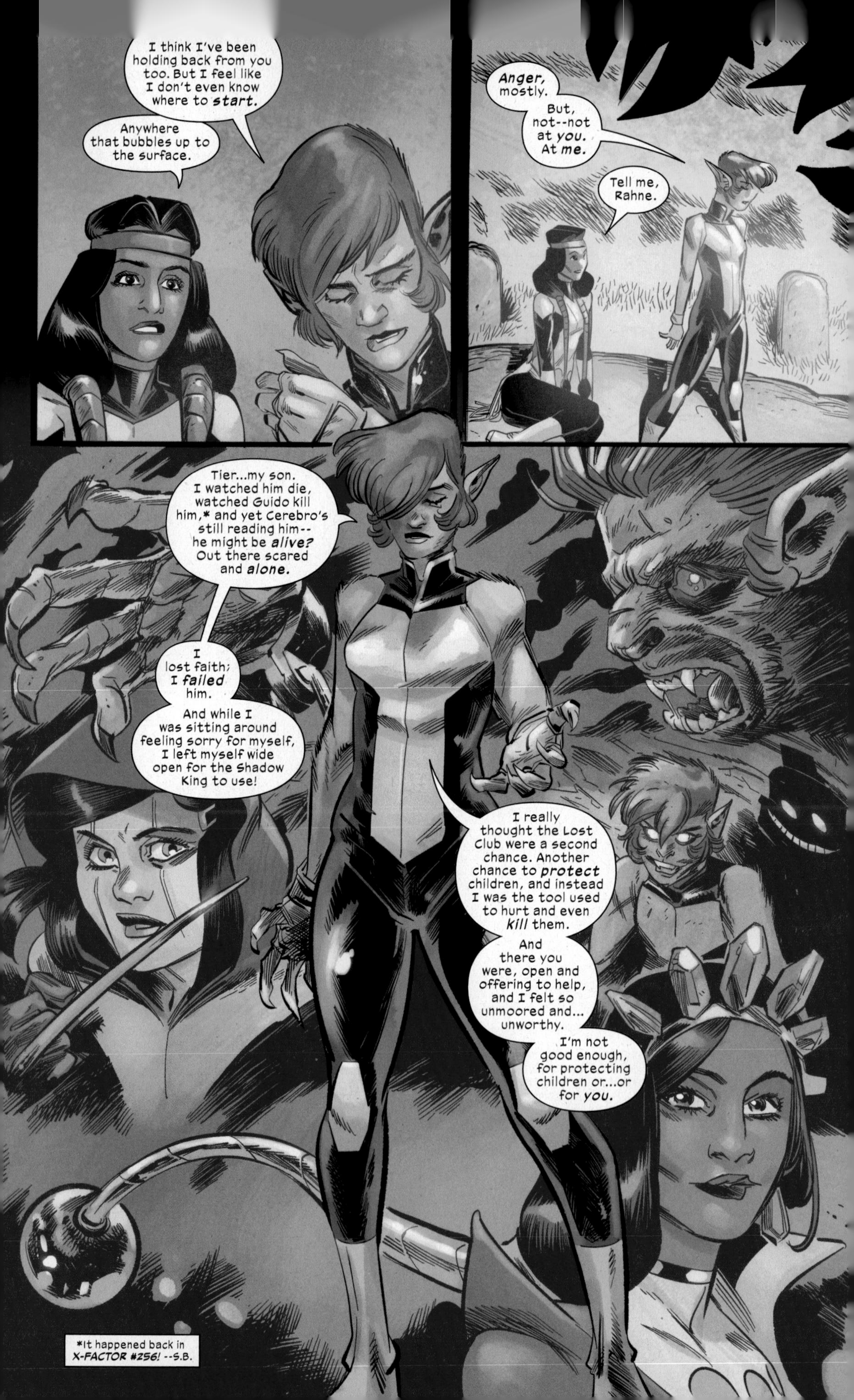
I think I've been holding back from you too. But I feel like I don't even know where to *start*.
Anywhere that bubbles up to the surface.
Anger, mostly.
But, not--not at *you*. At *me*.
Tell me, Rahne.
Tier...my son. I watched him die, watched Guido kill him,* and yet Cerebro's still reading him--he might be *alive?* Out there scared and *alone*.
I lost faith; I *failed* him.
And while I was sitting around feeling sorry for myself, I left myself wide open for the Shadow King to use!
I really thought the Lost Club were a second chance. Another chance to *protect* children, and instead I was the tool used to hurt and even *kill* them.
And there you were, open and offering to help, and I felt so unmoored and... unworthy.
I'm not good enough, for protecting children or...or for *you*.
*It happened back in *X-FACTOR #256!* --S.B.

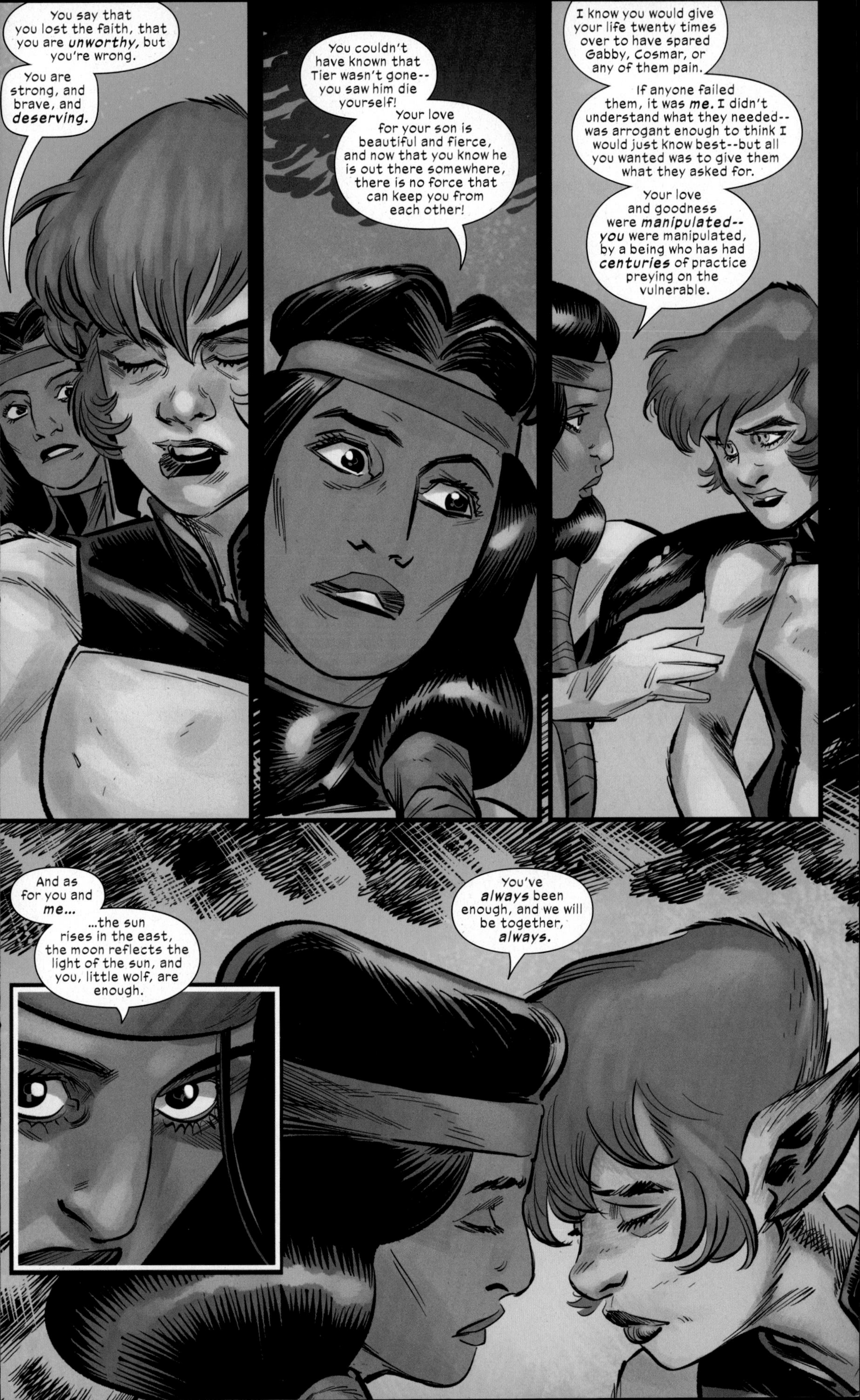
You say that you lost the faith, that you are *unworthy*, but you're wrong.
You are strong, and brave, and ***deserving.***
You couldn't have known that Tier wasn't gone--you saw him die yourself!
Your love for your son is beautiful and fierce, and now that you know he is out there somewhere, there is no force that can keep you from each other!
I know you would give your life twenty times over to have spared Gabby, Cosmar, or any of them pain.
If anyone failed them, it was **me.** I didn't understand what they needed--was arrogant enough to think I would just know best--but all you wanted was to give them what they asked for.
Your love and goodness were ***manipulated--*** ***you*** were manipulated, by a being who has had ***centuries*** of practice preying on the vulnerable.
And as for you and ***me...***
...the sun rises in the east, the moon reflects the light of the sun, and you, little wolf, are enough.
You've ***always*** been enough, and we will be together, ***always.***

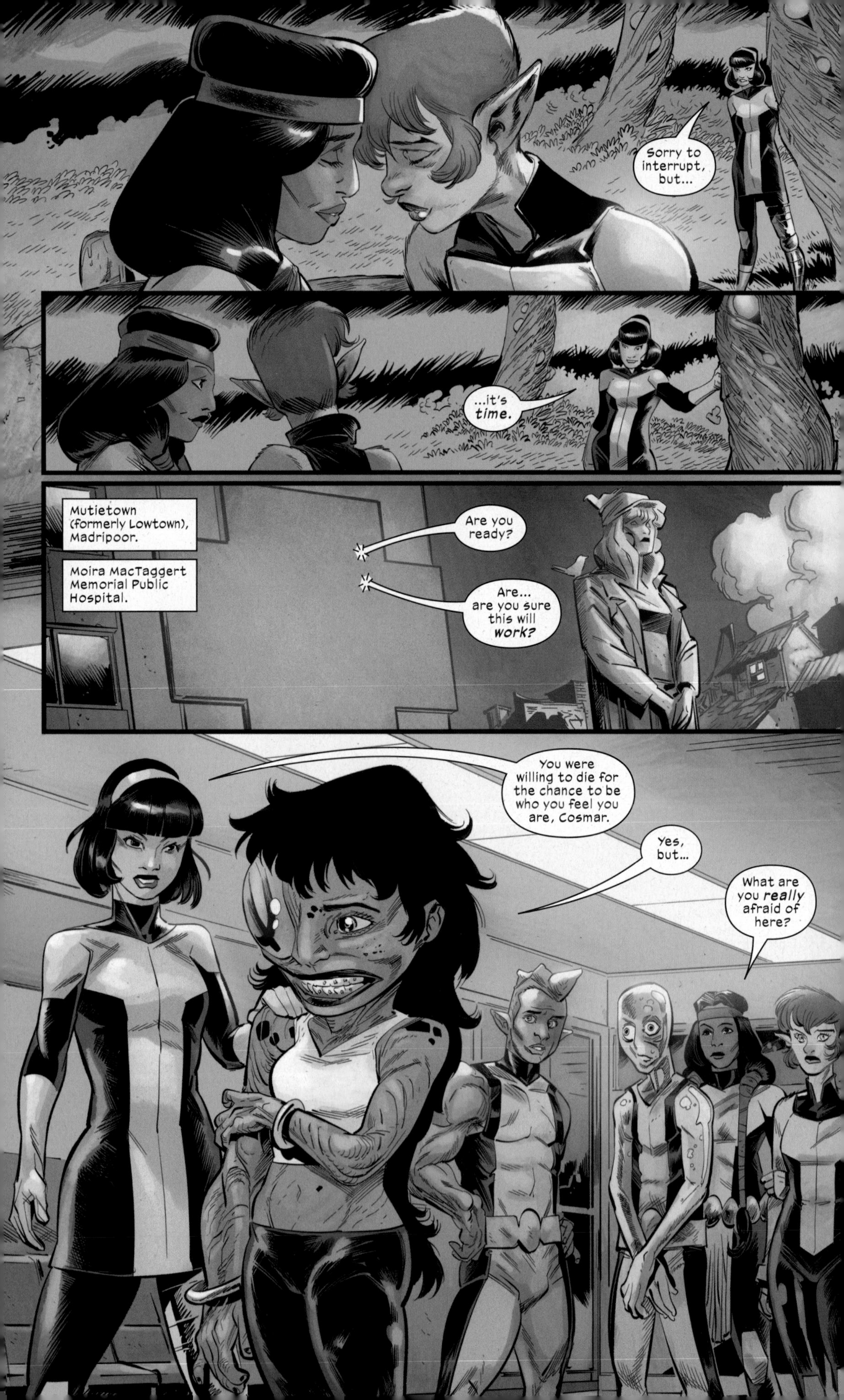
Sorry to interrupt, but...
...it's *time.*
Mutietown (formerly Lowtown), Madripoor.
Moira MacTaggert Memorial Public Hospital.
Are you ready?
Are... are you sure this will *work?*
You were willing to die for the chance to be who you feel you are, Cosmar.
Yes, but...
What are you *really* afraid of here?

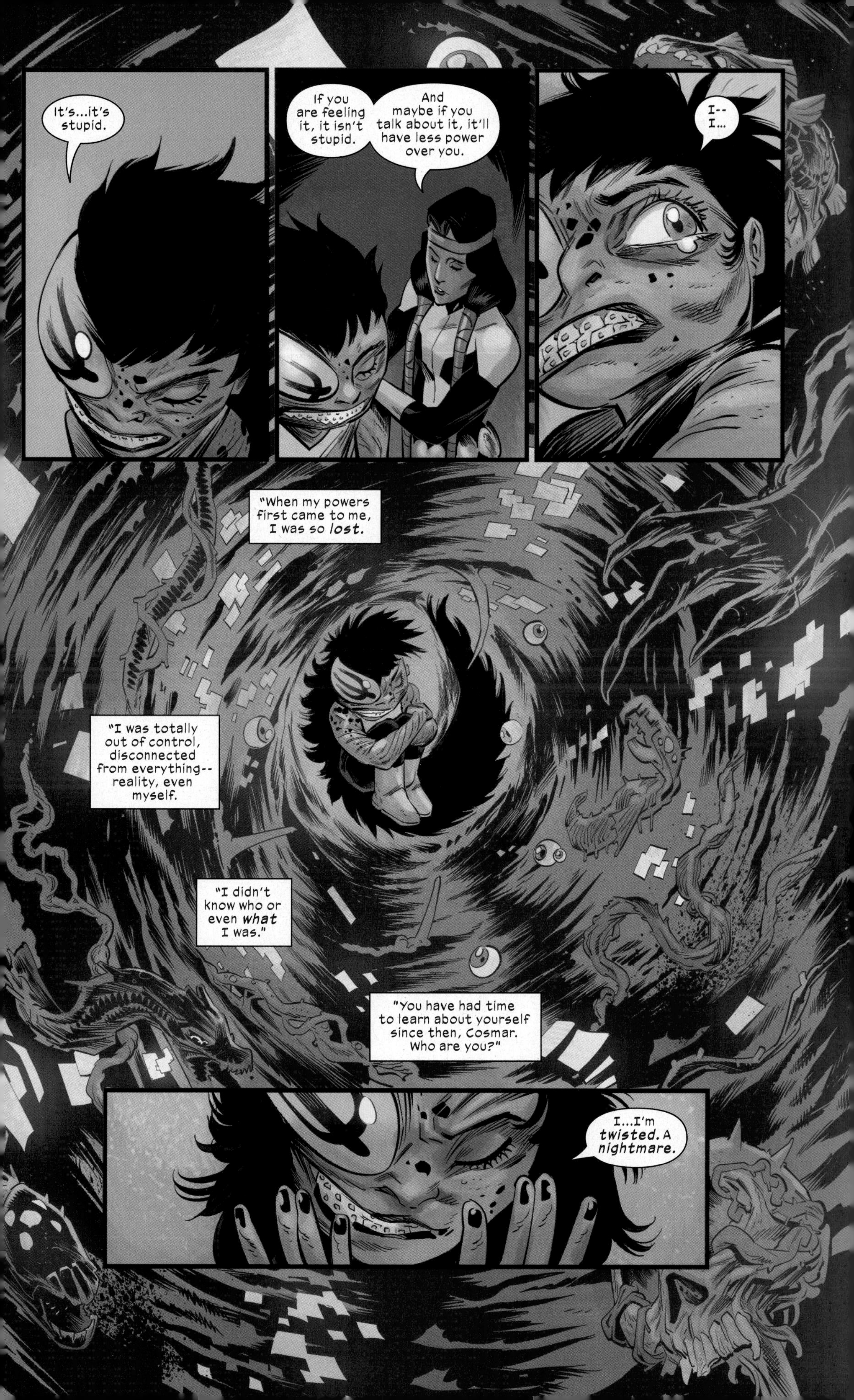

It's...it's stupid.
If you are feeling it, it isn't stupid.
And maybe if you talk about it, it'll have less power over you.
I-- I...
"When my powers first came to me, I was so *lost.*
"I was totally out of control, disconnected from everything-- reality, even myself.
"I didn't know who or even *what* I was."
"You have had time to learn about yourself since then, Cosmar. Who are you?"
I...I'm *twisted.* A *nightmare.*

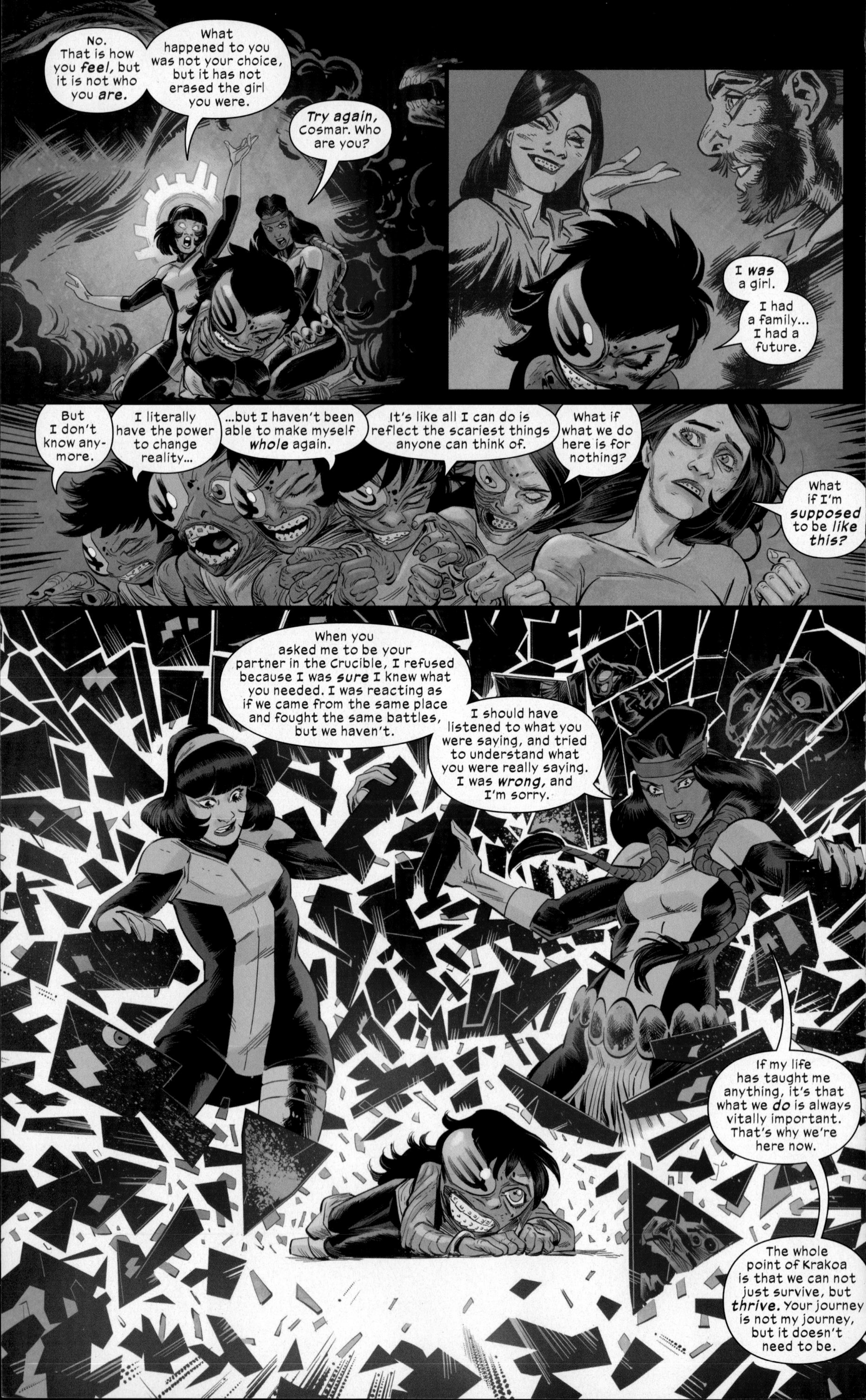
No. That is how you *feel*, but it is not who you *are.*
What happened to you was not your choice, but it has not erased the girl you were.
Try again, Cosmar. Who are you?
I *was* a girl.
I had a family... I had a future.
But I don't know any-more.
I literally have the power to change reality...
...but I haven't been able to make myself *whole* again.
It's like all I can do is reflect the scariest things anyone can think of.
What if what we do here is for nothing?
What if I'm *supposed* to be *like this?*
When you asked me to be your partner in the Crucible, I refused because I was *sure* I knew what you needed. I was reacting as if we came from the same place and fought the same battles, but we haven't.
I should have listened to what you were saying, and tried to understand what you were really saying. I was *wrong,* and I'm sorry.
If my life has taught me anything, it's that what we *do* is always vitally important. That's why we're here now.
The whole point of Krakoa is that we can not just survive, but *thrive.* Your journey is not my journey, but it doesn't need to be.

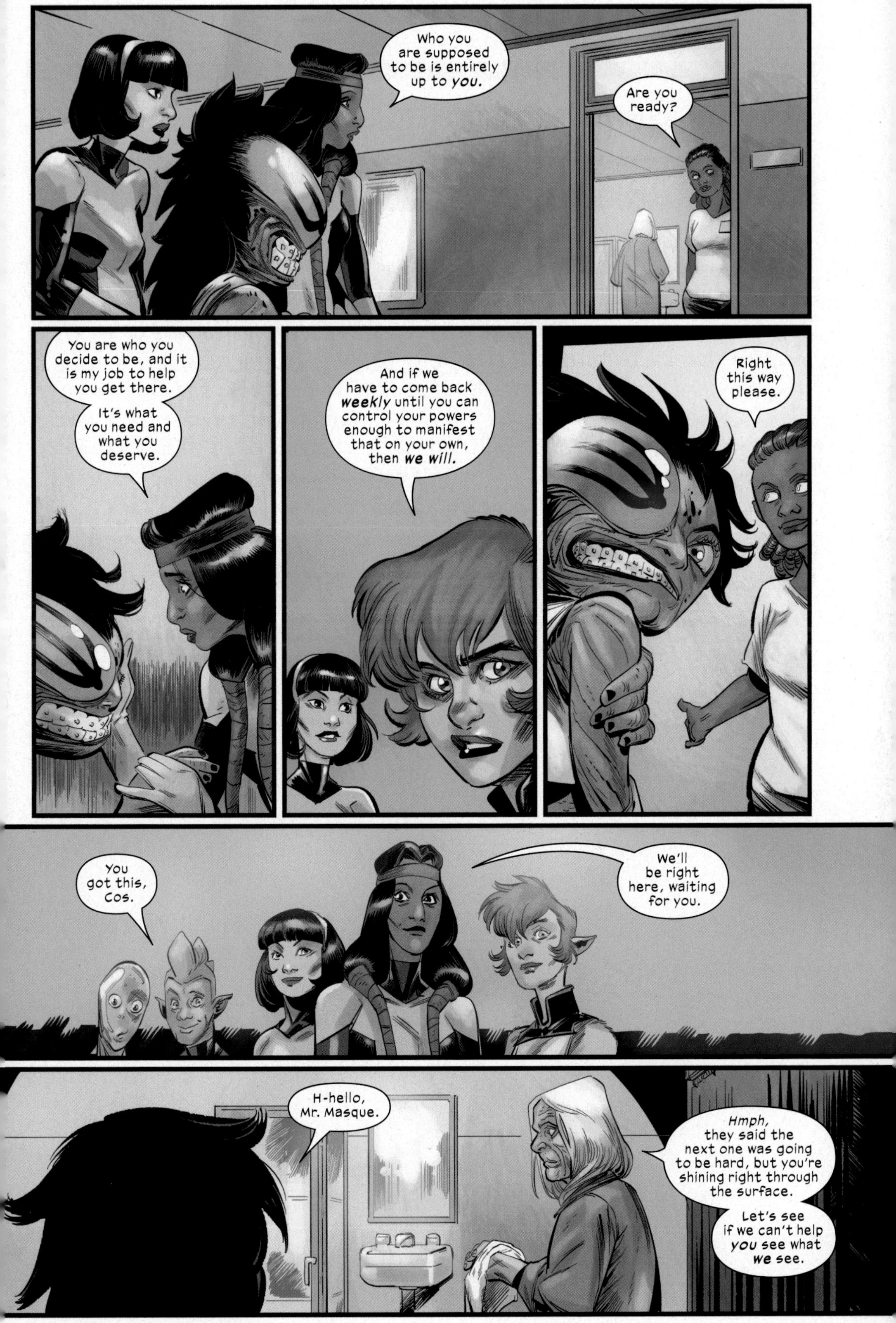

Who you are supposed to be is entirely up to *you.*
Are you ready?
You are who you decide to be, and it is my job to help you get there.
It's what you need and what you deserve.
And if we have to come back ***weekly*** until you can control your powers enough to manifest that on your own, then ***we will.***
Right this way please.
You got this, Cos.
We'll be right here, waiting for you.
H-hello, Mr. Masque.
Hmph, they said the next one was going to be hard, but you're shining right through the surface.
Let's see if we can't help ***you*** see what ***we*** see.

WARPATH JOURNAL, ENTRY 006

Write about one of your most treasured memories.

It is hard to fully put into words, not only because it feels as if it happened to someone else, but because it sounds so simple.

I was a child. My brother -- it hurt my neck to look up at him, he was so big -- decided that I must learn how to fish, so he took me. It was early summer, and there had been an unusual amount of rain, so the creeks and rivers were swollen with water. Trying to pull in a catch, I fell in. I was wearing boots with my pants tucked in, and they filled with water. I sunk like a stone. It was quiet down there...peaceful. Soon, I felt John's giant arm wrap around my chest and pull me up. I was not scared, because I knew that he would keep me safe.

If you could go back in time and talk to your younger self, what would you tell them?

Everything ends, but that does not take away meaning or value -- if anything, it makes life more precious.

―

―

―

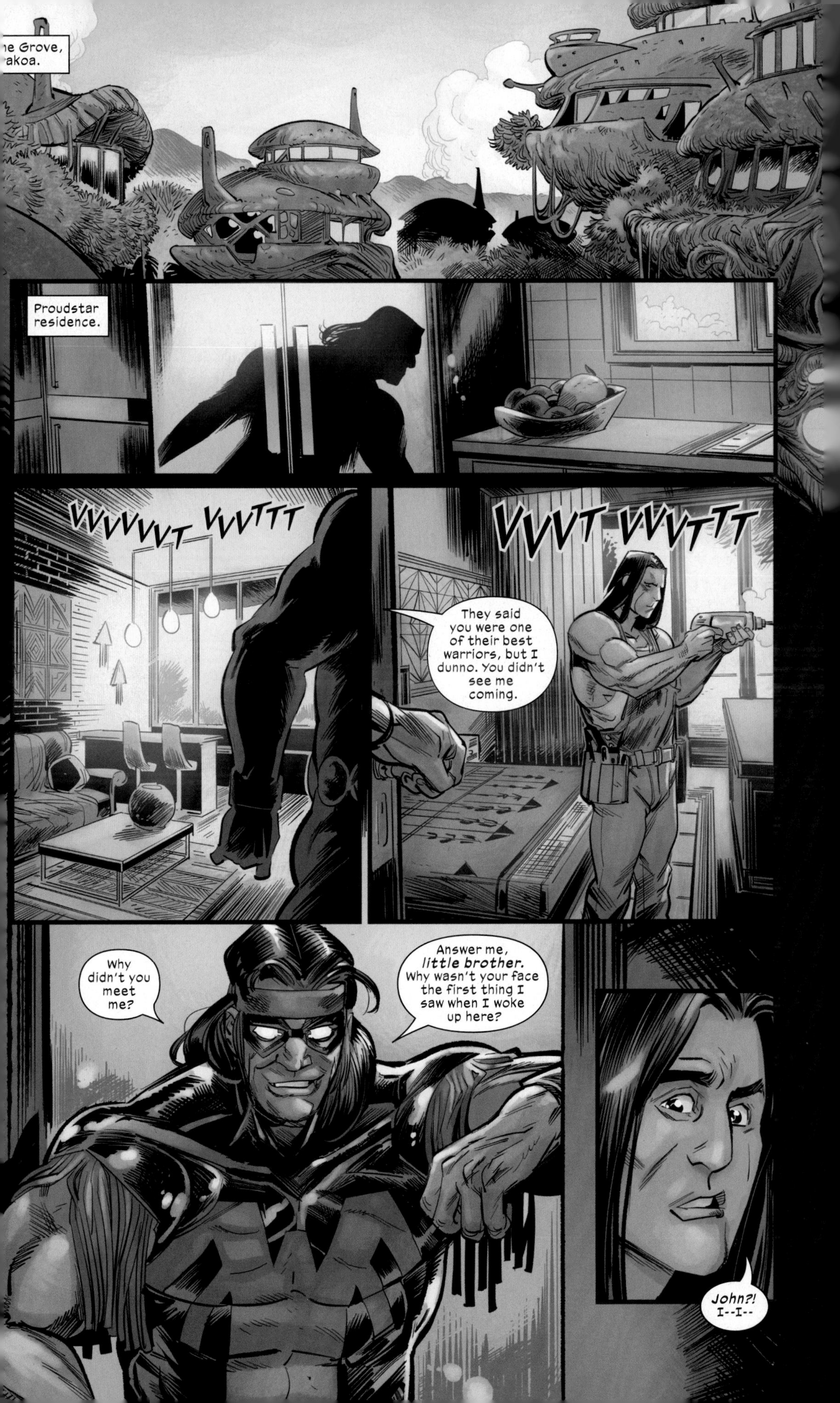

…e Grove,
…akoa.
Proudstar residence.
VVVVVVT VVVTTT
VVVT VVVTTT
They said you were one of their best warriors, but I dunno. You didn't see me coming.
Why didn't you meet me?
Answer me, *little brother.* Why wasn't your face the first thing I saw when I woke up here?
John?! I--I--

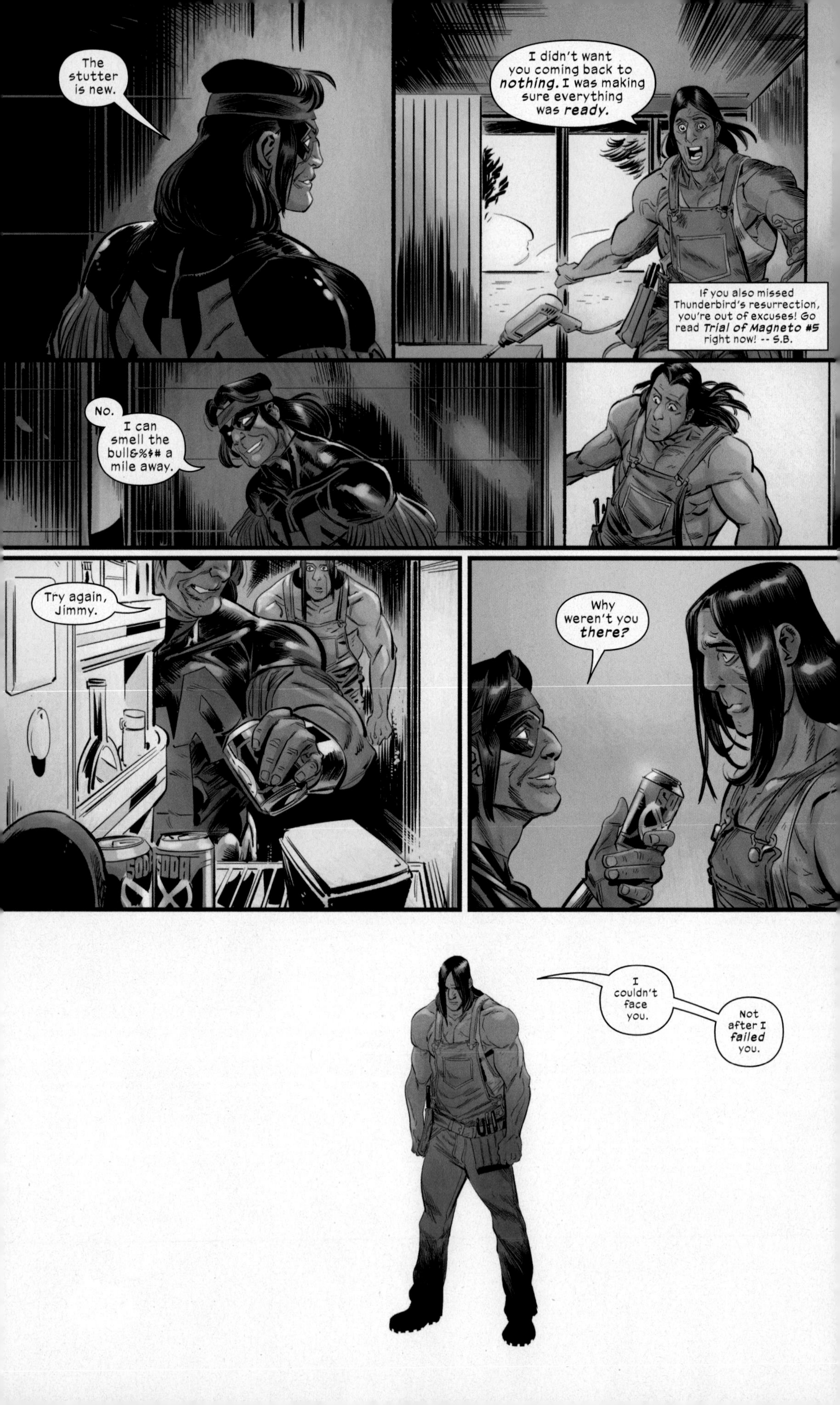
The stutter is new.
I didn't want you coming back to *nothing.* I was making sure everything was *ready.*
If you also missed Thunderbird's resurrection, you're out of excuses! Go read *Trial of Magneto #5* right now! -- S.B.
No.
I can smell the bull&%$# a mile away.
Try again, Jimmy.
Why weren't you *there?*
I couldn't face you.
Not after I *failed* you.

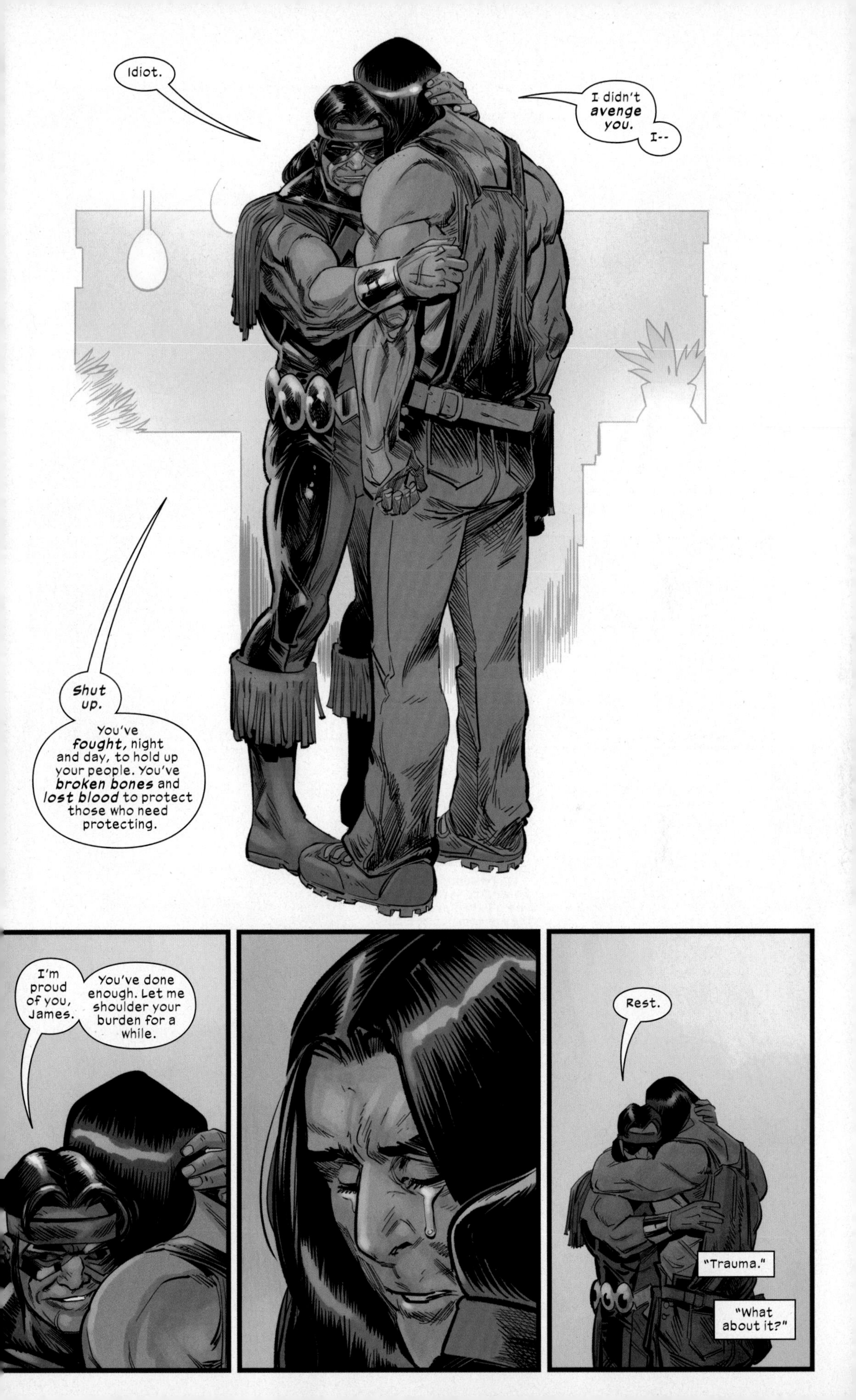
Idiot.
I didn't avenge you. I--
Shut up.
You've fought, night and day, to hold up your people. You've broken bones and lost blood to protect those who need protecting.
I'm proud of you, James.
You've done enough. Let me shoulder your burden for a while.
Rest.
"Trauma."
"What about it?"

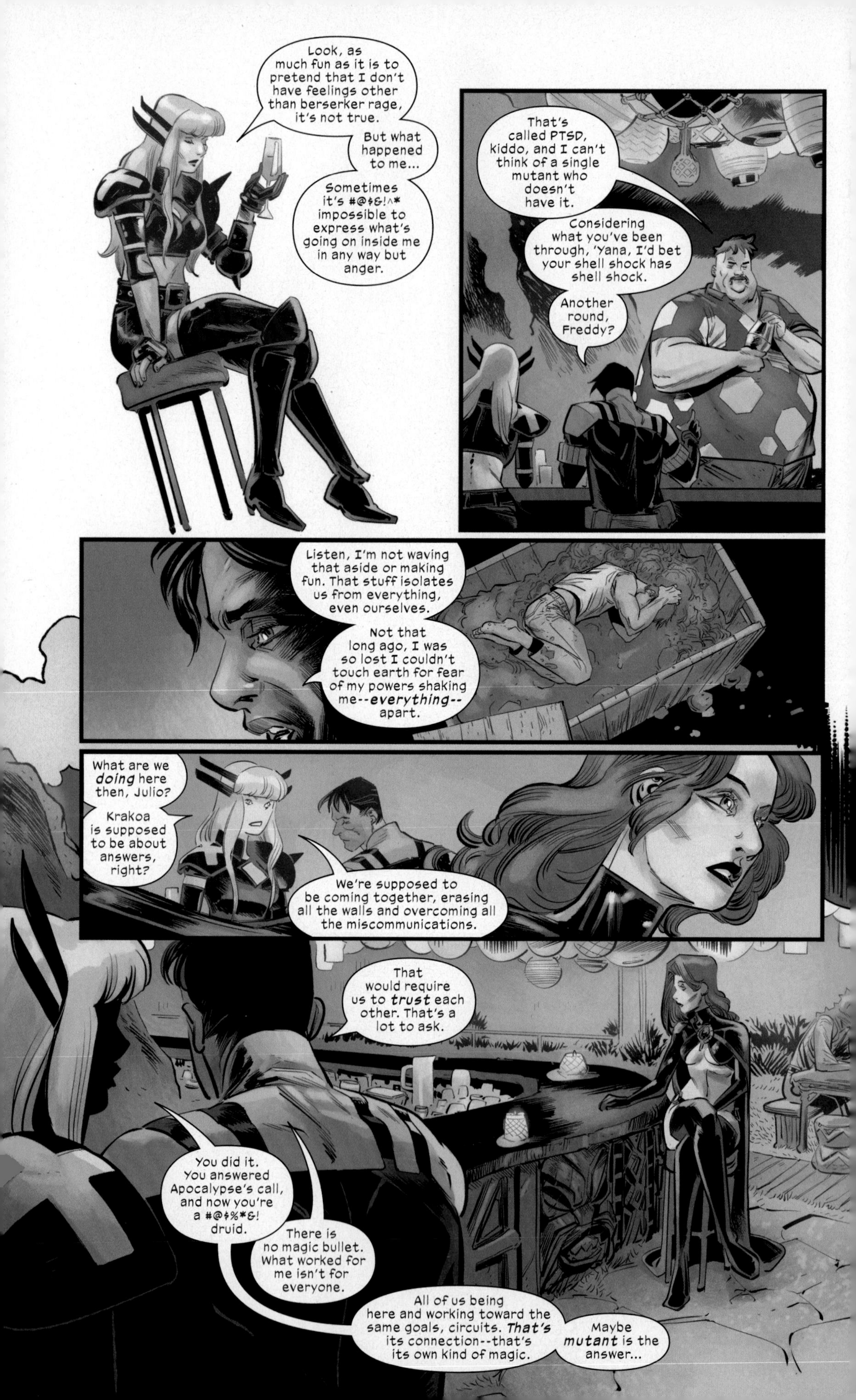
Look, as much fun as it is to pretend that I don't have feelings other than berserker rage, it's not true.
But what happened to me...
Sometimes it's #@$&!^* impossible to express what's going on inside me in any way but anger.
That's called PTSD, kiddo, and I can't think of a single mutant who doesn't have it.
Considering what you've been through, 'Yana, I'd bet your shell shock has shell shock.
Another round, Freddy?
Listen, I'm not waving that aside or making fun. That stuff isolates us from everything, even ourselves.
Not that long ago, I was so lost I couldn't touch earth for fear of my powers shaking me--*everything*--apart.
What are we *doing* here then, Julio?
Krakoa is supposed to be about answers, right?
We're supposed to be coming together, erasing all the walls and overcoming all the miscommunications.
That would require us to *trust* each other. That's a lot to ask.
You did it. You answered Apocalypse's call, and now you're a #@$%*&! druid.
There is no magic bullet. What worked for me isn't for everyone.
All of us being here and working toward the same goals, circuits. *That's* its connection--that's its own kind of magic.
Maybe *mutant* is the answer...

HUSK
REQUEST
FORM

NAME:

Martha Johansson/No-Girl

PROOF OF DEATH:

N/A *(see notes)*

MODIFICATIONS:

A fully hairless, transparent cranium

NOTES:

No-Girl technically has not died, though her physical body (save her brain) was destroyed by the U-Men. She has requested to be transferred to a new, full body, and that her mutant name be changed to fit who she feels she is...

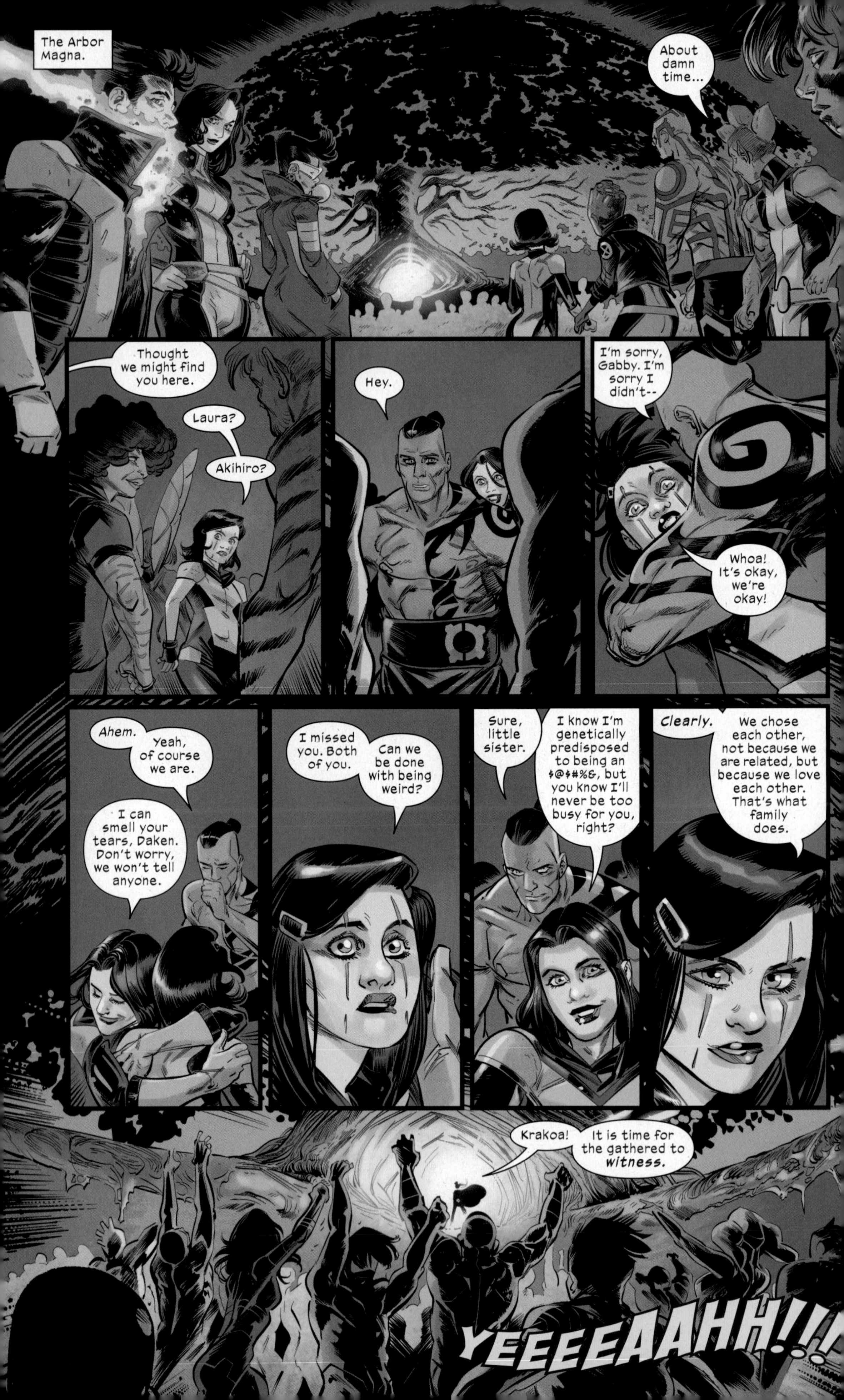

The Arbor Magna.
About damn time...
Thought we might find you here.
Laura?
Akihiro?
Hey.
I'm sorry, Gabby. I'm sorry I didn't--
Whoa! It's okay, we're okay!
Ahem.
Yeah, of course we are.
I can smell your tears, Daken. Don't worry, we won't tell anyone.
I missed you. Both of you.
Can we be done with being weird?
Sure, little sister.
I know I'm genetically predisposed to being an $@$#%&, but you know I'll never be too busy for you, right?
Clearly.
We chose each other, not because we are related, but because we love each other. That's what family does.
Krakoa!
It is time for the gathered to witness.
YEEEEAAHH!!!

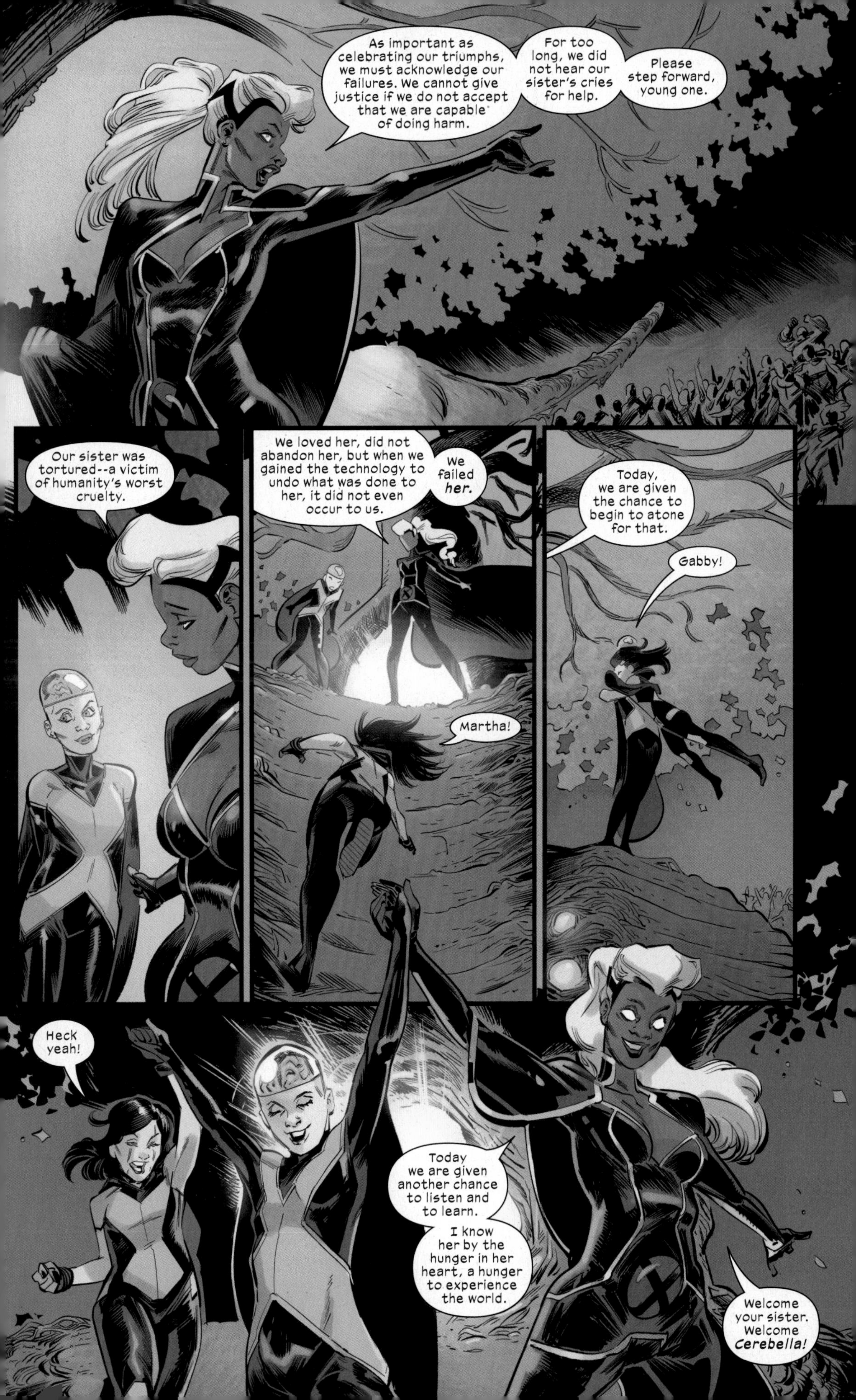
As important as celebrating our triumphs, we must acknowledge our failures. We cannot give justice if we do not accept that we are capable of doing harm.
For too long, we did not hear our sister's cries for help.
Please step forward, young one.
Our sister was tortured--a victim of humanity's worst cruelty.
We loved her, did not abandon her, but when we gained the technology to undo what was done to her, it did not even occur to us.
We failed *her.*
Martha!
Today, we are given the chance to begin to atone for that.
Gabby!
Heck yeah!
Today we are given another chance to listen and to learn.
I know her by the hunger in her heart, a hunger to experience the world.
Welcome your sister. Welcome *Cerebella!*

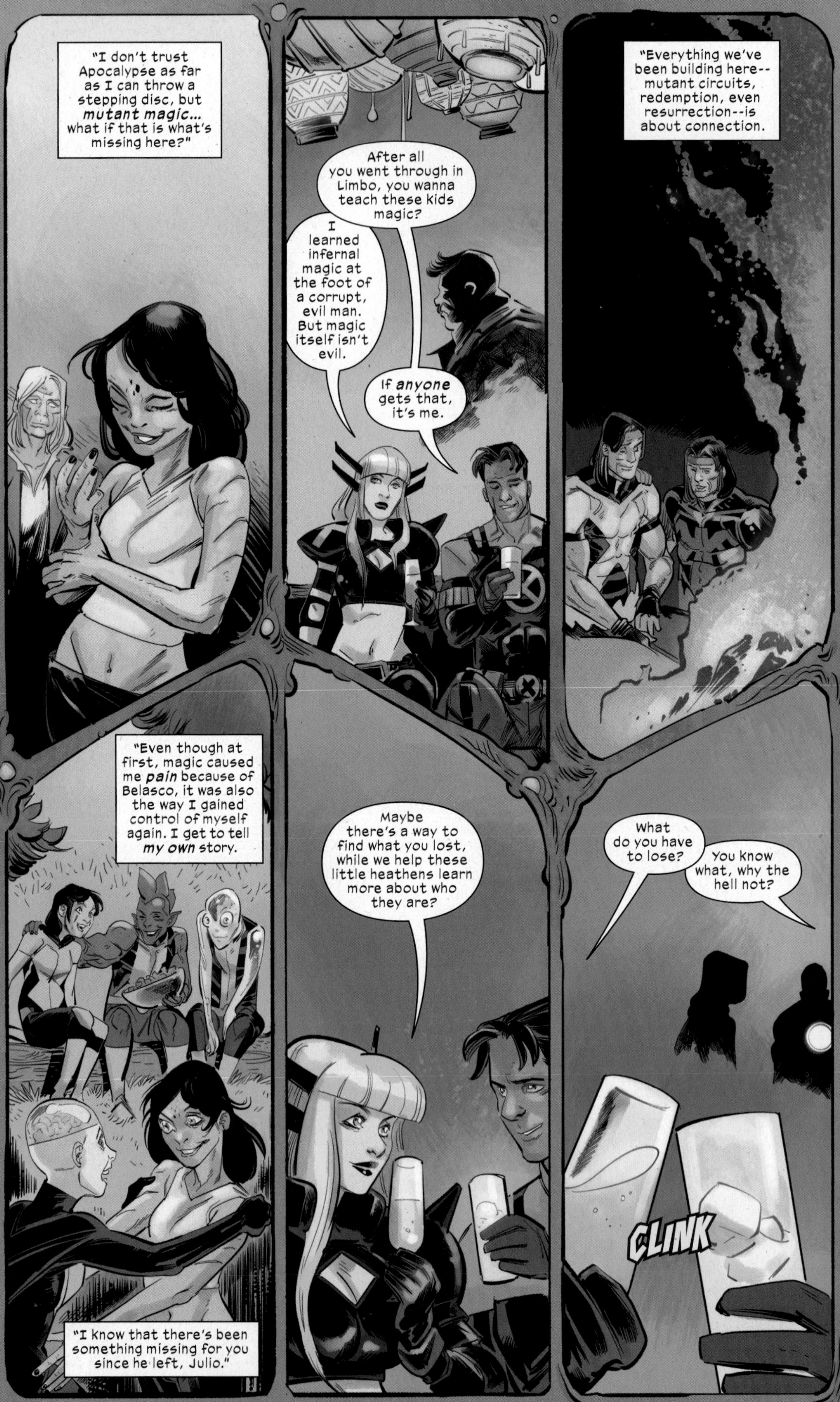
"I don't trust Apocalypse as far as I can throw a stepping disc, but mutant magic... what if that is what's missing here?"
After all you went through in Limbo, you wanna teach these kids magic?
I learned infernal magic at the foot of a corrupt, evil man. But magic itself isn't evil.
If anyone gets that, it's me.
"Everything we've been building here--mutant circuits, redemption, even resurrection--is about connection.
"Even though at first, magic caused me pain because of Belasco, it was also the way I gained control of myself again. I get to tell my own story.
"I know that there's been something missing for you since he left, Julio."
Maybe there's a way to find what you lost, while we help these little heathens learn more about who they are?
What do you have to lose?
You know what, why the hell not?
CLINK

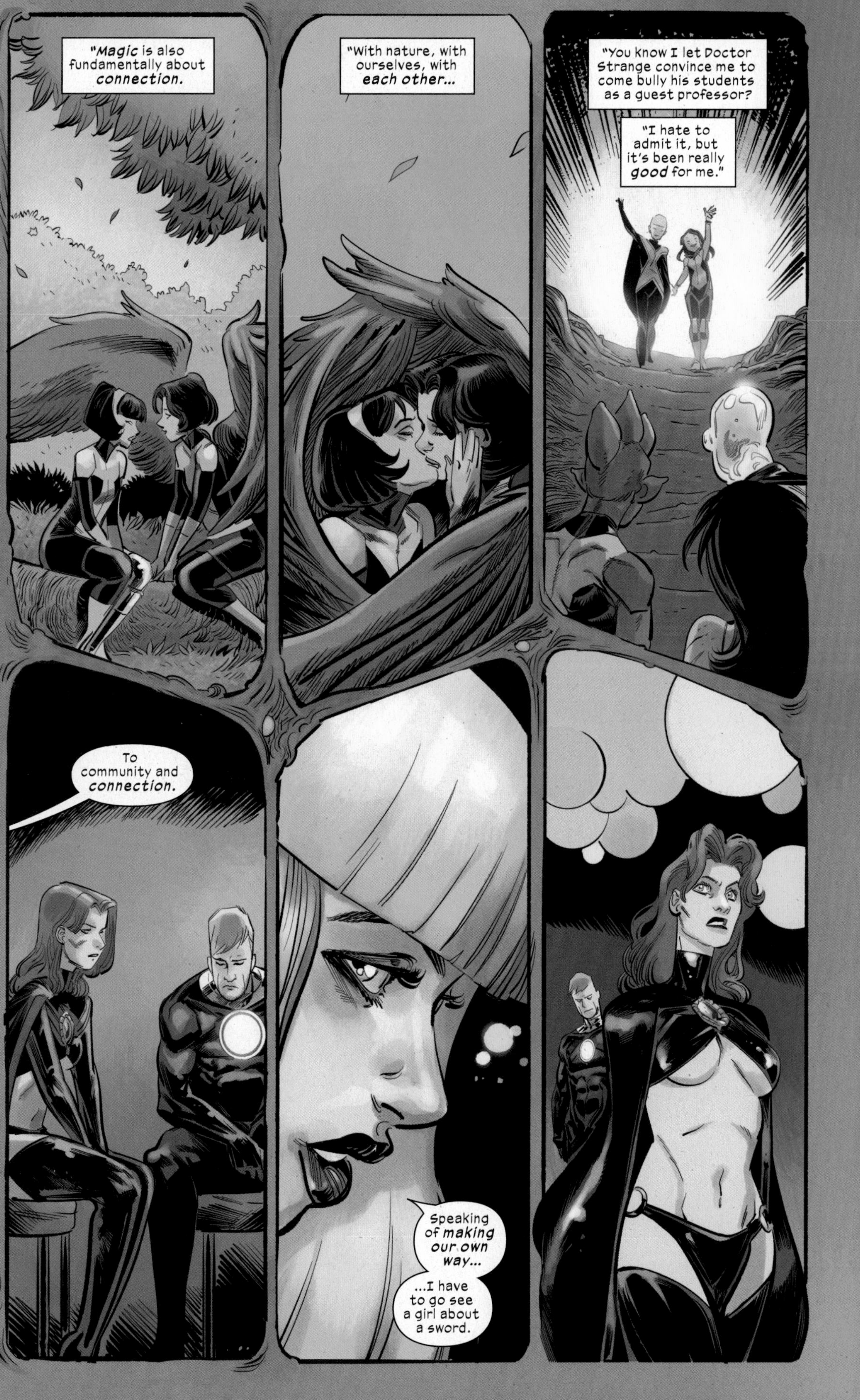
"Magic is also fundamentally about connection.
"With nature, with ourselves, with each other...
"You know I let Doctor Strange convince me to come bully his students as a guest professor?
"I hate to admit it, but it's been really good for me."
To community and connection.
Speaking of making our own way...
...I have to go see a girl about a sword.

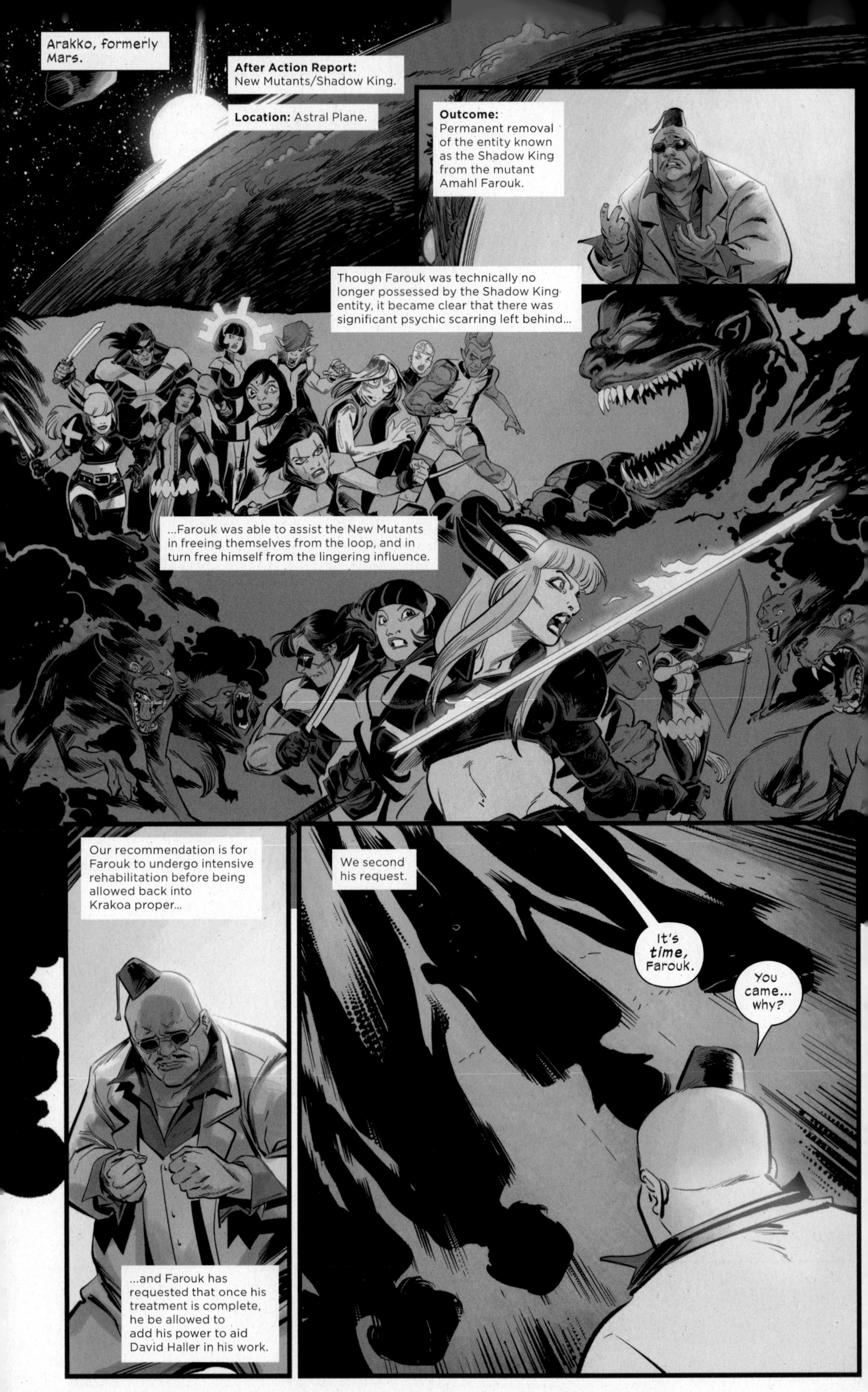
Arakko, formerly Mars.
After Action Report: New Mutants/Shadow King.
Location: Astral Plane.
Outcome: Permanent removal of the entity known as the Shadow King from the mutant Amahl Farouk.
Though Farouk was technically no longer possessed by the Shadow King entity, it became clear that there was significant psychic scarring left behind...
...Farouk was able to assist the New Mutants in freeing themselves from the loop, and in turn free himself from the lingering influence.
Our recommendation is for Farouk to undergo intensive rehabilitation before being allowed back into Krakoa proper...
...and Farouk has requested that once his treatment is complete, he be allowed to add his power to aid David Haller in his work.
We second his request.
It's *time*, Farouk.
You came... why?

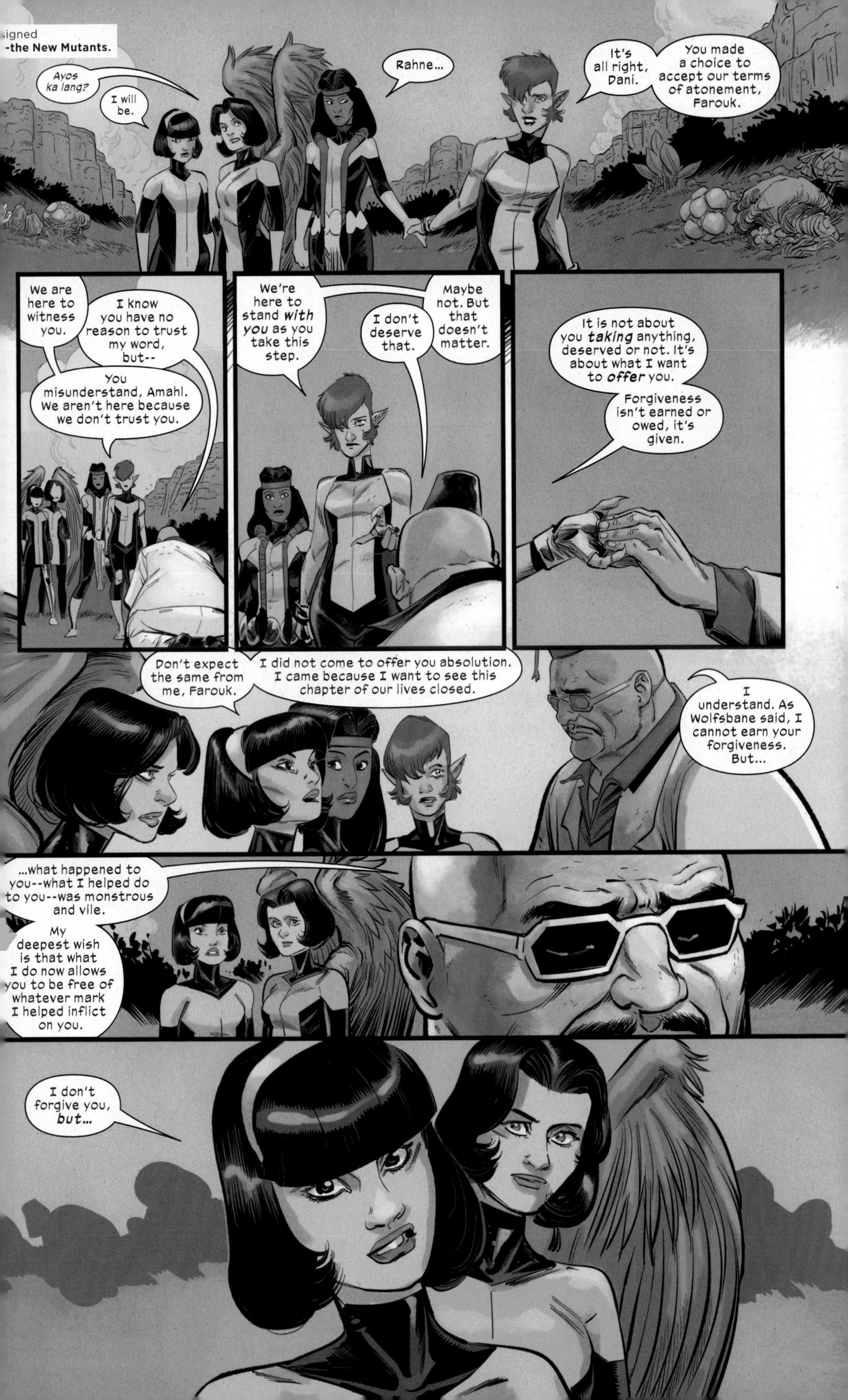
signed
-the New Mutants.
Ayos ka lang?
I will be.
Rahne...
It's all right, Dani.
You made a choice to accept our terms of atonement, Farouk.
We are here to witness you.
I know you have no reason to trust my word, but--
You misunderstand, Amahl. We aren't here because we don't trust you.
We're here to stand *with you* as you take this step.
I don't deserve that.
Maybe not. But that doesn't matter.
It is not about you *taking* anything, deserved or not. It's about what I want to *offer* you.
Forgiveness isn't earned or owed, it's given.
Don't expect the same from me, Farouk.
I did not come to offer you absolution. I came because I want to see this chapter of our lives closed.
I understand. As Wolfsbane said, I cannot earn your forgiveness. But...
...what happened to you--what I helped do to you--was monstrous and vile.
My deepest wish is that what I do now allows you to be free of whatever mark I helped inflict on you.
I don't forgive you, *but...*

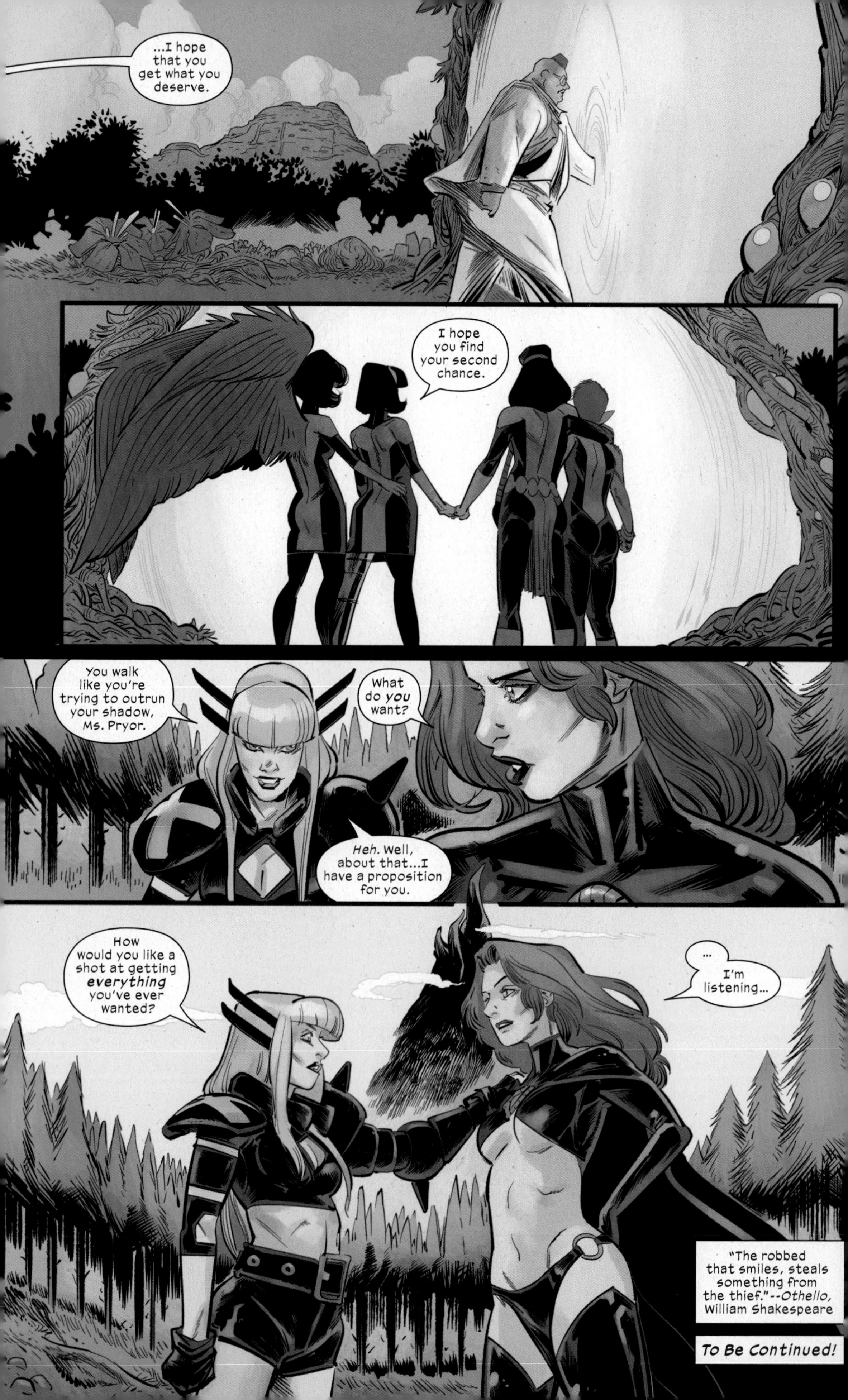
...I hope that you get what you deserve.
I hope you find your second chance.
You walk like you're trying to outrun your shadow, Ms. Pryor.
What do *you* want?
Heh. Well, about that...I have a proposition for you.
How would you like a shot at getting *everything* you've ever wanted?
... I'm listening...
"The robbed that smiles, steals something from the thief."--*Othello,* William Shakespeare
To Be Continued!

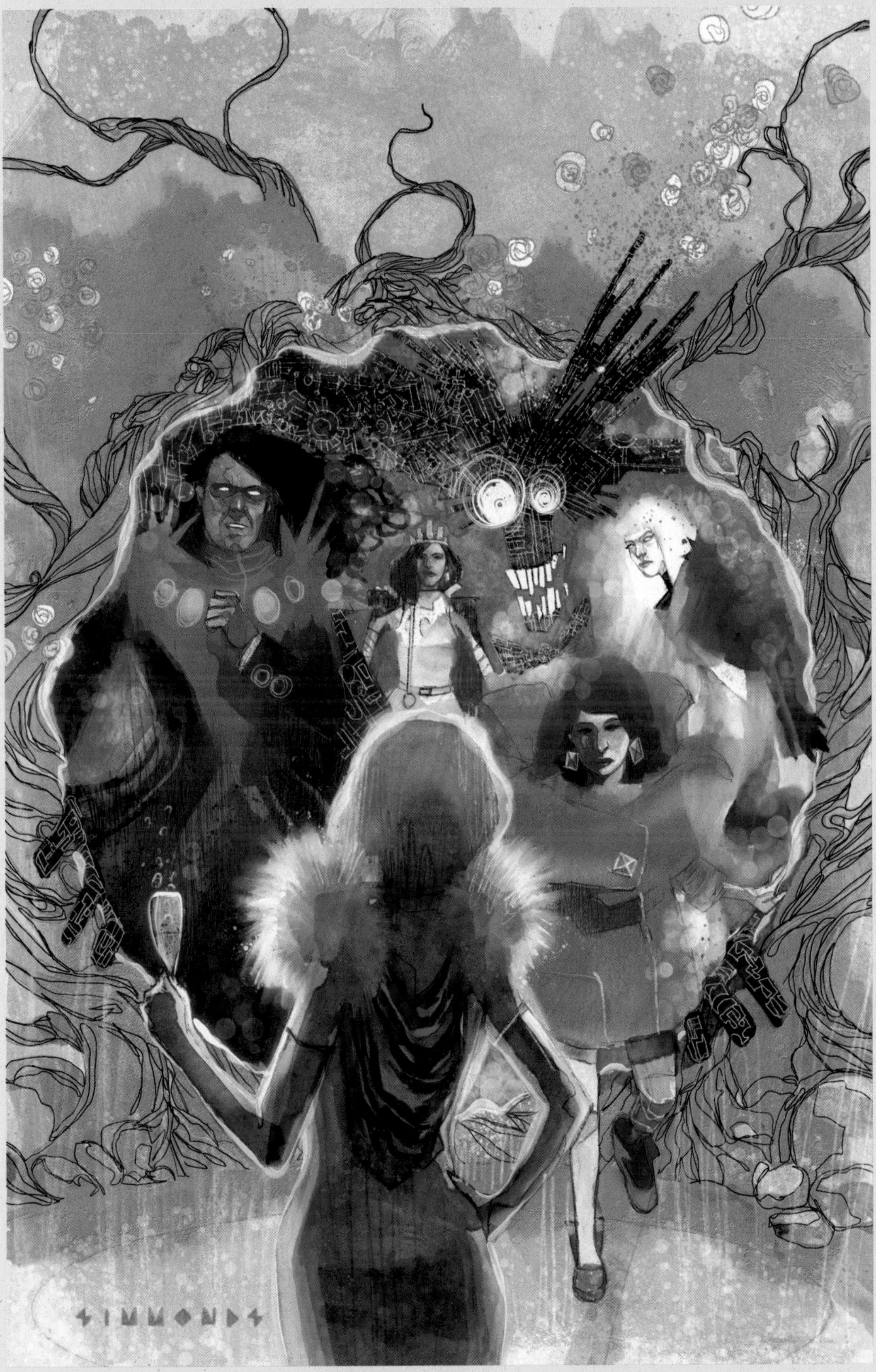
SIMMONDS

New Mutants #19 by Martin Simmonds

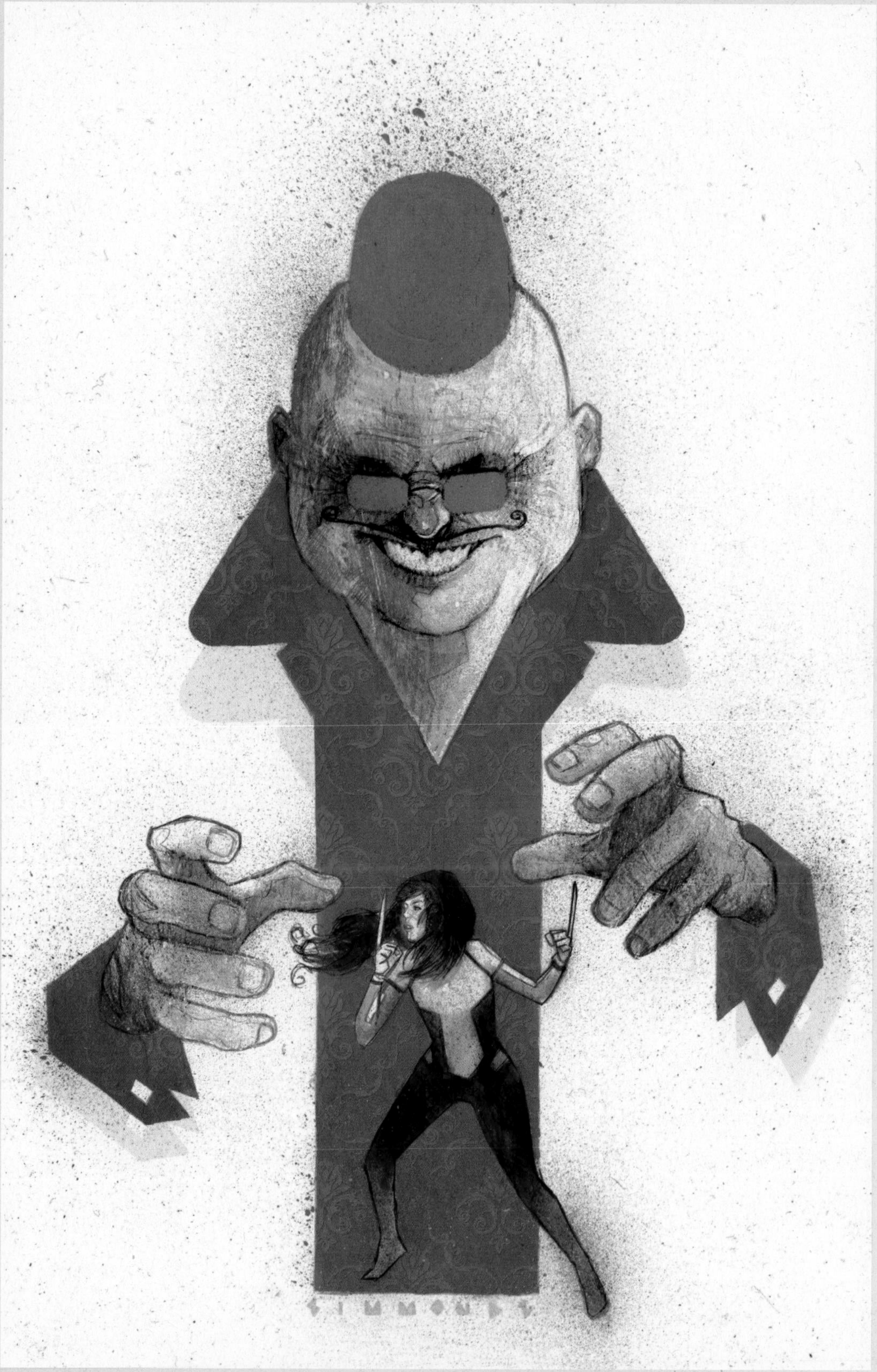
SIMMONDS

New Mutants #20 by Martin Simmonds

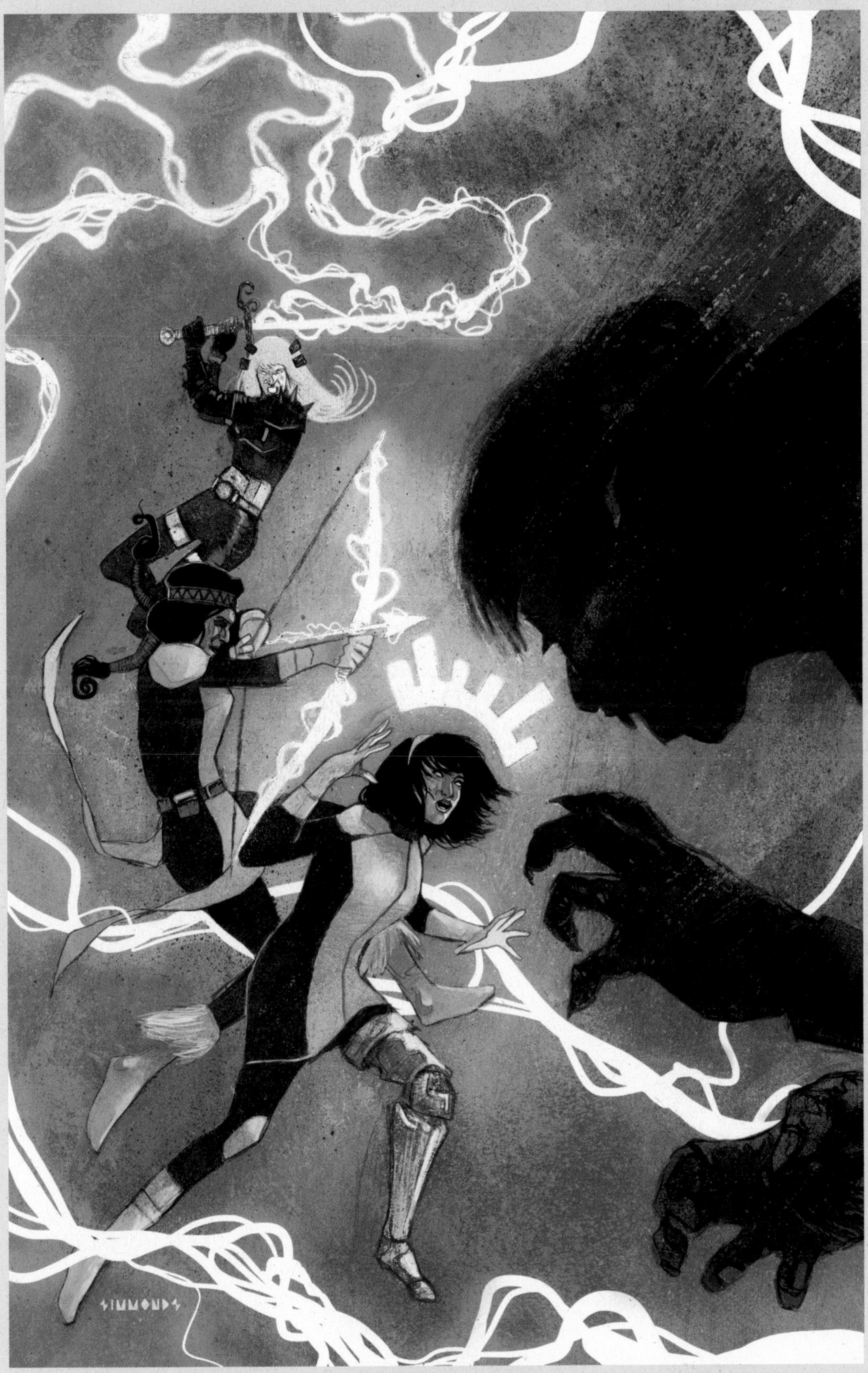
SIMMONDS

New Mutants #21 by Martin Simmonds

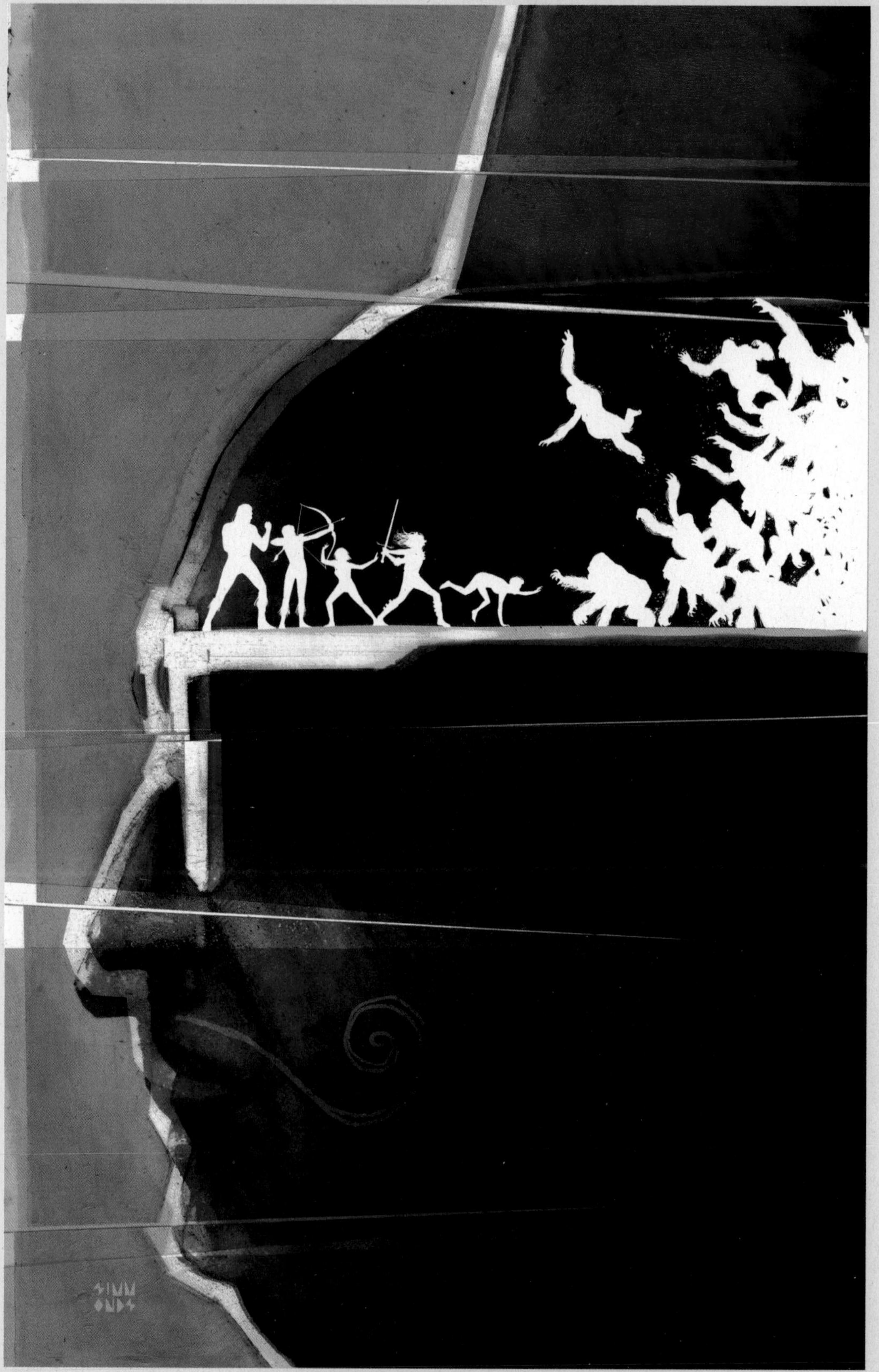

New Mutants #22 by Martin Simmonds

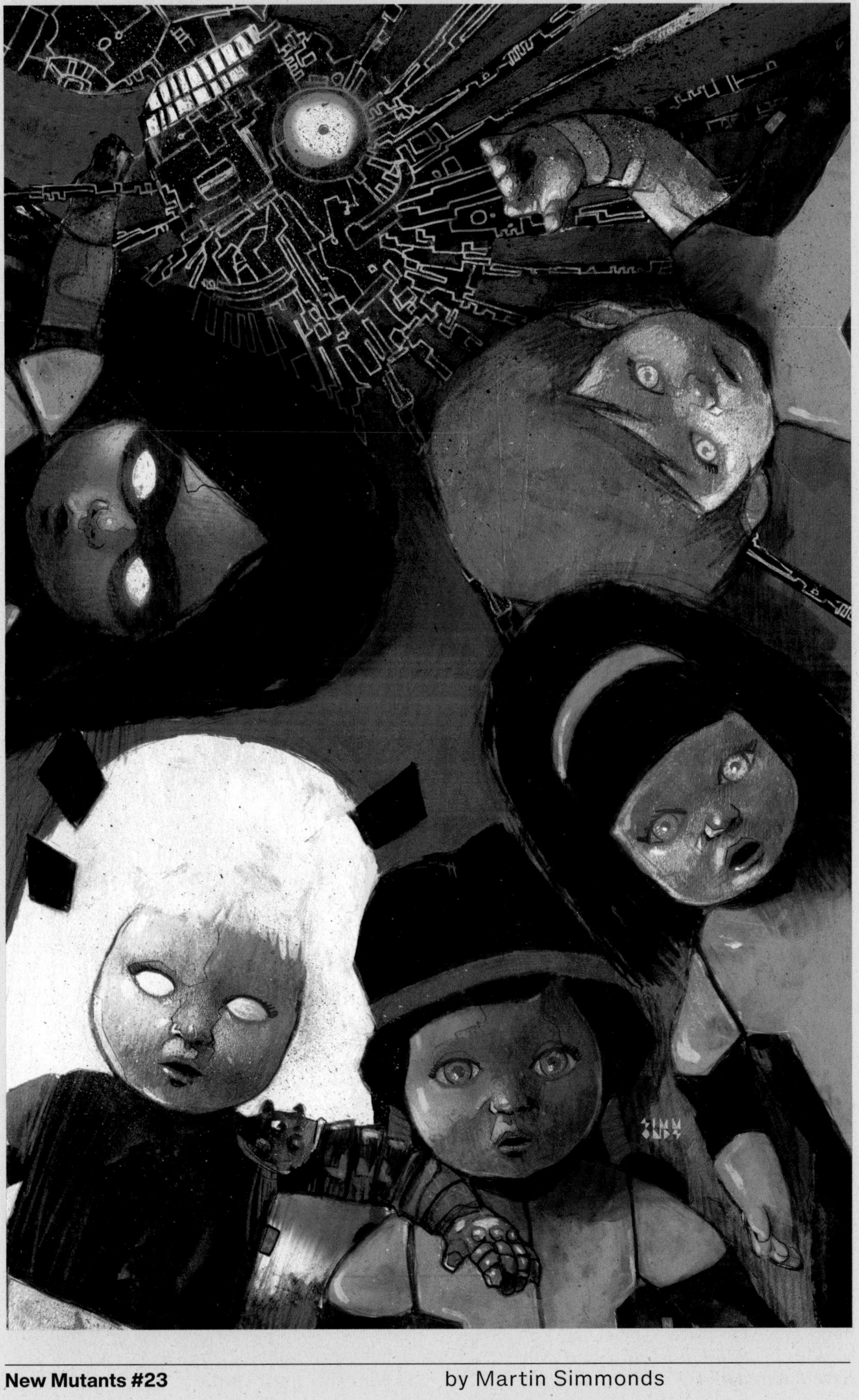

New Mutants #23 by Martin Simmonds

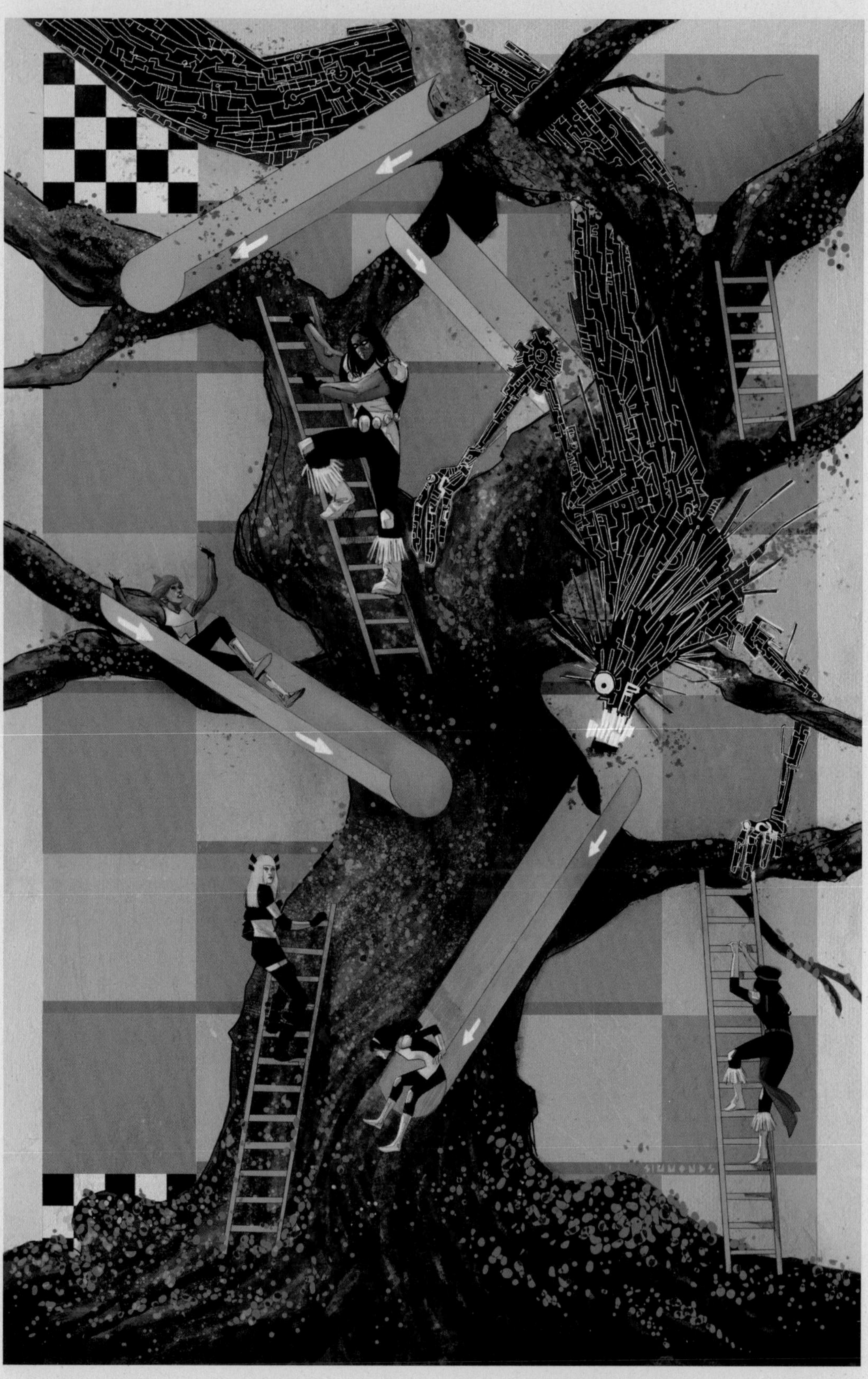
SIMMONDS

New Mutants #24 by Martin Simmonds

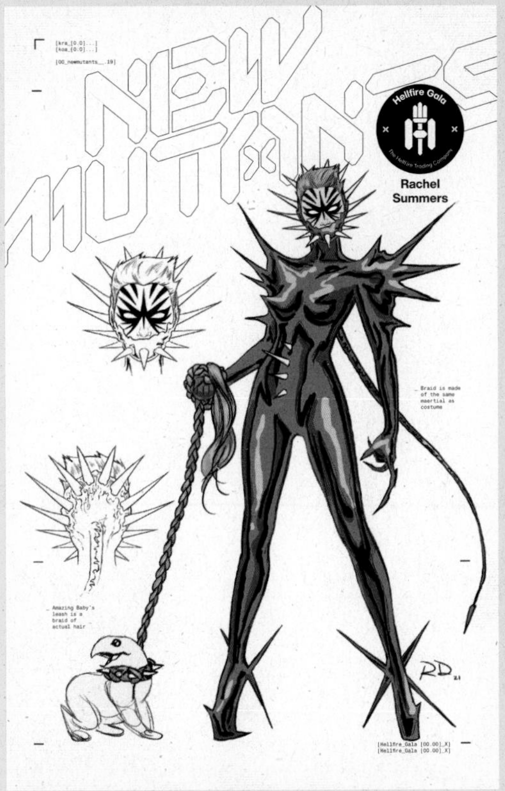
[kra_[0.0]...]
[koa_[0.0]...]
[00_newmutants__.19]
NEW MUTANTS
Hellfire Gala
The Hellfire Trading Company
Rachel
Summers
Braid is made of the same maertial as costume
Amazing Baby's leash is a braid of actual hair
RD 21
[Hellfire_Gala [00.00]_X]
[Hellfire_Gala [00.00]_X]

New Mutants #19 Design Variant
by Russell Dauterman

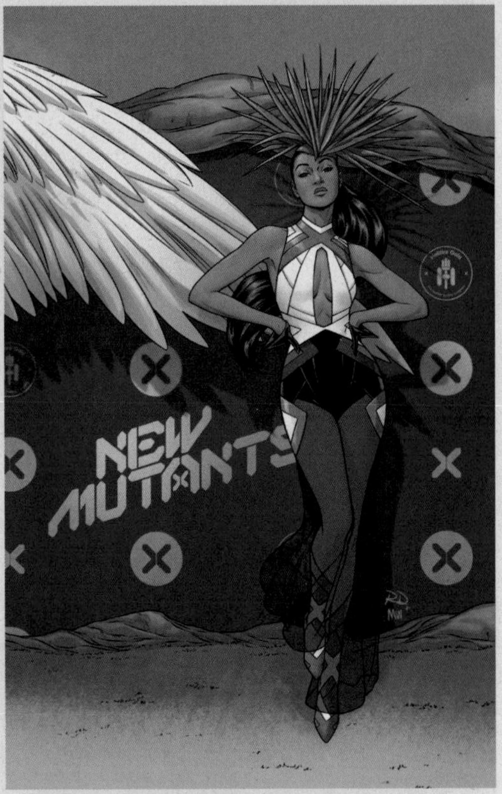
NEW MUTANTS

New Mutants #19 Connecting Variant
by Russell Dauterman
& Matthew Wilson

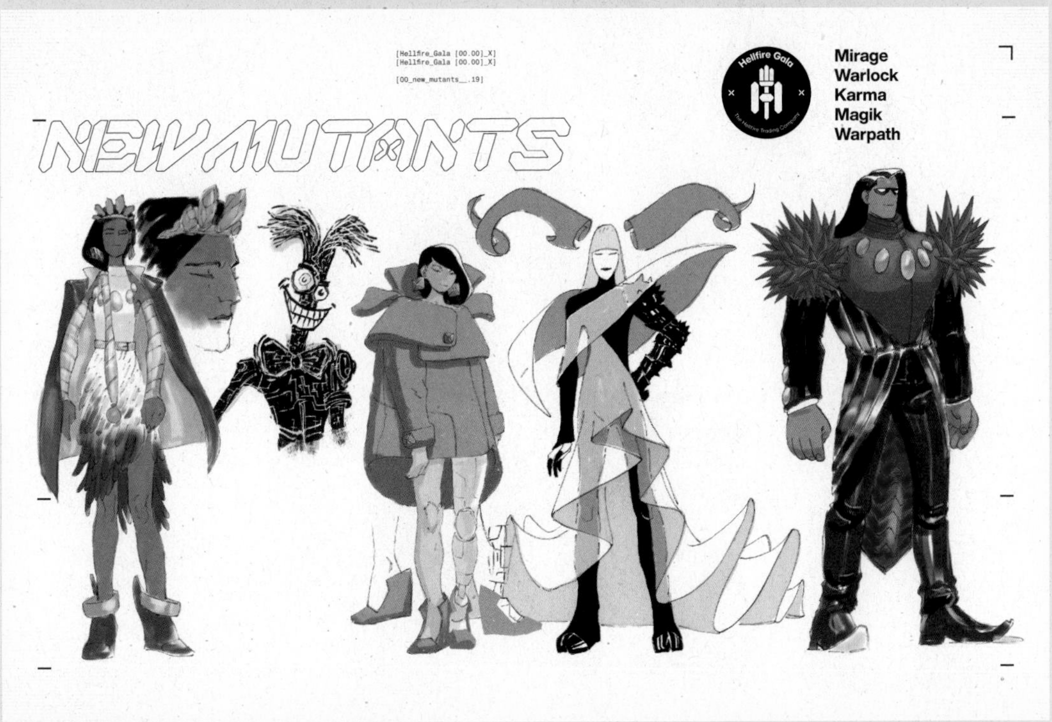
[Hellfire_Gala [00.00]_X]
[Hellfire_Gala [00.00]_X]
[00_new_mutants__.19]
NEW MUTANTS
Hellfire Gala
The Hellfire Trading Company
Mirage
Warlock
Karma
Magik
Warpath

New Mutants #19 Design Variant
by Alex Lins

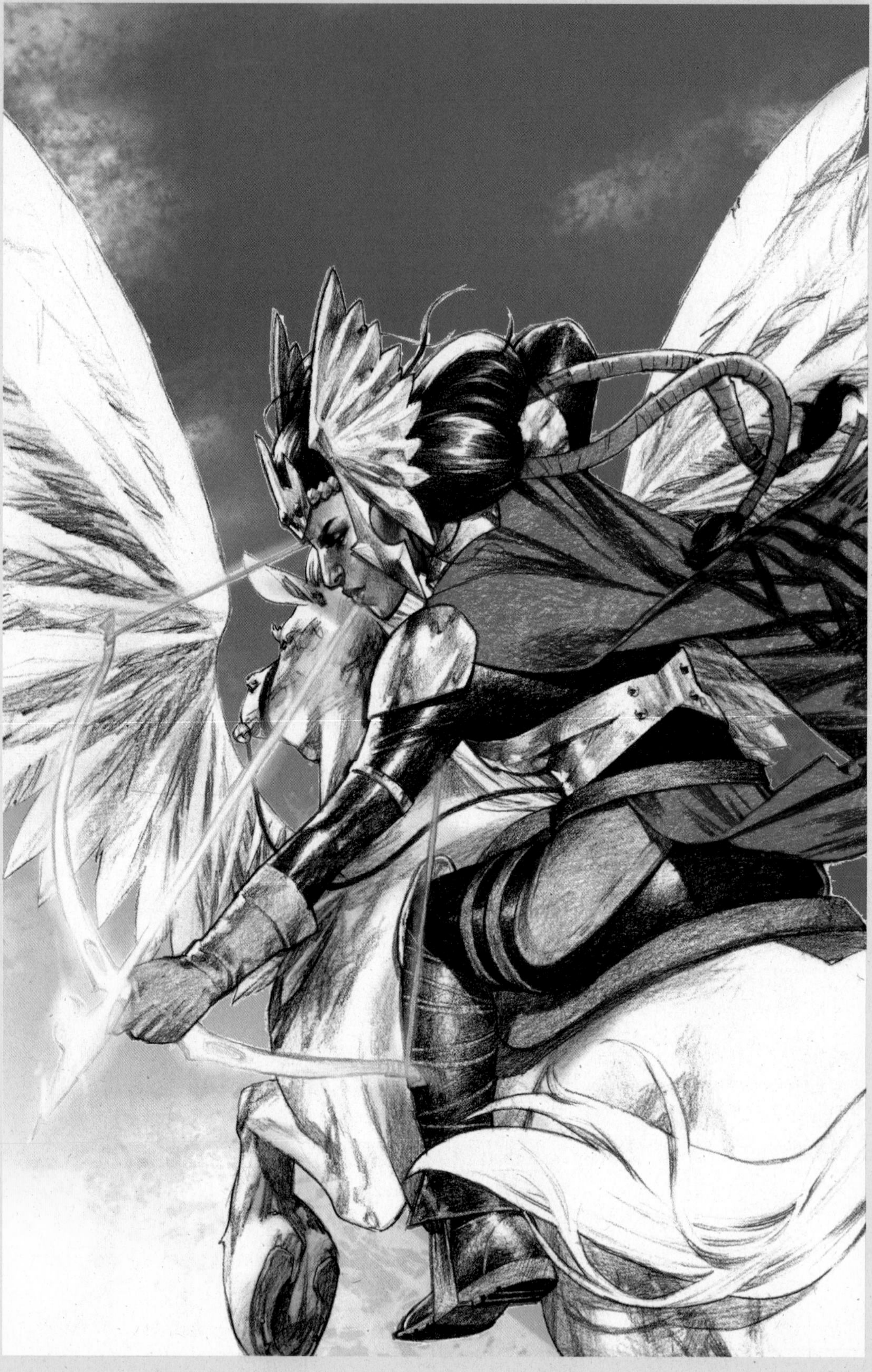

New Mutants #20 Variant by Davi Go

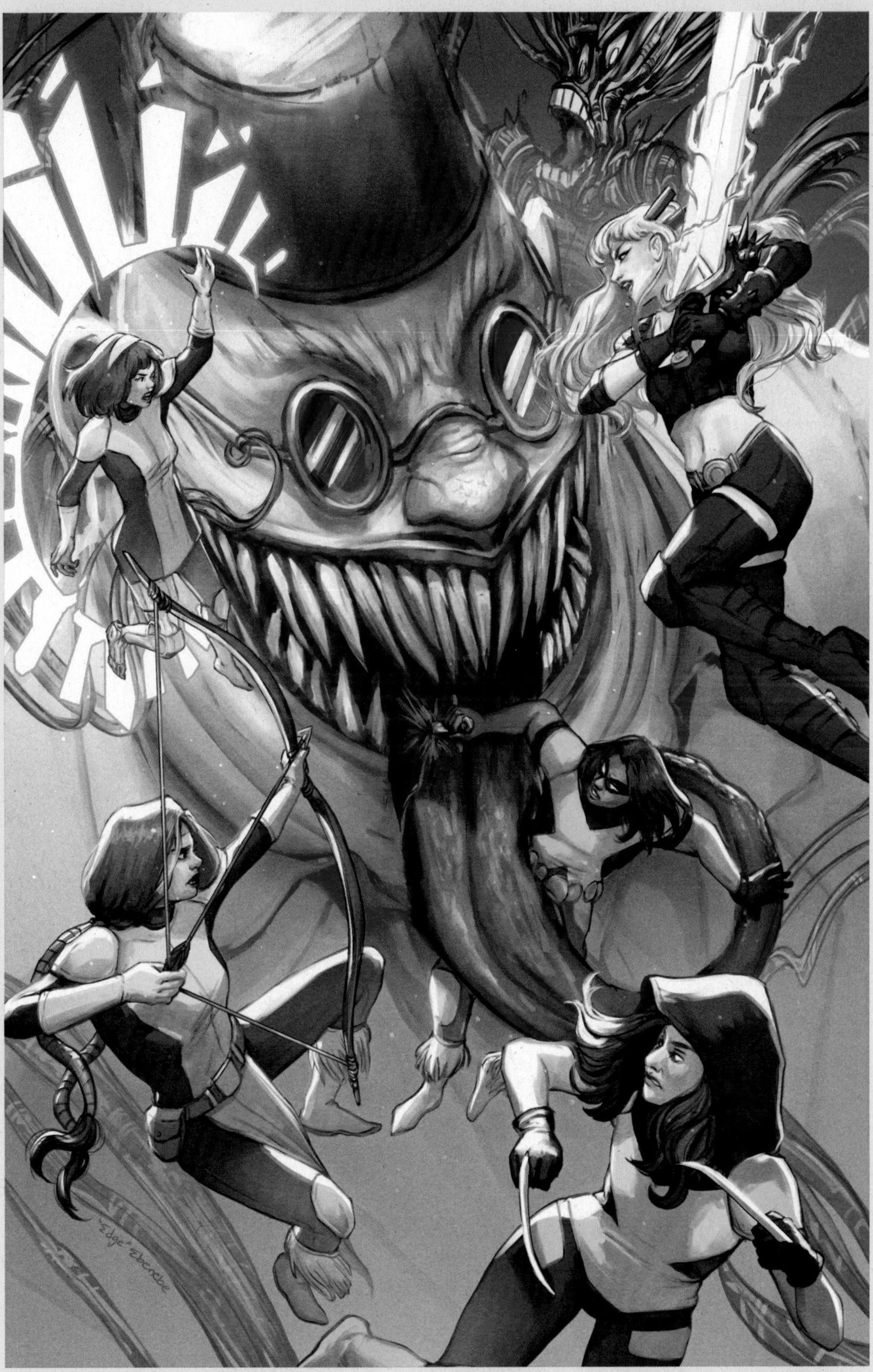

New Mutants #21 Variant by Edge

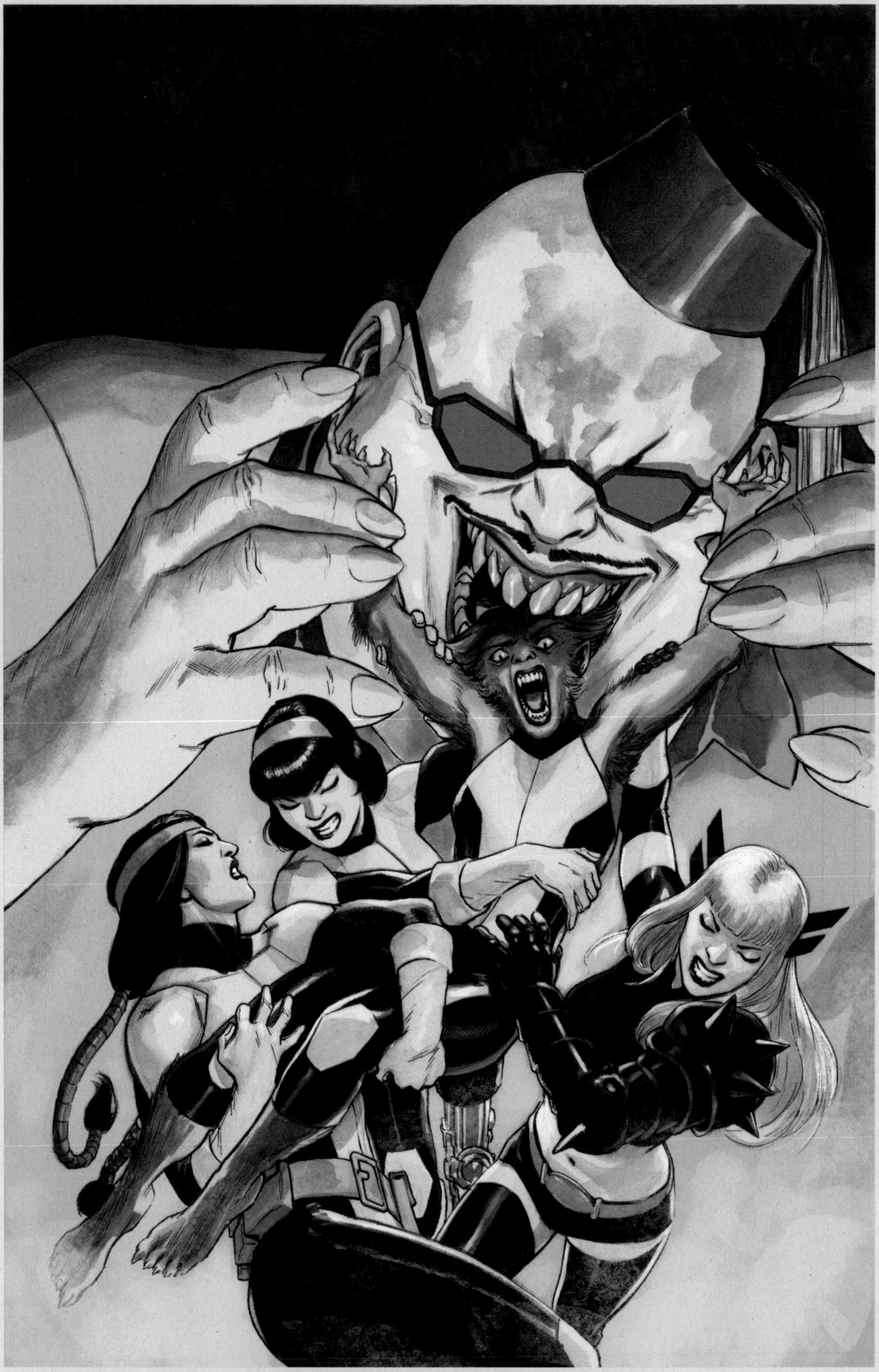

New Mutants #22 Variant by David Lopez

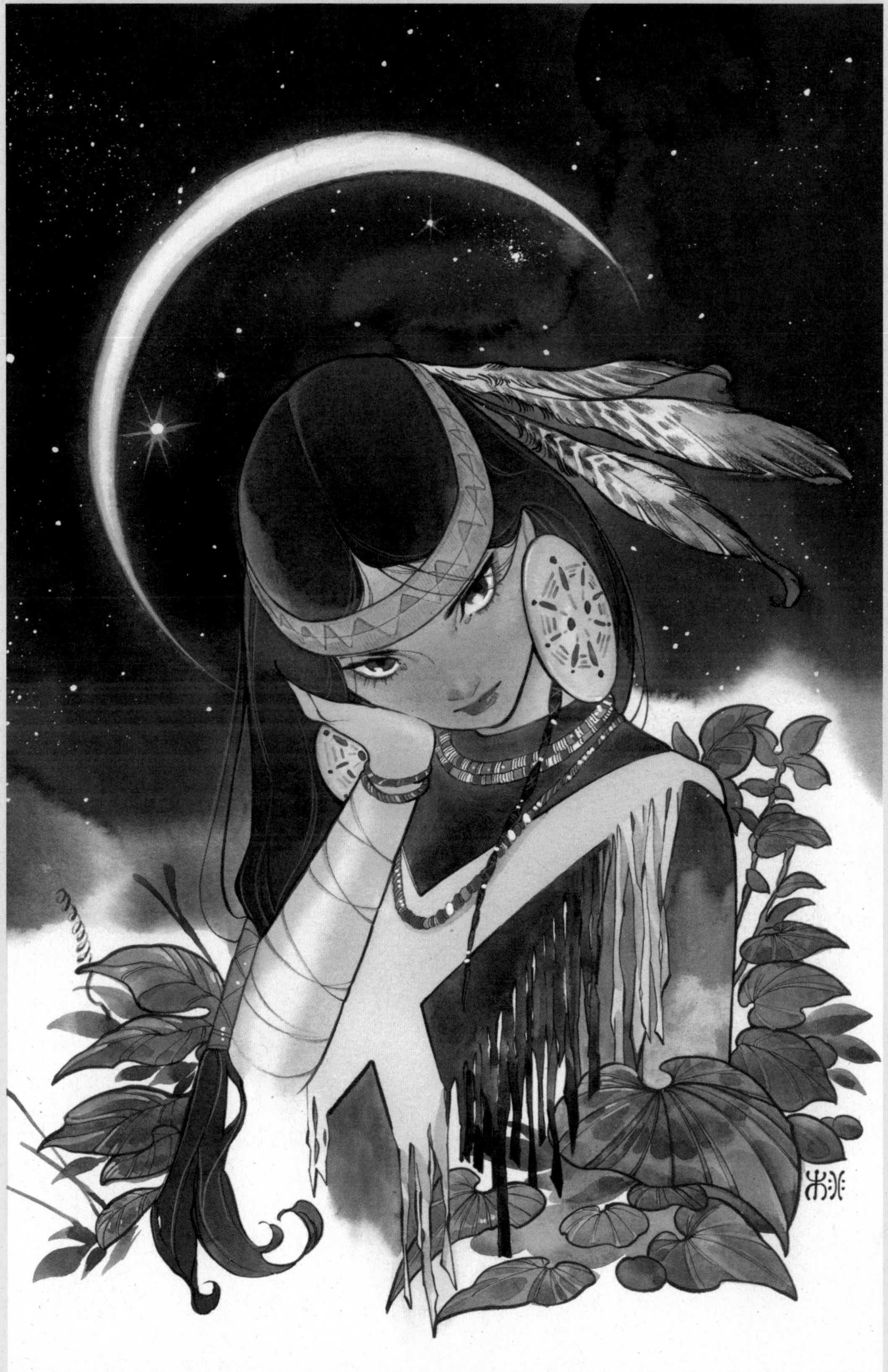

New Mutants #24 Variant by Peach Momoko

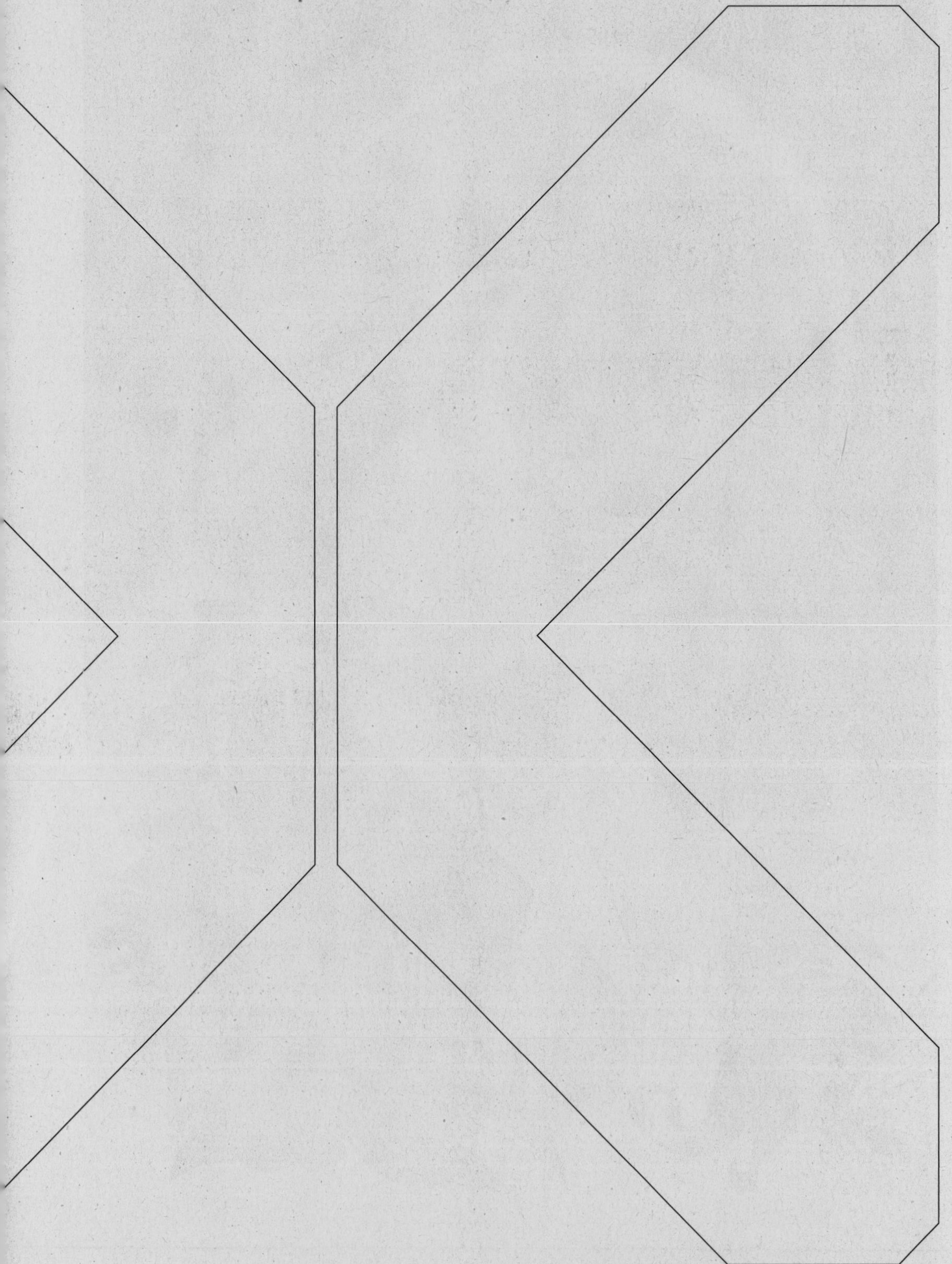